JOURNEY INTO
MYSTERY

THROUGH THE WORLD'S GREAT ENIGMAS

WHITE STAR PUBLISHERS

Contents

Foreword by Roberto Giacobbo — page 8
Introduction — page 10

1) **Loch Ness** UNITED KINGDOM — page 18
2) **Glamis Castle** UNITED KINGDOM — page 22
3) **Stonehenge** UNITED KINGDOM — page 28
4) **The Mysteries of Glastonbury** UNITED KINGDOM — page 32
5) **The Giant of Cerne Abbas** UNITED KINGDOM — page 38
6) **The Goseck Circle** GERMANY — page 42
7) **The Carnac Stones** FRANCE — page 44
8) **The Cathedral of Chartres** FRANCE — page 50
9) **The Secrets of the Popes** VATICAN CITY — page 56
10) **Castel del Monte** ITALY — page 58
11) **In Dracula's Court** ROMANIA — page 62
12) **The Pyramids of Visoko** BOSNIA — page 70
13) **The Oracle of Delphi** GREECE — page 72
14) **Atlantis** GREECE — page 78
15) **The Palace of Knossos** GREECE — page 82
16) **The Pyramid of Khufu** EGYPT — page 88
17) **The Sphinx** EGYPT — page 92
18) **Axum** ETHIOPIA — page 98
19) **Lalibela** ETHIOPIA — page 104
20) **The Ruins of Gedi** KENYA — page 112
21) **Great Zimbabwe** ZIMBABWE — page 116
22) **Noah's Ark** TURKEY — page 122
23) **Göbekli Tepe** TURKEY — page 124
24) **Har Megiddo** ISRAEL — page 130
25) **The Temple of King Solomon** ISRAEL — page 134
26) **The Dead Sea Scrolls** ISRAEL — page 138
27) **Petra, the Lost City** JORDAN — page 142
28) **Mohenjo-daro** PAKISTAN — page 150
29) **The Pillar of Ashoka** INDIA — page 156
30) **Mogui Cheng** CHINA — page 158
31) **The Pyramids of Xi'an** CHINA — page 162
32) **The Ruins of Yonaguni** JAPAN — page 166
33) **Angkor** CAMBODIA — page 170
34) **Uluru** AUSTRALIA — page 176

FOREWORD **ROBERTO GIACOBBO**

TEXT **GIULIO DI MARTINO**

Editorial staff
Valentina Giammarinaro
Giorgia Raineri

Graphic layout
Clara Zanotti

35) **Area 51** UNITED STATES	page 182	45) **Las Bolas** COSTA RICA	page 230
36) **The Sailing Stones** UNITED STATES	page 186	46) **El Dorado** BRAZIL	page 232
37) **The Disappearance of the Anasazi** UNITED STATES	page 190	47) **The Nazca Lines** PERU	page 234
		48) **Machu Picchu** PERU	page 242
38) **The Bermuda Triangle** ATLANTIC OCEAN	page 194	49) **Sacsayhuamán** PERU	page 248
39) **Chichén Itzá** MEXICO	page 196	50) **Lake Titicaca** BOLIVIA AND PERÙ	page 254
40) **The Magic of Cenotes** MEXICO	page 202	51) **Tiahuanaco** BOLIVIA	page 256
41) **Uxmal** MEXICO	page 208	52) **Easter Island** CHILE	page 262
42) **Teotihuacán** MEXICO	page 212		
43) **The Olmecs** MEXICO	page 218	INDEX	page 268
44) **Palenque** MEXICO	page 224	PHOTO CREDITS	page 270

FOREWORD
by Roberto Giacobbo

Federico Cesi was an important contributor to our knowledge. A boy who in 1603 – at the age of only 17 years – founded together with three friends an institution that would endure for centuries: the Accademia dei Lincei (literally, "the Academy of the Lynx-eyed," also referred to as the Lincean Academy), one of Italy's most prestigious cultural societies. The name was a tribute to the lynx, proverbial for its *piercing* gaze: accordingly, the gazes of its members were to go beyond the boundaries of *traditional* science. The objects of study for the Academy included all natural sciences, which were to be investigated with observations and experiments that were absolutely free, with no constraint related to office or authority. And it is in the same spirit that, for nearly 10 years, Giulio Di Martino has been traveling all over the planet together with me and my team, on the hunt for many of the unresolved mysteries bequeathed to us by science, archaeology, and history. After many years of broadcasting with RAI (Italy's biggest television company), we have produced many documentaries and pursued many amazing investigations: we dived off the coast of Japan to examine the submerged pyramids of Yonaguni; we scrutinized the timeless faces of the Moai on Easter Island; we descended to the depths of the earth and ascended to its most enigmatic peaks. We traveled on every means of transportation invented. We shared stories and food with men and women of every race and culture. Ever searching for answers, which often were larger than we are. This new journey, which Giulio undertook alone, brings as its accompanying gift the gazes, emotions, and astonishment of all the adventures experienced together. A volume made up of exciting images, but also of amazing stories, realized with curiosity and seriousness, with an intense desire to know, to explore as far as *the boundaries of knowledge*. Moreover, as the great Marcel Proust wrote: "The only real voyage of discovery consists not in seeking new landscapes, but in having new eyes." The eyes of a lynx.

INTRODUCTION

by Giulio Di Martino

"To those who never stop searching"

The most wonderful sensation we can experience is that of the mysterious. It constitutes the fundamental emotion at the basis of true art and true science. Anyone who has experienced it and who remains incapable of becoming excited is a sort of damaged ware, like an extinguished candle.
ALBERT EINSTEIN

I learned about Einstein's ideas on the university benches, in the theoretical physics department. But I could not imagine that my scientific degree would dissolve in an ocean larger than that of scientific research, or that I would end up immersing myself in the endless depths of the hunt for the great unresolved mysteries of history and archaeology. Ten years elapsed between travels and documentaries, theories and hypotheses, encounters and discoveries. Stories through images and words, attempting ever to shed light on the most obscure zones of our knowledge; to meet the challenge cast by the most enigmatic constructions on our planet;

to measure oneself with myths, legends, and civilizations remote from one another in time and space. To decipher a past that seems at times to recount a story different than the one we know. And after 10 years, this book. A journey within journeys.

A journey of discovery in 52 mysteries. Fifty-two, like the weeks that make up the year, or like the playing cards in a deck: the two different ways, in fact, that you can browse through this work. The first is to follow a "week by week" itinerary, leading along an ideal path, passing from one page to the following, from one mystery to the next, the one "bordering" on the previous.

So you can fantasize about departing on a year-long trip, crossing over the entire planet, following the traces of its greatest mysteries, stage after stage. Or you can "pick a card, any card" from the deck, letting it correspond to one of the 52 stories in this volume, to amaze you, to take you far away.

In recent years, one of the questions I have been most frequently asked is: "What has your most thrilling trip been, your most amazing mystery?" An easy answer is, paraphrasing the Turkish poet Nazim Hikmet, "Our most splendid journey is the one we have not yet taken." But that would be only a part – elegiac – of the truth. The other part is, rather, what pulsates in the memory.

First of all Rapa Nui, Easter Island. A small triangle of land lost in the Pacific Ocean, thousands of kilometers from everything.

And studded with enormous inscrutable stone faces.

Who do they represent? Why do the inhabitants of a place so separate from the rest of the world appear to have been "damned" into reproducing them? There is a precise point on the island, at the intersection between the edges of two craters, looking 300 m (984 ft) straight down over the ocean, where is easy to get overwhelmed by fantasies about ancient and unknown civilizations. And about what idea they could have had about the meaning of our existence.

You get a similar feeling on the tiny Isla del Sol in Lake Titicaca, a mirror of hypnotic, indescribably blue water. On its shores, the images in my head – slowed by the scarcity of oxygen – attempt to return back in time, to when the mysterious builders of Tiahuanaco erected, perhaps, the

_ (2-3)   The stone circle at Stonehenge, England, has been forever shrouded in mist and mystery.
_ (4-5)   The lost city of Machu Picchu is a jewel set among the Andean peaks.
_ (10-11) The Mayan calendar has a cyclical structure: it began on 11 August, 3114 BC and ends on 21 December, 2012.
_ (14-15) The eternal army of Xi'an has been protecting the secrets of the first Chinese emperor's tomb for centuries.
_ (16-17) The enigmatic face of the Sphinx on the Giza Plateau in Egypt seems to defy time and the truths of man.

capital of a vanished empire, on the shores of that enchanted lake. And then even further back, to millions of years ago, when the Andean uplands were, instead of 4000 m (13,123 ft) above sea level, at the bottom of the ocean, as their fossil seashells would appear to suggest.

Time is a concept you feel compelled, also, to consider while at the top of the steps of the marvelous Mayan pyramids in the Yucatán: beyond their aesthetic power, their secret tunnels, their hidden treasures, it is, above all, the obsession this people had about time that suggests you shift your gaze, change your focus. Each of their buildings or monuments seems, in fact, to have been built to measure, to relate, to calculate the passage of time and of the stars. Almost as though wanting to control it, to confine it in an eternal circumference it cannot escape: that is how their legendary calendar works. Cyclical, complicated, perfect. And destined to start up again on 21 December, 2012.

But the wildest and most poignant memory is connected with Uluru in the heart of the Australian desert. Which is perhaps just Nature at her purest. And even there, when the whole desert becomes dark with an implacable black, the gigantic sacred monolith continues to shine vividly its impossible red. A few minutes of genuine magic, and then everything disappears. You feel abandoned, lost in the darkness of a boundless solitude. And it's then that you can imagine what questions must have struck our ancient ancestors, those men who allowed us to become what we are today.

And maybe that is what travel is really for: finding new questions, rather than finding new answers. Like the scientists, as Einstein said, when they are confronted with the mystery. A vital and exhilarating thought: we have not yet figured it all out. Everything is not already here. It has not all been conceived already.

Some claim that we are safe as long as we still have a story to tell. I believe we are safe as long as there still exists a story to go looking for. As another Nobel laureate, José Saramago, wrote in his *Journey to Portugal*: "The journey never ends. Only travelers end. And they may be prolonged in memory, in the recalling, in the narrative. When the traveler sat on the sandy beach and said: 'There is nothing more to see,' he knew it was not true." It never is.

18

UNITED KINGDOM

Loch Ness

(57°18'N - 4°27'W)

THE MOST FAMOUS AND ELUSIVE MONSTER IN HISTORY SEEMS TO INHABIT ONE OF THE MOST BEAUTIFUL LAKES ON THE PLANET.

The Scottish highlands are without a doubt one of the most beautiful regions of Europe: the rugged mountains, the endless views, the yet untouched nature compose ancient and breathtaking scenery. The center's main region is Inverness, just a few kilometers from a freshwater lake that serves as the backdrop for one of the world's best-known legends, that of the Loch Ness monster. The lake, extending 37 km (23 mi), is one of the largest in the area, and it is in its very deep waters that an ancient and mysterious creatures supposedly lives. For about 80 years it has been chased after by thousands of curious visitors, as well as scientists, magnates, and researchers.

It all began on 2 May, 1933, when an article published in the *Inverness Courier* reported the first sighting of a strange animal in the lake. A couple, Mr. and Mrs. MacKay, claimed to have seen two disturbing humps emerging from the waters at Loch Ness. The episode is reminiscent of "the wild sea beast" described by St. Adomnán of Iona, a 7th-century Irish monk, in his work *Vita Columbae* (a hagiography of St. Columba). That creature came right out of the lake in 565 and it was expelled by St. Columba through the use of the cross and the famous phrase, "You shall go no further."

Six months after the 1933 appearance, the first photograph of the presumed Loch Ness monster was published, with the curved profile of the creature moving in front of the wave, raising several splashes of water. This, like all the following photographs and films, would fuel lively debates among experts, heated confrontations lasting up to the present day.

Among all the various shots of the mysterious creature, the one called "the surgeon's photo" became the icon of the legend. Robert Wilson took the photo in April, 1934, winning a place on various front pages of the times. But it was a fake, discovered 60 years later by researchers at the Loch Ness Centre, who tracked down the small model used by Wilson for orchestrating the hoax.

However, the other images remain controversial. The most famous, snapped in 1951 by Lachlan Stuart, is the one depicting three humps as they wind in and out of the surface of the lake. The first film was taken by Malcolm Irvine, showing nearly a minute of the presumed monster swimming below the surface of the lake. Also suggestive is the 1955 photograph taken by Peter MacNab, who immortalized something extremely long sliding along the surface of the Loch Ness waters near Urquhart Castle; owing to the view of the bastion in the frame, it is possible to estimate that the emerged part of the creature was about 20 m (65 ft) long.

In the 1950s, the popularity of the lake monster reached planetary levels. Curious people from all around the world came to Scotland to hunt for the mysterious creature, which was amicably dubbed Nessie.

_ (18-19) THE RUINS OF URQUHART CASTLE STAND AT WHAT IS PROBABLY THE MOST SUGGESTIVE AND SCENIC POINT OF THE ENTIRE COAST OF LOCH NESS. IN ANCIENT TIMES, IT WAS ONE OF THE MOST IMPOSING FORTRESSES OF MEDIEVAL SCOTLAND, AND IT IS RIGHT IN ITS VICINITY THAT THE MOST SIGHTINGS OF NESSIE HAVE OCCURRED, SUCH AS THE ONE IN 1955 BY PETER MACNAB.

_ (18 bottom) THE FAMOUS "SURGEON'S PHOTO": FOR MANY THIS REMAINS THE ICON OF THE LOCH NESS MONSTER. TAKEN BY ROBERT WILSON IN APRIL 1934, FOR MORE THAN HALF A CENTURY IT POPULATED PEOPLE'S IMAGINATIONS AND WAS THE SUBJECT OF MERCHANDISING OF MYSTERY. ONLY IN THE 1990S WAS IT DISCOVERED TO BE A WELL-CONCOCTED HOAX: THE SUBJECT OF THE PHOTO IS A SMALL WOODEN MODEL.

_ (20-21) Boston's Academy of Applied Sciences was the first to organize a scientific underwater expedition in 1970. The remote video cameras and sonar identified what seemed to be an aquatic creature several meters (yards) long lying on the bottom of the loch. In 1987, however, Project Deep Scan revealed that it was only a thick tree trunk covered with algae.

_ (21) The hunt for sightings of the monster knows no rest: from traditional binoculars of enthusiastic tourists to modern webcams installed along the coast of Loch Ness.

Another much-discussed film dating from 1960 was produced by a member of the RAF, Timothy Dinsdale; it showed a hump plowing through the water at great speed, leaving an impressive wake behind. The most recent film of Nessie was made in 2007; shot by Gordon Holmes, it shows a gigantic silhouette swimming in the lake. In August, 2009, even the public satellite images on Google Earth immortalized what seems to be an unknown aquatic creature.

There are those who believe the Loch Ness monster is a collective hallucination, others who believe it is a descendant of the ancient dinosaurs, others who believe it is a timeless monster, and still others who believe it is a series of jokes like Wilson's. In any case, the hunting expeditions seeking Nessie have continued for nearly 80 years, with remarkable deployments of increasingly advanced media and technologies. The entire lake has been scanned, monitored using underwater microphones, filled with enormous lures, repeatedly scanned with increasingly refined sonar, patrolled by submarines, and finally observed by satellites and webcams. Sometimes something unexplainable is recorded, while other times nothing out of the ordinary is found. But every time the case is declared closed, a new sighting calls everything back into question again. Like a monster that reappears from its secret lair after hibernation. Like a legend that can never die.

UNITED KINGDOM

Glamis Castle

(56°37'13"N - 3°0'10"W)

A MAGICAL PLACE, SHROUDED IN SCOTTISH MIST AND SUSPENDED AMID
SHAKESPEARE, CRUEL SECRETS, AND MYSTERIOUS GHOSTS.

In Scotland the idea of mystery immediately evokes ancient castles and ghost stories. And among all the legends of Scottish tradition, the prize for the most ghost-infested castle in Scotland goes without a doubt to Glamis Castle, owing to the sinister "Strathmore Curse" that hovers about the place. It all began in 1372 when Robert II of Scotland, the king who would found the House of Stuart, gave the castle to Sir John Lyon. But a spot of blood on the floor right at the entrance to the castle recalls that in 1034, King Malcolm II was brutally split in two here by the stroke of a claymore, the Scottish two-handed sword. No one has ever succeeded in removing the spot, and it may have been this that inspired Oscar Wilde's short story "The Canterville Ghost." However, Glamis's most famous ghost is that of Earl Beardie. Legend has it that one Sunday, Lord Beardie couldn't find anyone to play cards with (in fact, the Scottish church banned playing cards on the day of the Lord), and after he had maltreated several servants, he shouted that he would have played even "with the devil himself, until Judgment Day." At that moment, a stranger knocked at the castle and asked to play. The two closed themselves in a room, and no one ever heard anything more of Earl Beardie and the mysterious guest. But those living in the castle swear that during certain nights they have heard strange wails and the loud sound of dice. And many are convinced that they have met the spirit of Lord Beardie, tormented by endless gaming.

Glamis Castle is also the setting for William Shakespeare's *Macbeth*, the place where the protagonist, the general, supposedly assassinated King Duncan. But Macbeth is also the world's most feared drama – from the superstitious point of view – by theater companies; they do not even pronounce its name but rather refer to it as "the Scottish play." And performances of it have been marred by various misfortunes: 22 spectators died in riots stemming from the 1849 New York performance; three stage designers and costume designers died in a 1930 production; in 1948, an actress who was playing Lady Macbeth fell, during the sleepwalking scene, from a height of 5 m (about 16.5 ft). The production of the play has had its own package of fatal incidents and failures: sudden illnesses of actors, stages collapsing, stage weaponry causing actual wounds, entire electrical systems catching on fire. As though the prophecies of Shakespeare's fictional witches had cast a sinister shadow beyond the text.

And it was of witchcraft, in fact, that Janet Douglas, Lady Glamis, was accused in 1540. The castle was requisitioned by King James V and Lady Glamis was burned at the stake. The accusations were proved false and the castle was restored to the family, but ever since that time, the ghost, who became known as the Grey Lady, seemed to appear frequently to visitors to the castle. The family chapel annexed to Glamis Castle can host 46 people. But one of the places is always reserved for the Grey Lady, and no one, even today, dares sit in it.

There is also another female presence that many visitors through the centuries – even exceptional witnesses, such as the sister of the Queen Mother of England, who was born right at Glamis – have sworn having encountered along the corridors of Glamis Castle: the White Lady. Her story is unknown, but the different colors assigned to the two ancient ladies reflect the intensity of their presumed apparitions: the grey one is more subdued, sad, impalpable; the white, more vivid, aggressive, and brilliant.

But beyond these possible influences, the history of the inhabitants of Glamis Castle is marked by many dark events. The most terrible are doubtlessly those involving Count Patrick Strathmore, a dissolute and cruel man, during a war between Clan Lindsay and Clan Ogilvy. There came a point when he was asked asylum by the latter. Not being able to refuse them hospitality, he welcomed

_ (22-23) THE ACCESS TO GLAMIS CASTLE, A MILE LONG AVENUE: DEPENDING ON THE HOUR, THE COLORS OF THE ARCHITECTURAL COMPLEX AND ITS GARDENS PROVOKE QUITE DIFFERENT EMOTIONS. FROM THE MAGNIFICENCE OF THE DAY TO THE RESTLESSNESS OF THE SUNSET, ON TO THE MYSTERY THAT SEEMS TO ENWRAP THE ANCIENT WALLS AND THEIR SECRETS DURING THE NIGHT.

_ (24) THE LARGE SUNDIAL STANDS IMPOSINGLY IN THE CASTLE GARDENS, A FEW STEPS FROM THE ENTRANCE. BUILT IN 1671, AND STANDING 7 M (23 FT) HIGH, IT IS ONE OF SCOTLAND'S LARGEST SUNDIALS. BUT THERE ARE 83 MORE SUNDIALS THROUGHOUT THE GARDENS OF GLAMIS: A CURIOUS OBSESSION FOR THE SCANNING OF TIME IN THIS ENCHANTED PLACE.

them, but then he walled them up in a secret room, where they supposedly died of hunger and privation, after having fed upon one another. Supposedly even today you can hear desperate moans coming from inaccessible places in the castle.

There is another disquieting legend regarding the same Patrick: in another room in the castle, he supposedly locked up for life a child that was born with too much hair and with other never-revealed deformities; this child became known as the monster of Glamis, and he, as well, is mentioned in regard to many repeated sightings.

For centuries, guests, patrons, and researchers have been chasing after the castle's secret rooms. During a famous reception, the guests were asked to hang a towel out of every window they came across. When they met together outside the castle, they noted that in fully seven windows (but in other versions of the tale, the windows number two or 11), no towel was hanging: a clear sign that some secret rooms existed. The castle is open to the public today: it can be visited, and the most courageous can spend the night there. Lovers of mystery can even decide to celebrate their weddings here, in spite of the centuries-old "Strathmore Curse."

(24-25) THIRTEEN TOWERS, SPIRES THAT RISE INTO THE SKY, HUNDREDS OF ROOMS, SOME PERHAPS STILL SECRET: THE ARCHITECTURE OF GLAMIS CASTLE RECOUNTS AN ENDLESS SERIES OF INTERVENTIONS OVER THE CENTURIES, INCLUDING ALTERATIONS, ADDITIONS, AND RESTORATIONS. LIKE THE GREAT TOWER OF THE EAST WING, ADDED IN 1435.

_ (26-27) IN KING MALCOLM'S ROOM, THERE IS A BLOOD STAIN ON THE FLOOR THAT SEEMS IMPOSSIBLE TO REMOVE, IN SPITE OF NUMEROUS ATTEMPTS OVER THE CENTURIES. THE BILLIARD ROOM IS HOME TO SOME CHARMING AND QUITE RARE TAPESTRIES FROM THE 17TH CENTURY.

_ (27 top) THE DINING ROOM AT GLAMIS CASTLE HAS A MAGNIFICENT PANEL OF FINEST ENGLISH OAK. ITS CEILING IS DECORATED WITH A STUNNING COMPOSITION.

_ (27 bottom) EVEN TODAY, THE ROYAL APARTMENTS HOST THE BEDROOM OF THE QUEEN MOTHER OF ENGLAND, ELIZABETH BOWES-LYON, WHO SPENT PART OF HER CHILDHOOD HERE AT GLAMIS CASTLE.

_ (28-29) SUNRISE AND SUNSET ARE PERHAPS THE TIMES WHEN STONEHENGE REACHES THE MAXIMUM OF ITS EVOCATIVE POWER. IT IS THE PRECISE ALIGNMENT OF THE STONES WITH THE RAYS OF LIGHT ON SPECIFIC DAYS OF THE YEAR THAT RENDERS THIS CROMLECH SO FASCINATING AND MYSTERIOUS.

_ (28 bottom) STONEHENGE HAS INSPIRED MANY ARTISTS THROUGH THE COURSE OF THE CENTURIES, SUCH AS ROBERT HAVELL SENIOR, WHO MADE THIS PRINT IN 1815.

Stonehenge

(51°10'44"N - 1°49'35"W)

ONE OF THE MOST FAMOUS ICONS OF MYSTERY, IMMERSED
IN THE ANCIENT MISTS OF THE LEGENDARY DRUIDS.

One of the greatest enigmas of archaeology is undoubtedly in England, on Salisbury Plain. Stonehenge is a circle of megalithic stones built 5000 years ago. Its name derives from the combination of the words *stone* and *henge* (derived from the Old English *hung*, meaning "hanging" or "suspended"): the suspended stones. Questions about their origin and purpose have forever obsessed scientists and researchers: the treatises, books, studies, and hypotheses on the function of Stonehenge are, quite simply, countless.

The megaliths arranged in a circle display an alignment with the summer solstice, which suggests a link with ancient astronomical knowledge. But there is much more: the prestigious astronomer and mathematician Fred Hoyle hypothesized in 1972 that the entire complex was a refined astronomical calculator. The 56 holes present in the ground would allow precise calculations of the phases of the moon; the ditches would represent the orbits of the sun and moon just as they appeared to the prehistoric men who erected the complex. The astronomic knowledge assumed by Hoyle's hypothesis would be unthinkable for a civilization living 5000 years ago.

But Stonehenge's strength lies in its magical dimension: it was here that the ancient Celtic Druids officiated at their sacred rituals, and it is here, even today, that the priests of Wicca and other neo-pagan cults celebrate their occult ceremonies. Moreover, the figures of King Arthur and the legendary wizard Merlin are also linked with Stonehenge.

An ancient manuscript still conserved at the library of Corpus Christi College, Cambridge, depicts the circle of stones, embellished by a striking caption: "Stonehenge, near Amesbury in England. In 483 Merlin the Magician bore the Giants' Dance to Stonehenge."

British historian Geoffrey of Monmouth, in his *Vita Merlini* (or *The Life of Merlin*) from 1150, tells how the circular complex – called *Chorea Gigantum*, the Giants' Dance – was transported by means of gigantic beings from Africa as far as Mount Killaraus in Ireland. Then by magic, Merlin transported it over the sea to Salisbury plain: "... Merlin the Magician carried King Uther Pendragon, father of King Arthur, to Stonehenge, and told him: 'this monument shall be the testimony of your victory and that of Emrys. You owe it to the memory of your brother. But realize that it will be said that it is the Giants' Dance and that spirits come to this place, among the stones, every night, awaiting the light that will ignite the morning and give new life to the world.' "

Stonehenge marks a turning point in the construction of megalithic sites. Here, in fact, for the first time, the stones are linked together by a method referred to as the "mortise and tenon" joint: a true revolution for the presumed time of its construction, which highlights the importance and the technological advancement of the construction at the site. The mortise and tenon joint is a solution derived from the world of carpentry: a hole receives a piece specifically shaped to fit it.

But this is not all: the site also is composed of 43 (originally there were probably 80 or 90) so-called *bluestones*, by virtue of the color that they take on in contact with water; these are masses the like of which are not found within a radius of at least 240 km (150 mi), weighing more than a tonne. One wonders how these stones could have been brought to Stonehenge from such a great distance, and why for centuries it was believed that they had miraculous powers.

It probably took centuries to build Stonehenge. Its extremely heavy stones needed to travel hundreds of kilometers and it required a logistic organization involving various generations of ancient Britons. Why all this huge expenditure of energy? Perhaps Stonehenge has yet to reveal its true secret.

A fascinating new hypothesis was formulated in 2003 by Mike Parker Pearson, director of the Stonehenge Riverside Project.

_ (30 top) SEVERAL PROPOSALS HAVE BEEN MADE FOR THE VARIOUS RECONSTRUCTIONS OF THE STONEHENGE CIRCLE. THE MOST RELIABLE THEORIES HYPOTHESIZE THREE DIFFERENT BUILDING PHASES: THE FIRST DATING BACK TO 3100 BC, THE SECOND OCCURRING A CENTURY LATER, AND THE LAST BEGINNING AROUND 2600 BC AND TERMINATING AROUND 1600 BC. DIFFERENT PEOPLES HAVE MADE DIFFERENT USES OF THIS SACRED PLACE.

_ (30-31) WHEN WALKING THROUGH THE CROMLECH ON FOOT, IT IS POSSIBLE TO BECOME DISORIENTED BY THE PLACEMENT OF THE STONES, BUT A VIEW FROM ABOVE IMMEDIATELY HONORS STONEHENGE'S PERFECT ARCHITECTURAL DESIGN. THE RUINS, IN FACT, APPEAR ARRANGED ALONG AN EXACT CIRCUMFERENCE. A PROJECT CONCEIVED AND BEGUN OVER 5000 YEARS AGO.

Surveys and excavations carried out by the five universities involved in the project have pointed the finger at nearby Durrington Walls, a ring about 20 times as wide as that of Stonehenge that is only 3 km (1.9 mi) away. Inside it is a series of wooden circular monuments and, as at Stonehenge, an avenue that connected it to the River Avon.

But while 52 burial places have been found at Stonehenge, none at all have been found at Durrington Walls. All this has led to the suggestion that Stonehenge represented the city of the dead and of ancestors, while Durrington Walls represented that of the living. Stone would represent a hardening through eternity, and wood, the deterioration and impermanence of life.

The connection between the two sites is strengthened by the presence of roads connecting them to the River Avon: 3 km (1.9 mi) of road flanked by ditches and embankments. A ritual and metaphoric procession, realized by men of genius from ancient times whose thoughts we are not yet able to decipher.

UNITED KINGDOM

The Mysteries of Glastonbury

(51°8'41"N — 2°41'55"W)

THE LEGENDARY AVALON IS TO BE FOUND? IS THIS THE PLACE ABOUT WHICH THE ENTIRE KING ARTHUR LEGEND TURNS?

Avalon is the island sung about in many legends, the dwelling of Merlin the Magician, of Morgan le Fay, and of Vivian, the Lady of the Lake. It is the place where the legendary King Arthur was supposedly buried, where the Holy Grail itself might possibly be hidden. A mythical place, one that fog conceals from the eyes of all, except that there is evidence that suggests a different and incredible story.

For thousands of years, the island of Avalon was supposedly circular, surrounded by a shallow inland sea. Covered by a forest of oaks and elms, with a few patches of wild apple trees, it was formed of four hills, one of which, the Tor, towered over the others. Two springs issued forth from the foot of this hill; with its 158 m (518 ft) height, the hill was the only thing visible when the fog came up. With the passing of time, the island disappeared from history and vanished into its perennial mists, entering into legend.

And yet there are some people who believe that at Glastonbury it is possible to find traces of the existence of an actual Avalon. All the elements of the descriptions appear, somehow, to be present. Glastonbury is a small city in Somerset in southwestern England. One of its hills has been considered to be magic ever since ancient times, and the inhabitants call it the Tor. Centuries ago, seven enormous concentric terraces were carved into its sides, as well as a series of gates opening onto empty fenced areas, on up to the tower of St. Michael's Church rising at the top. The meaning of this complex remains unclear. Other controversial elements are the sources of Glastonbury, only 50 m (164 ft) distant from each other: the White Spring and the Blood Spring. The names are connected with the water issuing forth, milky white from the one, reddish from the other.

_ (32-33) WHEN THE TYPICAL SOUTHERN ENGLAND FOG RISES, THE HILL OF GLASTONBURY SEEMS TO LOSE ITS TIES WITH THE SURROUNDING COUNTRYSIDE. FROM A DISTANCE, IT LOOKS LIKE A FANTASTICAL ISLAND FLOATING IN THE CLOUDS, A VISION THAT EVOKES THE LEGENDARY ISLAND OF AVALON.

Moreover, the zone was rich with yew trees, rendering the place highly suggestive. According to tradition, an apple tree grows upon every enchanted island, and the name Avalon could mean "apple orchard": in Welsh, the word for apple is *aballon*. But in addition to the yew and apple trees at Glastonbury are two other venerated trees: ancient oaks named Gog and Magog, which have forever been considered the traditional point of access to Glastonbury. The sun's rays at dawn on the summer solstice transit the imaginary line joining the Tor with the two trees, as do the sun's rays at sunset on the winter solstice, confirming the importance of these trees. In the 18th century, they were part of a long avenue of oaks made by the Druids.

Chalice Hill is another of Glastonbury's hills, and another point of reference in the alignment of solstices. As its name would indicate, the hill is connected with the legend of the Holy Grail, supposedly hidden there by Joseph of Arimathea. It is said that when he thrust his staff into English soil, the Glastonbury Thorn sprang forth. It still flowers today at Christmas and Easter, and actually belongs to a species originating in the Holy Land. The last abbot of Glastonbury, Michael Whiting, before being killed by Cromwell's men in 1539, supposedly entrusted to his monks a wooden cup described as "the most precious treasure in the abbey," to be concealed in a safe place. Could this possibly be the chalice buried at Chalice Hill?

One fundamental detail keeps Glastonbury from being likened to the legendary Avalon: Glastonbury is not an island. But perhaps it might have been in the past.

_ (34) THE HILL OF GLASTONBURY HAS SEVEN LARGE TERRACES, WHOSE FUNCTION HAS NOT YET BEEN MADE CLEAR. SOME BELIEVE IT REPRESENTS AN INITIATORY JOURNEY: THE ACTUAL PEAK OF THE TOR OR, METAPHORICALLY, HEAVEN.

_ (34-35) THE CHURCH OF ST. MICHAEL, ON THE TOP OF THE TOR, WAS BUILT ON THE RUINS OF A FORT DATING FROM THE 5TH CENTURY AD. IT WAS DESTROYED BY A VIOLENT EARTHQUAKE IN 1275, AND AFTER ITS RECONSTRUCTION IT REMAINED ACTIVE UNTIL THE SUPPRESSION OF THE MONASTERIES IN 1539. THE TOWER DOMINATING GLASTONBURY TODAY IS A MODERN ESTORATION.

The region of Glastonbury is called Somerset, "the summer land," probably because during winter it could not be inhabited as it was submerged. For centuries, the entire area was supposedly an enormous marsh, as also demonstrated by the recent discovery of an ancient village on stilts. Thus, many centuries ago, Glastonbury appeared like an island enveloped by mists, just like the legendary Avalon. English historian Geoffrey of Monmouth narrates in his *Historia Regum Britanniae* that the body of King Arthur was borne to Glastonbury and buried there. In 1190, the presumed tomb of King Arthur was discovered after a Welsh bard revealed the secret of the burial to King Henry II. The tomb was discovered right in Glastonbury, in a pit adjacent to the St. Mary Chapel. The monks even created a false lead cross with the Latin inscription *Hic iacet sepultus inclitus Rex Arturius in insula Avalonia* ("Here lies the famous King Arthur, buried on the island of Avalon."). A false cross that since that time has drawn thousands of pilgrims from all around the world: men and women who visit Glastonbury and imagine it is the mythical Avalon, suspended in the mists of legend.

_ (36 top) TREES PLAY AN IMPORTANT ROLE IN THE HISTORY OF GLASTONBURY: IN ADDITION TO THE HAWTHORN (ALSO CALLED "HOLY THORN," SAID TO BE BORN FROM THE STAFF OF JOSEPH OF ARIMATHEA, AND WHICH BLOOMS ONLY AT EASTER AND CHRISTMAS), AN OLD OAK TREE SEEMS TO BE WHAT REMAINS FROM THE LEGENDARY GOG AND MAGOG, THE TREES THAT WERE PART OF THE DRUIDIC PATHWAY TOWARD THE TOR.

_ (36 bottom) CHALICE HILL IS A SOFT ROUND HILL FLANKING THE TOR. MANY RESEARCHERS IDENTIFY THIS AS THE PLACE CHOSEN BY THE LEGENDARY KNIGHTS OF THE ROUND TABLE, UNDER ORDERS OF KING ARTHUR, TO BURY AND HIDE THE HOLY GRAIL.

(36-37) GLASTONBURY ABBEY IS ONE OF THE MOST CHARMING PLACES IN ALL OF SOUTHERN ENGLAND. THE VIEW THAT ONCE EXTENDED FROM THE NORTH TRANSEPT TOWARD THE CHOIR NOW CROSSES SOME RUINS THAT HAVE BECOME AN ICON OF THE AREA ITSELF. INSIDE, ACCORDING TO LEGEND, THE BODIES OF KING ARTHUR AND HIS WIFE, GUINEVERE, MAY BE BURIED.

UNITED KINGDOM

The Giant of Cerne Abbas

(50°48'49"N   -   2°28'29"W)

A MYSTERY CARVED IN THE CHALK, AS LARGE AS AN ENTIRE ENGLISH HILLSIDE.

The county of Dorset in southern England, with its rolling hills and spellbinding cliffs adorned with nostalgic, solitary lighthouses, has inspired dreamers, writers, and creative people for generations. Its Jurassic Coast is also a unique heritage for geologists, with its 95 km (60 mi) of coastline in which fossils from every age are embedded, telling – like a monumental stone book – of the last 180 million years of our planet.

And right on one of the hills of Dorset, that of Cerne Abbas, a very ancient rebus appears engraved, remaining to be deciphered. It is known as "the giant of Cerne Abbas," or also "the rude giant": it is a pictogram in chalk portraying an imposing nude man brandishing an enormous club. Engraved in the belly of the hill, with channels 30 cm (12 in) deep and equally wide, the huge figure reaches 55 m (188 ft) in height and 51 m (167 ft) in width, allowing it to be seen from all the surrounding valleys. The club alone, which the giant bears in his fist, reaches 37 m (121 ft) in length. The impressive engraving stands out in vivid white, owing to the chalk found just beneath the soil on the hill of Cerne Abbas.

The impressive figure embraces within itself many mysteries: who made it, and in what era, and what was it supposed to represent? The main dispute is about the era of its creation. One possible clue comes from another similar hill, that of Uffington, upon which a powerful white horse is engraved, 114 m long and dug more than 1 m (3.3 ft) deep into the soil of the hill. The Uffington White Horse has in fact been dated to the Bronze Age, about 3000 years ago. Could the giant have been its contemporary?

The construction technique would suggest yes, but the problem lies in the historical sources: the oldest existing testimony of the "giant" dates only to 1694, when the parish of Cerne Abbas commissioned a cleaning and new engraving of the colossal chalk figure for three shillings. A study conducted by a team of archaeologists in 2008 indicated that a part of the ancient engraving was probably lost: in his left arm, the giant probably was holding a mantle or the skin of an animal. This detail has led to the elaboration of various fantastical theories: on the one hand, there are some who see this as confirmation that the pictogram is an ancient representation of a prehistoric hunter; on the other, there are those who see it as the solution to a rebus engraved over two centuries ago. The skin in the left arm could in fact be that of the legendary Nemean Lion, defeated by Hercules in the first of his 12 labors, which would make the Giant of Cerne Abbas a representation of the Greco-Roman mythological hero.

In keeping with this line of interpretation, the pictogram could be a caricature of Oliver Cromwell, the leader of the Republican revolution from the mid-17th century, who was mockingly dubbed "England's Hercules" by his detractors. The commissioner of the figure, then, could have been Baron Denzel Hollis, owner of the land and outspoken enemy of Cromwell.

Whatever its origin, the giant has watched over the local community since it was engraved into the hill at Cerne Abbas; it has become part of the folklore and legends of all of Dorset. The figure was concealed only for a brief period, during the Second World War. The British did not want to concede such an easily recognizable landmark to the Nazi Luftwaffe pilots.

Today the Giant of Cerne Abbas is worshipped by neopagan sects, and fertility ceremonies for those unable to have children are celebrated around his phallus. Some couples have even challenged cold full moon nights (as well as British laws) to make love right on the grass composing the giant's genitals, hoping for his powerful, ancient, mysterious blessing.

_ (39) AN AERIAL VIEW PRESENTS US WITH A COMPLETE IMAGE OF THE GIANT OF CERNE ABBAS. A SORT OF MONUMENTAL FRESCO MORE THAN 50 M (164 FT) WIDE AND TALL. THE WHITE IS DUE TO THE CHALK THAT COMPOSES THE UNDERGROUND LAYER OF THE HILL, WHICH IS CARVED TO A DEPTH OF FULLY 30 CM (1 FT) IN ORDER TO MAINTAIN THE VIVIDNESS OF THE COLOSSAL PHALLIC DESIGN.

_ (40-41) THE WHITE HORSE OF UFFINGTON, WHICH IS ALSO CARVED INTO THE HILL, IS LOCATED NOT FAR FROM THE GIANT OF CERNE ABBAS. SCIENTIFIC TESTS ACCURATELY TRACE IT BACK TO ABOUT 3000 YEARS AGO. NOT ALL, HOWEVER, ARE CONVINCED THAT THE PREHISTORIC ANIMAL PORTRAYED IS ACTUALLY A HORSE. AMONG THE MANY HYPOTHESES, THE MOST INTERESTING IMAGINES IT AS A MYTHOLOGICAL DRAGON.

GERMANY

The Goseck Circle

(51°12'01"N — 11°51'51"E)

THE OLDEST SOLAR OBSERVATORY EVER FOUND, OLDER EVEN THAN THE LEGENDARY STONEHENGE.

The state of Saxony in eastern Germany is an aristocratic land, rich with castles, libraries, and art galleries. But the greatest of its treasures is not conserved in any collection or museum; instead, it is engraved deep into the countryside and it is considered the most ancient astronomical observatory of Europe. It is known as Goseck Circle, named for the nearby town in the Burgenlandkreis district. But it has also been dubbed the "German Stonehenge" since it opened to the public in 2003.

The complex is a set of concentric trenches dug into the ground to form a circle 75 m (246 ft) in diameter. Inside, two circular palisades open only at the points of three gates precisely arranged for observing the movements of the sun and stars. The structure would appear to date from the Neolithic period: some artifacts found in the area set the clock back to 5000 BC, fully 2000 years before Stonehenge. And yet, according to official archaeology, the prehistoric man of that period did not possess the mathematical or astronomical knowledge to realize Goseck Circle, let alone use it as an observatory. The incredible German structure seems to want to force us to rewrite history, or to formulate science-fiction hypotheses.

Some pilots discovered the Circle in 2002 as they were flying over Saxony. They noted how the grain was growing in accordance with a strange circular geometry. Originally it consisted of four concentric circles, a tumulus, a ditch, and two wooden palisades at human height, open at three series of gates: one facing southeast, one facing southwest, and one facing north. A person standing at the center of the circle on the day of the winter solstice 7000 years ago would have seen the sun rising and setting through the two gates facing toward the south. There still is no explanation for the gate facing north.

But Goseck is only the oldest and the most important of an incredible series of similar prehistoric sites scattered throughout the area: more than 200 observatories are distributed throughout Germany, Austria, and Croatia. In this very ancient site, however, it was not just the stars in the heavens that were observed. In this sacred complex, mysterious and forgotten ceremonies took place. Archaeological excavations here have unearthed human bones and skeletons of decapitated animals, probably traces of sacrifices in honor of divinities from an unknown past.

The Goseck Circle seems to resolve another mystery of the past: that of the legendary Nebra Sky Disk. In 1999, an incredible circular metal object was discovered at Nebra, Germany, inside some stone tombs: a bronze disk with a diameter of 32 cm (12.6 in) onto which plaques of gold are attached, depicting the sun, moon, and a series of seven stars — which some researchers have identified as the constellation of the Pleiades — as well as 23 additional stars that have not been identified. Also present are three plaques in the form of an arc, two of which describe the movements of the sun. The third plaque represents a watercraft, which might refer to the ancient legend of the solar bark responsible for the heavenly journey of the sun by night. The artifact is 3600 years old and is considered the world's first map of the stars. The town of Nebra is only 25 km (15.5 mi) from Goseck Circle: the enigmatic disk could represent a synthesis of all the knowledge of the priests who observed

_ (42 and 43) THE GOSECK CIRCLE IS ABOUT 7000 YEARS OLD. THE CIRCULAR STRUCTURE THAT HAS BEEN RECONSTRUCTED HAS A DIAMETER OF 75 M (246 FT) AND IS COMPOSED OF TWO CONCENTRIC RINGS OF WOODEN PALISADES, 2.5 M (8.2 FT) HIGH, OPENING AT THREE GATES.

_ (42-43) IT IS NOT CLEAR WHY THE SITE OF GOSECK WAS ABANDONED. ARCHAEOLOGISTS HAVE FOUND TRACES OF CARBONIZED HUMAN AND ANIMAL REMAINS, A DETAIL THAT SUGGESTS THE ANCIENT CIRCLE MAY HAVE BEEN USED FOR PERFORMING SACRIFICES.

and studied the heavens from the center of the complex at Goseck. In light of these considerations, the barbaric image commonly attributed to ancient central-northern Europe, always depicted as backward and a far cry from Greece or Egypt, needs to be totally reviewed. Does history need to be rewritten? The answer to this question appears to be concealed in the 200 astronomical observatories abandoned in the cold lands of central northern Europe.

FRANCE

The Carnac Stones

(47°35'31"N   -   3°5'5"W)

AN "ARMY" OF STONE THAT HAS BEEN CLOSING ITS RANKS IN BRITTANY FOR CENTURIES, ALMOST AS THOUGH GUARDING A SECRET, STILL INVIOLATE.

In Brittany to the northwest of France stands the largest complex of megaliths on the planet. Nearly 3000 gigantic stones embedded in the ground, sometimes in circles, sometimes in alignments. Whoever realized these cyclopean works, and what their purpose may have been, remain unresolved enigmas. They are known as the megaliths of Carnac, taking their name after a small village in the middle of this incredible book of stone. The entire zone doubtlessly has a millennial history, one that has not yet been entirely reconstructed. One of the most ancient stone constructions in Europe, the tumulus of Kercado, is located right here in the midst of these prehistoric masses, and as early as 10,000 BC, ancient fishermen were burying their dead here.

One can encounter mysterious monuments of every shape and size: in addition to these suggestive alignments, one can also find gallery tombs, dolmens, isolated menhirs, circular tumuluses. From the tumulus of Saint-Michel is possible to embrace with one's gaze the entire expanse of megaliths on the one side and the tumultuous Brittany coast on the other. The alignment of Le Ménec, preceded by a huge cromlech exceeding 100 m (328 ft) in diameter, is impressive with its 11 parallel rows of monoliths; then, to close the alignment, there is another cromlech of 90 m (295 ft). Not far away are 10 more rows, formed by monoliths varying from 6.5 m (21.3 ft) at the beginning to 60 cm (2.0 ft) at the end: it is the Kermario alignment, translating as "village of the dead." Lost among the various menhir compositions, the colossal "Manio Giant" stands out, an imposing menhir of nearly

_ (44-45) THE ALIGNMENT OF LE MÉNEC, 11 CONVERGENT ROWS OF MENHIRS, OCCUPIES AN AREA 100 M (328 FT) WIDE AND MORE THAN 1 KM (0.6 MI) LONG. THE WESTERN END HAS A CROMLECH OF 71 STONE BLOCKS, WHILE THE ONE AT THE OTHER END IS TOO DAMAGED TO BE INTERPRETED.

6 m (19.7 ft). The third large alignment, then, is that of the Kerlescan, or the "place of cremation," pointing to the east and consisting of 13 parallel rows of 555 stones. The impressive total is about 3000 menhirs, arranged in platoons of 10 or more lines stretching over a length of more than 3 km (1.9 mi). And many have been lost, destroyed, or stolen over time.

There are many hypotheses regarding the ancient men who built all these monuments, and just as many fantasies of those who view this as a sacred place, magical and rich in spiritual energies. According to Professor Alexander Thom, Carnac would be an astronomical clock of colossal proportions, created by prehistoric men to predict seasons and lunar cycles. If this were true, the geometric, algebraic, and astronomic knowledge possessed by these men from the Neolithic era must have been inconceivable. The center of the astronomic complex would have been the Mané-er-Hroek monolith – the "stone of the fairy" – now lying on the ground, struck by lightning in the 18th century. Carved from a single block of granite, and 20 m (65.6 ft) or more in height, it would have been visible within a radius of 13 km (8.1 mi). At any point within the area of the Carnac alignments, it would have been possible to use as a visual reference for sighting the movements of the moon or the sun, for example, or for predicting phenomena such as eclipses. But there are some who maintain that the enormous area of land and the thousands of standing monoliths would have constituted an excessively oversized work for such a purpose. Another widely accepted hypothesis is one that views this as a

_ (46-47) DAWN RISING ON THE KERMARIO ALIGNMENT REVEALS ITS INTERESTING STRUCTURE: AN AVENUE EXTENDING FOR 1120 M (0.7 MI), COMPOSED OF 1029 MENHIRS, ARRANGED ALONG 10 ROWS OF INCIDENT STRAIGHT LINES. KERMARIO IS ONLY 400 M (1312 FT) AWAY FROM THE ALIGNMENT OF LE MÉNEC, AND HIS NAME IN THE BRETON LANGUAGE MEANS "THE VILLAGE OF THE DEAD."

civilization obsessed with the cult of the dead: the original 5000 stones would have been tributes to the dead, rising from a place characterized by a particularly mystical aura, which, according to devotees of neopaganism, would still be perceptible even today. There are even those who believe that it could be an articulate and enormous sacred area, in which the rows would represent access roads to consecrated circles. Inside these, ancient and mysterious ceremonies would have taken place, the memory of which is now lost. To this day, the name of the civilization that might have created this cult center remains unknown, as do the names of the gods they worshipped. Lastly, a colorful local legend has it that the alignments of Carnac are the remains of a contingent of Roman soldiers who were magically transformed into stone by St. Cornelius, a pope who lived in the 3rd century, to save Brittany from invaders.

_ (47) THE LARGEST STONES OF THE ALIGNMENT OF LE MÉNEC REACH 4 M (13 FT) IN HEIGHT AND ARE LOCATED NEAR THE WESTERN EDGE OF THE COMPLEX. THE ROCKS GRADUALLY BECOME SHORTER, REACHING 60 CM (24 IN), THEN INCREASE IN SIZE AGAIN UNTIL REACHING THE EASTERN BORDER. DAWN IS CERTAINLY THE MOST SUGGESTIVE MOMENT FOR ADMIRING THEM.

48

_ (48-49) THE MYSTERIOUS TUMULUS OF GAVRINIS WAS FOUND ON THE SMALL DESERTED ISLAND OF THE SAME NAME IN BRITTANY. IT IS A STONE BURIAL CHAMBER DATING FROM THE NEOLITHIC PERIOD: A CIRCULAR STRUCTURE OF 100 M (328 FT) IN DIAMETER HOSTING A GALLERY WHERE 29 STONES BEAR MYSTERIOUS SYMBOLIC ENGRAVINGS.

_ (49) IT HAS BEEN CALCULATED THAT A TOTAL OF 2934 MENHIRS ARE PRESENT TODAY AT CARNAC. THE TALLEST REACH UP TO 7 M (23 FT) IN HEIGHT, WHILE THE SMALLEST ARE LESS THAN A TENTH OF THAT SIZE. BUT WHAT WAS THEIR TRUE FUNCTION: FUNERARY MONUMENTS OR ASTRONOMICAL MECHANISMS?

FRANCE

The Cathedral of Chartres

(48°26'50"N - 1°29'16"E)

A MASTERPIECE OF ARCHITECTURE WITH SUGGESTIVE ECHOES OF THE TEMPLARS AND OF THE LEGENDARY ARK OF THE COVENANT.

In 1135, the Cistercian monks began constructing the Cathedral of Our Lady of Chartres (Notre-Dame de Chartres) in the village of Chartres, 95 km (60 mi) southwest of Paris. The religious building presents an architectural plan and intersections that are absolutely unique. The Cistercian order was closely linked to that of the Knights Templar through the figure of Bernard of Clairvaux. And the Knights Templar were the keepers of the knowledge – along with many other secrets – relating to the construction of the cathedrals. Among the Templars' many objectives, however, was also that of gathering and conserving the relics of Christianity, and in this, Chartres may also have played a very important role.

The first phase of work on the Cathedral of Chartres terminated in 1240, 105 years after the start of construction, even though it still lacked the towers and other details. The solemn consecration took place in 1260.

One of the most astonishing elements of Chartres is a labyrinth found on the floor of the cathedral. The number of stones composing it is equal to the number of days of human gestation. For many scholars, this labyrinth would represent an *initiatory journey*: to traverse it from the outside toward the center signifies metaphorically to grow spiritually and be born into a new life. But not only this: the path, which continually varies in distance, becoming closer and farther from the destination, is an allegory of how tortuous the road to enlightenment is and how it puts to the test the true desire to achieve it. The 261 m (856 ft) of pathway inside the labyrinth were to be traveled on the knees, wearing a rosary around the neck and praying ceaselessly. Even today it is possible to witness such a practice performed by spiritual groups on the day of the summer solstice, June 21. The exact same labyrinth can be found at Alatri, not far from Rome, but instead of the large rose motif present at Chartres, a depiction of Christ appears at the center of the Alatri maze.

The mysteries of Chartres are not limited to the labyrinth, but involve all its dimensions: the great central nave, 74 m (243 ft) long, is crossed by an imaginary line, 37 m (121 ft) long, running through the choir. Adding 74 and 37, we obtain 111. This number also appears in many other sites of the Templars; it inextricably links Chartres with Castel del Monte in Puglia and with the pyramid of Cheops in Egypt: all three great monuments, in fact, are located on a straight line that unites them, and in all three the number 111, along with its two elective addends, 74 and 37, recurs in various architectural elements.

Chartres is the only Gothic cathedral that still conserves its original stained-glass windows. They are certainly an artistic masterpiece, a collection unique to the world, with more than 4000 personages represented. Light is one of the great protagonists of the cathedral's magic atmosphere: whether the outside light is dim or bright, the windows seem to glow with the same luminosity. In both daylight and dusk, the windows seem to diffuse the same enchanted aura within the interior of Chartres.

_ (50) IN THE MAGNIFICENT STAINED GLASS WINDOW OF SAINT APOLLINAIRE, A HOLE WAS DELIBERATELY LEFT BY THE BUILDERS: ON THE EXACT DAY OF THE SUMMER SOLSTICE, THE RAYS OF SUN PASSING THROUGH IT REFLECT UPON A STONE THAT IS DIFFERENT FROM THE OTHERS (OBLIQUE AND LIGHT-COLORED) ON THE FLOOR OF THE WEST NAVE. WAS THIS JUST A GAME OF THE DESIGNER OR A CLUE TO BE DECIPHERED?

_ (50-51) THE CATHEDRAL OF OUR LADY OF CHARTRES HAS A TWOFOLD LINK WITH LIGHT. BESIDES THE WINDOW OF ST. APOLLINAIRE, THE OTHER STAINED GLASS WINDOWS ALSO SET OFF A LITTLE BIT OF "MAGIC": REGARDLESS OF THE DEGREE OF LIGHT OUTSIDE THE BUILDING, FROM DAWN TO DUSK, THE WINDOWS ALWAYS SHINE WITH THE SAME INTENSITY FOR SOMEONE STANDING ON THE INSIDE.

_ (52 and 53) THE PICTURESQUE NORTH PORTAL OF THE CATHEDRAL SHOWS DIFFERENT SCENES, SOME FROM THE OLD TESTAMENT AND OTHERS FROM THE LIFE OF THE VIRGIN MARY. ONE OF THE MOST THRILLING PORTRAYS ABRAHAM GRASPING THE ARMS OF HIS SON ISAAC, READY TO SACRIFICE HIM. THE MAGNIFICENT STATUES WERE ALL CREATED BETWEEN 1205 AND 1210. BUT THE PORTAL IS ALSO CALLED THE PORTAL OF THE COVENANT SINCE IT DEPICTS THE LEGENDARY ARK OF THE COVENANT, UNDER WHICH AN ENGRAVING READS: HIC AMITTITUR ARCHA FEDERIS, OR "THE ARK WAS SENT HERE."

_ (54-55) THE FAMOUS LABYRINTH AT CHARTRES IS ONE OF THE CATHEDRAL'S MAJOR ATTRACTIONS: ITS NUMBER OF STONES IS THE SAME AS THE NUMBER OF DAYS OF A WOMAN'S GESTATION, SO TRAVERSING THEM IS A CLEAR SYMBOLIC JOURNEY FOR BEING REBORN TO A NEW LIFE. EVEN TODAY, DURING THE SUMMER SOLSTICE, MANY MEN AND WOMEN TRAVEL ITS 261 M (856 FT) WHILE PRAYING.

Some think that this effect is due to an external iridescence of the glass, to the secret components with which it was produced. There is also an enigma that no one has yet been able to decipher: in the window of Saint Apollinaire, a small circular space left without stained glass allows a ray of direct light to filter through. This would not be so strange except for the fact that, exactly on the day of the summer solstice, the ray goes to strike the only oblique stone on the floor, in the west end of the nave, one that is whiter than the others, causing to shine a small, golden-colored metal plate inserted especially at that point on the stone. In a cathedral, where nothing is left to chance, and where symbols and metaphors chase after one another, this ancient and sophisticated play of ancient engineering cannot be without significance. No one has yet managed to explain it.

Some have imagined that the great secret of Chartres concerns the legendary Ark of the Covenant: in fact, on a column in the north portal of the Cathedral, there is a representation of the Ark and its sacred contents. And immediately below, an engraving in Medieval Latin reads *Hic Amittitur Archa Federis*, which can be interpreted as "the Ark has been sent here." Perhaps even directly through the order of the Knights Templar. Could it still be buried beneath the splendid and majestic crypt of the mysterious Cathedral of Our Lady of Chartres?

VATICAN CITY

The Secrets of the Popes

(41°54'8"N - 12°27'12"E)

IN THE HEART OF THE ETERNAL CITY, AN ANCIENT SECRET ARCHIVE CONTAINS DOCUMENTS THAT REVEAL SHOCKING PROPHECIES.

The Vatican is the heart of Christianity, in Rome, the Eternal City. It is the smallest independent state in the world, but it certainly does lie at the center of history. Its marvelous buildings, the artistic masterpieces that adorn them, the relics contained within them: everything points to the sacred, but also to the power, spiritual and otherwise, that these locations have emanated for centuries. And also to the intrigues and the many secrets hidden in the boundless Vatican libraries.

One of the most incredible pages relating to the Vatican is the prophecy – made by a saint – about the end of the Catholic Church itself: the prophecy of St. Malachy. His most disturbing passage reads: "During the last persecution of the Holy Roman Church, Peter the Roman will sit, and he will shepherd the flocks among many tribulations; once these have passed, the City of Seven Hills will collapse, and the Dreadful Judge will judge his people. Amen."

According to legend, St. Malachy received a vision indicating all the popes who, from that day forward, would rise to the papal throne. This occurred in 1148 but the manuscripts were published only in 1595, as the *Prophetia de summis pontificibus*, drawn up by the Benedictine monk Arnold Wion. It is a list of 112 popes: to each pope, one line is dedicated, a few words in Latin anticipating his election. The list begins with Celestine II and seems to end right at Benedict XVI. The first pope on the list, Celestine II, is announced with the phrase *Ex castro Tiberis*, which one can translate as "from a castle on the Tiber": the pontiff, indeed, was a native of Città di Castello ("the city of the castle"), the first Umbrian center in the upper valley of the Tiber River.

For Lucius II, the prophecy announces: *Inimicus expulsus*, meaning "the enemy expelled," and the surname of the future pope was nothing other than Caccianemici (literally, "enemy-chaser"). The famous Celestine V was prophesied by the phrase *Ex eremo celsus*, "elevated from the hermitage": Pietro da Morrone was indeed a hermit.

Even if the coincidences seem impressive, we must always remember that there is a broad margin of personal discretion in the retrospective interpretation of a prophecy. The 107th pope predicted by St. Malachy is identified by the phrase *Pastor et Nauta*, "shepherd and mariner." Angelo Roncalli was a man of humble origins (*pastor*) and he was Patriarch of Venice, the city on the water. Number 108 is prophesied as *Flos Florum*, that is, "the flower of flowers." In the coat of arms of Giovanbattista Montini, the future Pope Paul VI, three lilies appear; this plant has always been called "the flower of flowers." In 1978, it was Albino Luciani who rose to the papal throne: his pontificate, however, lasted only 33 days, and for him, St. Malachy had predicted: *De medietate lunae*, which some have interpreted as "the time of one moon," just the duration of his papacy. The next 27 years were those of John Paul II, who is announced in the prophecy as *De Labore Solis*, which can be translated as "by the effort of the sun." Some people have interpreted the prophecy with the consideration that Karol Wojtyla was the pope who visited more countries than any other. Lastly, for the final pope predicted by the sayings of Malachy, we read the phrase *Gloria Olivae*. The interpretation in relation to

_ (56) THE PROPHET MALACHY APPEARS IN THE GOLDEN ALTARPIECE AT THE BASILICA OF SAN MARCO IN VENICE.

_ (56-57) THE SECRETS OF THE VATICAN HAVE ALWAYS GIVEN RISE TO THE MOST INCREDIBLE FANTASIES. IN PARTICULAR, THE COLLECTION OF DOCUMENTS KEPT IN THE SECRET VATICAN ARCHIVES APPEARS TO CONTAIN VERY OLD AND UNSETTLING PROPHECIES.

Pope Benedict XVI is still confused. Benedict XVI is thus the last pope to whom the prophecy dedicates just one line. Then would come the time of Peter the Roman, and with him, the end of the Catholic Church. He could be a Roman priest, a cardinal operating in Rome, or even a pope who takes the name of Peter II. According to this hypothesis, just as Peter received the mandate from Jesus to build his Church, so would Peter II return the Church to Christ. A circle that closes itself perfectly.

That is, assuming you want to believe in the prophecies of the saint.

58

Castel del Monte

(41°5'5"N - 16°16'16"E)

IN SOUTHERN ITALY, HALFWAY BETWEEN FRANCE AND EGYPT, A MAJESTIC AND INCOMPREHENSIBLE EDIFICE CHALLENGES HUNTERS OF SECRETS.

Castel del Monte is one of the most enigmatic castles in the world. Built on top of a hill 465 m (about 500 yards) high, it lies on the imaginary line connecting Jerusalem with Rome. In the 13th century, this is how far the Holy Roman Empire extended, governed by Frederick II of Swabia, the ruler known as *Stupor mundi*, "the wonder of the world." It is uncertain when the castle was built – it is assumed to have been built between 1230 and 1240 – just as its intended purpose is unknown. There are no moats or drawbridges for defending against enemy attacks, nor are there spaces for lodging garrisons, stocks, kitchens, or storerooms. Some have advanced the hypothesis that it might have been a hunting lodge, or a stopover place from which the sovereign departed on his hunting trips, but there remains the stumbling block of the excessive majesty of the building. Many agree, however, that Frederick II had built it in keeping with a quite precise, secret design. Nothing here seems to have been left to chance, beginning even with the choice of location. Castel del Monte is located about halfway between the Cathedral of Chartres and the great pyramid of Cheops, exactly along the line that unites them. Considering that it is the last of the three monuments to have been built, could this be pure coincidence?

But that is not all: the plan of the castle is octagonal; there are eight towers, each also of octagonal plan. On each of the two floors are eight rooms with windows facing onto an inner courtyard, also octagonal, and at the center of this there was originally a basin, also with eight sides. On the external portal and at the entrances to the various rooms are representations of various types of flowers in groups of eight. There are also petals in groups of eight on the capitals of the rooms, and other details of the construction represent the number eight in an obsessive manner. No explanation has yet been found for the recurrence of this number.

Frederick II of Swabia was attracted by the Orient. Even though he ruled the Holy Roman Empire, he was excommunicated twice and waged war against the papacy. His court, a rare example of magnificence, was frequented by poets, magicians, and alchemists. For the esoteric tradition, the octagon was the figure that united earth and heaven. Historically, in baptisteries, usually of octagonal plan, this form was a tribute to the relationship between the infant and God. There is also another number that recurs and that would seem to link the Castel del Monte with ancient Egypt. The number 111 (calculated in cubits, the unit of measure of the Egyptians) turns out to be one of the key numbers in the great pyramid of Giza, along with its two addends, 74 and 37 (the same numbers often return in the

_ (58-59) WHEN LOOKING FROM AFAR AT CASTEL DEL MONTE, WE IMMEDIATELY PERCEIVE ITS SINGULARITY: WHY WOULD SUCH AN IMPOSING CASTLE HAVE NO SYSTEM OF DEFENSE? WHY IS IT PERCHED ON TOP OF A HILL WITHOUT ANY PROTECTION? AND WHERE ARE ALL THE NECESSARY ANCILLARY STRUCTURES FOR GARRISONS AND STAFF?

_ (58) INITIAL LETTER WITH FREDERICK II, KING OF SICILY, MINIATURE FROM A CHRONICLE FROM 1344. DUKE OF SWABIA, KING OF GERMANY, EMPEROR OF THE ROMANS, KING OF JERUSALEM. BELONGING TO THE HOHENSTAUFEN FAMILY AND DESCENDANT OF THE ALTAVILLA DYNASTY, HE WAS KNOWN AS "STUPOR MUNDI" OR "PUER APULIAE," MEANING, RESPECTIVELY, WONDER OF THE WORLD AND BOY OF PUGLIA.

_ (60-61 and 61) THE ENTIRE STRUCTURE OF CASTEL DEL MONTE DISPLAYS A MANIFEST OBSESSION FOR GEOMETRY: FROM ABOVE AND FROM INSIDE ITS COURTYARD, IT IS EASY TO APPRECIATE THE DOUBLE OCTAGON THAT CHARACTERIZES THE ENTIRE ARCHITECTURAL PROJECT. AND THAT IS NOT ALL: THE EIGHT TOWERS SURROUNDING IT HAVE AN OCTAGONAL BASE, AND EACH FLOOR CONTAINS EIGHT ROOMS.

mysterious Cathedral of Chartres). The sum of the widths of the six visible faces of each of the eight towers of Castel del Monte is equal to 37 Egyptian cubits, and the sum of the lengths of the walls of the courtyard is equal to 111 Egyptian cubits. And not only did Frederick II use numbers that were dear to the Egyptians, but he also took inspiration from their method of construction. In fact, on particular days, the shadows projected by the sun indicate quite precise points. And furthermore, 26 December, 1194 is the date of the birth of Frederick II, who lived for 56 years; six façades for each of the eight octagonal towers make 48, which, when added to the eight outer walls, give 56, the exact number of years that the emperor lived.

Simply games with numbers? Perhaps. But there are some who believe that the impressive construction was an enormous safe erected to enclose a legendary object: the Holy Grail. The entire castle would represent the legendary lost chalice. When Frederick II died in 1250, he was robed, as he had asked to be, in the habit of the Cistercian monks, the order that built the Temple of Chartres and inspired the Knights Templar. For some, this would be a further indication that the sacred relic had passed through or is still hidden within the emperor's spectacular castle.

ROMANIA

In Dracula's Court

(45°30'54"N - 25°22'2"E)

AMID HISTORY AND LEGEND, TRANSYLVANIA IS HOME TO SEVERAL PLACES THAT WERE THE SCENES OF PRINCE VLAD'S CRUEL ATROCITIES.

Created by Irish writer Bram Stoker in 1897, Dracula is one of the symbolic personages of the horror genre. Ever since the day his eponymous novel was published, many researchers have attempted to identify real traces of his story, to identify what actually existing person might have inspired Stoker's vampire, and to determine the location of his sinister castle.

The vampire is one of the oldest figures in mythology. In ancient Babylonia, in Egypt, in South America, nearly all civilizations have tales of undead creatures who chase after living beings. But Stoker chose Romania as the location for his novel. The reason for this choice may be based on its unique combination of elements: wilderness, Gothic cities, and a bloodthirsty prince. Romania is a very mysterious place, perhaps the most enigmatic of Europe. And in this region, Dracula is not only a character in a novel, but his name also refers to a murderer in the flesh, a notorious nobleman who lived in the 15th century, Vlad III Dracula. Nicknamed Vlad Tepes – Vlad the Impaler – he was the son of Vlad Dràcul, an obscure member of the Order of the Dragon, and in those times, the word for dragon translated as "devil." The members of this order wore long black cloaks and red caps.

Vlad was born around 1431 at Sighişoara, which today is one of the best-conserved medieval fortresses of Europe, called the "Pearl of Transylvania." The house where Vlad was born is known today by the name of Casa Dràcul, and it is marked by a sign and the emblem of the Dragon. The medieval fresco inside is the only known portrait of Vlad Dràcul. Just three doors ahead, in the belly of a gigantic bell tower, there is a museum conserving chilling examples of some of Vlad's favorite torture instruments.

The mad exploits of Dracula were already being recounted in the mid-15th century. The protagonist, who actually lived, was a warlord, the prince of Wallachia, a region now in Romania. Already in life he was considered a bloodthirsty monster, and his reputation grew with the passing of time. Crowds filled the streets throughout Europe to hear the latest macabre exploits of Dracula, famous for his perverse pleasure in personally torturing and killing his enemies. There are numerous traits in common between the character of Dracula, created by Bram Stoker, and Vlad III, the primary of which was an obsession for other people's blood.

Wallachia was the kingdom of Vlad Dracula, and perhaps the realm of the true vampire: today Targovişte, the capital and fortress of Vlad Dracula, is in ruins. The most imposing structure still standing is the Tower of Chindia, built by the prince himself. It was probably here that he plotted some of his bloodiest revenge. The prisoners who were spared impalement were sent to build the dark Poenari Castle 80 km (50 mi) away. This was an ancient fortress that Vlad had decided to restore in order to make it his own citadel. Defined as "the citadel of the prince of darkness," this was the real lair of Dracula.

However, Bram Stoker set his novel along Borgo Pass, a very old road in an enchanting mountain region, the area

_ (62-63) THE FALLING OF DUSK IGNITES FANTASIES AND ANIMATES THE SINISTER LEGENDS OF TRANSYLVANIA. THE ARCHITECTURE OF BRAN CASTLE COINCIDES WITH THE DESCRIPTIONS OF THE RESIDENCE OF DRACULA, THE FAMOUS VAMPIRE CREATED BY BRAM STOKER. THE FOREST, FURTHERMORE, FEEDS THE POWERFUL AURA OF THE BUILDING'S RESTLESSNESS.

_ (64) BRAN CASTLE DOMINATES THE CITY OF BRAȘOV. BY DAY, ITS CHARACTERISTIC ROOFS EVOKE FAIRY-TALE SCENARIOS, UNLIKE THE NIGHT. THE ENTIRE BUILDING STANDS ON WHAT WAS ONCE A FORTRESS FOR THE ORDER OF TEUTONIC KNIGHTS. THE CURRENT STRUCTURE DATES BACK TO 1377. LOOKING AT IT FROM ABOVE, HOWEVER, WE NOTE THAT THE MAJOR RIVER APPEARING IN BRAM STOKER'S NOVEL IS ABSENT.

_ (65) THE MOST FAMOUS PORTRAIT OF VLAD III DATES FROM 1560 AND IS CONSERVED AT AMBRAS CASTLE IN INNSBRUCK, AUSTRIA. IT IS A COPY OF AN ORIGINAL PORTRAIT PAINTED WHILE VLAD WAS STILL LIVING. THE LEGENDARY PRINCE OF WALLACHIA, ALSO KNOWN AS VLAD TEPES (VLAD THE IMPALER, IN ROMANIAN), WAS IN FACT BORN AT SIGHIȘOARA ON 2 NOVEMBER 1431 AND DIED ON 16 DECEMBER 1476, PROBABLY AT GIURGIU.

of the lower Carpathians. The rugged mountains looming on the horizon evoke an eerie atmosphere, but in reality, no traces of the castle of Dracula exist.

Stoker's description actually resembles the architecture of Bran Castle, which stands out over the Gothic city of Brașov: appearing by day as an enchanting castle, by night, it looks like a sinister hideout. The narrow stairway and the forest surrounding the manor bring goose bumps to many. Today Bran Castle is one of Romania's national monuments. Rising from the ruins of an ancient fortress of the Teutonic Knights, it was built in 1377. But certain details do not correspond to the refuge of Dracula described by Stoker: for example, there is no great river flowing near the castle. Certainly the tangled forests and gothic landscapes of Transylvania have fueled the portrait drawn by Stoker of the realm of Dracula. But which is the true Castle of Dracula and where the real tomb of Vlad Tepes can be found remain mysteries still a mystery.

AVEIDA·DVX·WALA

_ (66 top, bottom and 67) WHETHER OR NOT IT TRULY IS THE CASTLE DESCRIBED IN DRACULA BY BRAM STOKER, BRAN CASTLE IS DOUBTLESSLY ONE OF THE MOST BEAUTIFUL CASTLES IN EUROPE, AND THOUSANDS OF TOURISTS FROM ALL AROUND THE WORLD VISIT IT EACH YEAR. ALL IN SEARCH OF THRILLS CONNECTED WITH THE SINISTER LEGEND OF THE VAMPIRE COUNT. YOU CAN STROLL THROUGH ITS LONG WALKS AND VISIT THE OLD ROOMS THAT HOSTED THE COURT OF VLAD III OF WALLACHIA. ITS MASSIVE TOWERS ARE CONNECTED BY DOZENS OF CORRIDORS, WHICH WERE ALSO USED FOR STORING GUNPOWDER. TODAY IT HOUSES A FINE COLLECTION OF ART AND FURNISHINGS OWNED BY QUEEN MARY, ALONG WITH WEAPONS AND ARMOR DATING FROM THE 14TH THROUGH 19TH CENTURIES.

(68 top and bottom) VLAD TEPES WAS BORN IN THE THREE-STORY HOUSE AT PIATA MUZEULUI 6, IN SIGHIŞOARA, IN 1431. TODAY THE HOUSE WHERE HE WAS BORN, STILL SHOWING ITS ORIGINAL CHARACTERISTIC PAVEMENT MADE FROM RIVER STONES, HOSTS A FAMOUS BEER PARLOR AND RESTAURANT. THE INTERIOR OF WHAT IS CALLED CASA VLAD DRACUL CAN BE VISITED. THE FATHER OF VLAD III, IN THE VERY YEAR HIS SON WAS BORN, WAS INVESTED AS A MEMBER OF THE ORDER OF THE DRAGON BY SIGISMUND, THE HOLY ROMAN EMPEROR.

(68-69) TÂRGOVIŞTE WAS ONE OF THE RESIDENCES OF VLAD TEPES; HIS BUST STILL STANDS NEAR THE RUINS. INSIDE CHINDIA TOWER (ALSO CALLED SUNSET TOWER), BUILT FOR VLAD III HIMSELF, A PERMANENT EXHIBITION SHOWS THE SEQUENCE OF EVENTS AND THE ATROCITIES PERPETRATED BY THE BLOODTHIRSTY PRINCE OF WALLACHIA.

_ (70-71) THE AREA OF VISOKO COULD BE AN ANCIENT SACRED CENTER: THERE ARE IN FACT SEVEN PYRAMIDS WHOSE PRESENCE HAS BEEN SUGGESTED IN THE AREA. THE THREE LARGEST, CALLED THE PYRAMIDS OF THE MOON, OF THE SUN, AND OF THE DRAGON, ARE SITUATED AT THE VERTICES OF A PERFECT EQUILATERAL TRIANGLE. THE ONE PRESUMED TO BE UNDER KRIZ HILL IS THE PYRAMID OF THE MOON.

The Pyramids of Visoko

(43°59'33"N - 18°10'21"E)

A CONTROVERSIAL EXCAVATION CAMPAIGN IN BOSNIA-HERZEGOVINA SUGGESTS THAT THE LARGEST PYRAMIDS OF EUROPE MAY BE HIDDEN BENEATH THREE GREEN HILLS.

In the heart of Bosnia-Herzegovina, a few kilometers from the capital, Sarajevo, rise three hills that for years have been provoking fierce debate in the archaeological world. Bosnian-American archaeologist Semir Osmanagi claims that in 2005 he discovered the largest and most ancient pyramids on our planet. According to the archaeologist, the three hills rising around the village of Visoko would in fact be colossal pyramids, covered by centuries-old layers of vegetation. Proceeding with excavation is not easy, not only because of the hostility on the part of the academic world toward Osmanagiæ's hypothesis, but also because numerous minefields are present in the zone, a sad legacy of the civil war from the 1990s. The entire site has been dubbed "the Valley of the Pyramids," and the emerging archaeological structures have been called the Pyramids of the Sun, of the Moon, and of the Dragon. In order to understand the scope of the alleged discovery, the Pyramid of the Sun, once "liberated" from the hill, would reach 220 m (722 ft) in height, higher than the Great Pyramid of Khufu (Cheops) in Egypt.

Osmanagi says, "This is the largest complex ever built upon our planet. In the valley of Visoko, there are three large four-sided pyramidal structures. The construction of the pyramids was realized in accordance with these very principles. We must, however, succeed in demonstrating that these monuments are human artifacts. The blocks of stone recovered from the site are cement, cement of an excellent quality, even better than what we produce today. The fact that it has resisted for several thousands of years demonstrates that it is material of a superior quality."

Satellite imagery has, shown how the three hills appear to be hiding some structures of pyramidal inspiration and how they appear to be oriented in accordance with the cardinal axes. But if the monumental complex discovered actually does exist on Bosnian ground, it remains to be revealed who could have produced it and when. In this zone, there are no traces of a civilization capable of constructing such monuments during the period of the presumed dating of the site, that is, 10,000 BC.

Osmanagi also affirms, "As our geological and archaeological research gradually proceeds, we find growing evidence demonstrating the human matrix of these immense monuments. The enormous slabs of sandstone are clearly worked by human hand. I think it would be obvious even to the eyes of a five-year-old child. About 1 m (3.3 ft) deep, under a layer of earth, we have found sandstone slabs arranged in perfect order. Furthermore, when we performed material analysis on it, we discovered that it is an adhesive connective material, the presence of which is also been found in the Pyramids of the Sun and of the Moon. This means that the three Bosnian pyramids were built by the same hand, using one same adhesive material."

Moreover, the points at which the three hills rise form the vertices of an equilateral triangle, which indeed causes one to think of an architectural design of human matrix. And it is not the only coincidence, as Osmanagi explains: "When we began baring the walls and terraces of these monuments, we discovered an interesting rectangular structure on the Pyramid of the Moon. It is singular to note how these two pyramids, together with that of the Dragon, are arranged in such a manner as to form a triangle, each about 2.2 km (1.4 mi) from the others. What is the probability that nature could have produced these three hills, having exactly the same design – four sides, a triangular form, a flat summit, a perfect orientation with the cardinal points – and with the three together forming an equilateral triangle? I would say none. And then, near the top of the pyramid, we find more sandstone. The position of the sandstone slab is vertical and, as we know, nature does not put things vertically."

It is suggestive to visit the excavations at Visoko, to walk on the pavements: the stones unearthed make one dream of and imagine unknown realities. But there are also some who shout "sacrilege!" Garrett Fagan of Pennsylvania State University, declares, "They should not be allowed to destroy genuine sites in the pursuit of these delusions [...] It's as if someone were given permission to bulldoze Stonehenge to find secret chambers of lost ancient wisdom underneath." Fantasy or reality? The upcoming years will tell us whether we have to rewrite the history of archaeology and of the ancient civilizations that have preceded us.

_ (72-73) THE SANCTUARY OF THE ORACLE OF DELPHI, ORIGINALLY DEDICATED TO GAIA, RISES ON THE SLOPES OF MOUNT PARNASSUS. ACCORDING TO ANCIENT GREEK LEGENDS, IT WAS ON ITS SUMMIT THAT THE MARRIAGE TOOK PLACE BETWEEN EARTH AND HEAVEN, BETWEEN GAIA AND URANUS. IN OVID'S METAMORPHOSES, THE PEAK OF THIS MOUNTAIN WAS "THE ONLY PLACE ON EARTH THAT THE WATERS COULD NOT COVER" DURING THE FLOOD CAUSED BY THE GODS.

_ (73) A KYLIX – THE TYPICAL GREEK WINE CUP MADE OF CERAMIC – DATING FROM BETWEEN THE 6TH AND 5TH CENTURIES BC, SHOWS AEGEUS, KING OF ATHENS, AS HE CONSULTS THE ORACLE OF DELPHI AND THE PYTHIA. THE ORACLE'S POWER WAS VIRTUALLY LIMITLESS AS THE KINGS OF DIFFERENT NATIONS BOWED TO ITS PROPHECIES AND SIGNS.

The Oracle of Delphi

(38°29'N - 22°30'E)

IN ANCIENT TIMES, SOVEREIGNS AND COMMANDERS CAME TO THIS PLACE TO KNOW THEIR FUTURE; ARTISTS AND POETS CAME TO RECEIVE INSPIRATION.

The Greek site of Delphi, built beginning in the 7th century BC, was considered the *omphalos* or navel of the then-known world: according to myth, Zeus chose it as such because two eagles that he had set in flight from two extreme ends of the earth came to land there at the same time. And the traveler who visits the valley of Delphi today cannot help but notice the presence of the ancient divinities in one of the world's most famous sacred areas, one of the greatest centers of ancient Greece.

Omphalos is also the name of the stone (now conserved in the Museum of Delphi) beside which the priestess of Apollo was able to predict the future. There are many mysteries contained within the numerous variants of the myths connected with the Oracle of Delphi.

In order to understand the origin of the name Delphi, we must refer to the myth. A Homeric hymn tells how the god Apollo transformed himself into a dolphin (*delphis*, in fact, in Greek), jumped onto a ship sailing from Crete and forced the sailors to land at Crisa, the port closest to the Valley of Delphi, and become his priests. According to other myths, Delphine/Daphne ("the bloody one") was the name of the prophetess of Mother Earth (Gaea) from whom Apollo usurped the art of predicting the future, by desecrating her temple, killing her, and taking possession of the art of divination. Plutarch, the Greek historian who was also a priest of the Delphi sanctuary in the times of Roman domination, tells of a mysterious ancient rite that appears to refer to this myth. In his work *The Obsolescence of Oracles*, Plutarch writes: "Every nine years on the threshold of the Temple of Delphi, a hut was built in the style of a royal residence, and a night attack was simulated [...] The table on which they had arranged the first fruits was overturned, the hut was set on fire, and the men bearing torches went away without looking back. Then the young man who had led the assault made his way to Tempe to purify himself, and he returned from there in triumph crowned with laurel and with a branch of laurel in hand…"

According to myth, the first sanctuary was erected with beeswax and feathers; the second was made of ferns; the third, with branches of laurel; the fourth was erected in bronze, by Hephaestus, with birds of gold singing at the top of it; the fifth, of stone, was destroyed by fire and then reconstructed in its definitive form.

It is certain that a female divinity, represented in many statuettes found in the deepest layers of archaeological excavations, was venerated at Delphi since the end of the 14th century BC (fully seven centuries before the construction of the sanctuary). An ancient shrine dedicated to Mother Earth was founded by the Cretans. Hellenic peoples who migrated from the north and arrived at Delphi eventually replaced the cult of Mother Earth with that of Apollo.

At the time of the Greek colonization of the Mediterranean, each city state consulted the Oracle to know how and where to implement its own campaigns of conquest. At Delphi each city erected its own Thesaurus (literally, "treasure store"), a building for depositing offerings, leading to rivalry in generosity.

_ (74-75) IN GREEK MYTHOLOGY, CASTALIA WAS A NYMPH WHOM APOLLO TRANSFORMED INTO A SPRING AT DELPHI. WHOEVER DRANK FROM HER WATERS, OR MERELY LISTENED TO THEIR SOUND, WOULD BE INSPIRED BY THE POETIC GENIUS. THIS WAS THE POINT WHERE THE PYTHIAN GAMES HAD THEIR START, AS LEGEND IDENTIFIED THIS PLACE AS THE SCENE OF THE KILLING OF THE MONSTER PYTHON, THE DRAGON-SERPENT.

_ (75) THE OMPHALOS STONE, FOUND IN THE TEMPLE OF APOLLO, IS CONSERVED AT THE ARCHAEOLOGICAL MUSEUM OF DELPHI. MANY BELIEVE IT IS A REPLICA OF WHAT WAS FOUND IN THE ADYTON, WHICH LITERALLY MEANS "PLACE WHERE IT IS FORBIDDEN TO ENTER." IN RELIEF, THE WEAVINGS OF THE WOOL BLANKET THAT COVERED THE ORIGINAL OMPHALOS. RECENT THEORIES, HOWEVER, SITUATE IT ON THE VERTEX OF THE "COLUMN OF THE DANCERS."

The precious ex-votos testified to the devotion of faithful cities and individuals to the oracle. Thus, in a short time, the sanctuary of Apollo became an international observatory that, through its very powerful college of priests, conditioned foreign politics of the time.

The power of the oracle was enormous: it was capable of triggering conflicts and wars. When the Pythia, the prophetess of the god, inhaled fumes from the crevice where the mythological serpent Python was killed, and then chewed laurel leaves (a plant sacred to Apollo), she went into a trance and began issuing prophecies in the abstruse and confused language of the oracle.

Foreigners as well went to consult the oracle of Apollo: Croesus, the king of Lydia, offered precious metals (of such a fabulous weight as to arouse astonishment) when he went to ask the prophetess whether he should fight against the king of Persia. The Pythia prophesied that if he crossed the River Halys, a great empire would fall. Galvanized by this response, Croesus forgot to ask which empire, and embarked upon war: the great empire that fell, however, was his own.
Moreover, every prophecy is, by its very nature, ambiguous.

There remains yet the mystery of the intoxicating and divinatory properties of the fumes released from the crevice – mentioned by Diodorus and Plutarch – which were perhaps composed of hydrocarbon gases and are still perceptible. And perhaps still capable of inspiring new oracles.

(76-77) THE SANCTUARY OF ATHENA PRONAIA (WHICH MEANS "BEFORE THE TEMPLE," REFERRING TO THE TEMPLE OF APOLLO) IS SURELY THE MOST SUGGESTIVE ELEMENT OF THE ENTIRE COMPLEX. BUILT IN THE 6TH CENTURY BC, IT IS A DORIC TEMPLE CHARACTERIZED BY COLUMNS RISING OVER 4.5 M (14.7 FT). THE TEMPLE WAS DESTROYED BY A VIOLENT EARTHQUAKE IN 373 BC.

_ (77 top) THE THEATER AT DELPHI WAS BUILT IN THE 4TH CENTURY BC. IT IS STILL VISIBLE TODAY OWING TO THE MAJOR RESTORATION COMPLETED IN 160 BC BY EUMENES II OF PERGAMUM. THE ANCIENT THEATER WAS BUILT ON THE HILL TO ALLOW SPECTATORS TO ENJOY THE VIEW OF THE ENTIRE SANCTUARY AND THE UNDERLYING VALLEY. ITS 35 ROWS COULD ACCOMMODATE 5000 PEOPLE.

_ (77 bottom) IN THIS PLACE CHAEREPHON, A PUPIL OF SOCRATES, ASKED THE ORACLE IF HIS MASTER WAS WISEST. THE PYTHIA RESPONDED THAT THERE WAS NO ONE WISER THAN SOCRATES. ONLY AFTER LONG THOUGHT AND INQUIRY DID SOCRATES UNDERSTAND THE MEANING OF THE DIVINE RESPONSE, APPARENTLY SHOCKING: IT WAS THAT HE WAS WISEST BECAUSE "HE KNEW THAT HE DID NOT KNOW."

GREECE

Atlantis

(36°23'17"N - 25°27'35"E)

THE LEGENDARY LOST CONTINENT DESCRIBED BY PLATO COULD HAVE MANY TIES WITH THE MARVELOUS ISLAND OF SANTORINI.

Atlantis is the myth of myths. Legend has it that a very ancient and incredibly involved civilization inhabited our planet before any other known civilization. And it disappeared in a cataclysm that annihilated the continent, plunging all traces of it forever into the abyss. Moreover, all our knowledge derives from what the inhabitants of Atlantis succeeded in passing down to us.

We owe the name of Atlantis to Plato: the legendary vanished civilization is cited in two famous dialogues of the Greek philosopher. In *Timaeus*, written around 360 BC, we read: "Before that narrow strait known as the Pillars of Hercules, there was an island. And this island was larger than Libya and Asia together, and from that one could pass to other islands, and from these, to the mainland opposite. [...] In later times [...], there were earthquakes and extraordinary cataclysms, so that in the course of one day and a dreadful night [...] everything, as a whole, sank into the earth. And thus swallowed up by the sea, Atlantis vanished." Also in Plato's writings, there is a careful description of the capital of the Lost Continent: "While all around the city there was a plain embracing the city, and this in turn was surrounded by mountains sloping down to the sea, flat and smooth, all elongated, 3000 stadia long (about 555 km or 345 mi) on two sides, and at the center, 2000 stadia (about 370 km or 230 mi) from the sea all the way down. [...] At a distance of about 50 stadia (9 km or 5.7 mi), there was a mountain of moderate size on each side [...]. The island, where the abode of the kings was located, had a diameter of 5 stadia (a little less than 1 km, about half a mile)." In *Critias*, a dialogue that unfortunately was not completed, Plato furthermore dates the existence of Atlantis to about 11,000 years ago, when Poseidon "enclosed the hill [...] by alternating three stretches of sea and land in concentric circles of different widths, of which two were land and three were water." At the center of the capital of Atlantis rose the imposing temple of Poseidon, all covered with silver, and housing the majestic statue of the god of the sea and his chargers, as high as the temple itself, and all golden.

At a distance of over 2000 years, Plato's text triggers fantasies and inspires the greatest treasure hunt in progress on our planet. Plato is considered a reliable author, his stories were taken as historical reality, as done by Crantor of Soli, the first philosopher to provide commentaries on Plato's works. From that point, the island of Atlantis, vanished 11,000 years earlier, has been imagined and situated almost everywhere on the planet: from the peaks of the Bolivian highlands to the depths of the Atlantic Ocean Ridge; from the glaciers of Antarctica to the warm waters of the Caribbean. Atlantis is everywhere, like all archetypes that pass through cultures and peoples distant from one another in time and space. But the theory most dear to Plato's descendants situates Atlantis in Greece itself. And in particular, in the archipelago of the Cyclades, at an island that was called Thera in ancient times, today known as Santorini.

Santorini is one of the most suggestive islands in the world: its present structure is all that remains after a series of volcanic explosions, the most clamorous of which is said to have devastated the entire Mediterranean Sea. The explosion of Thera hurled about 18 cu km (4.3 cu mi) of magma into the ancient heavens: the dating of artifacts discovered enwrapped within this mortal rain of lava situates the eruption around the year 1456 BC. The same date was hypothesized by geologist Angelos Galanopoulos, who even set the explosive volcano in relation to various events described in the Bible: some earthquakes, the mythical opening of the waters of the Red Sea, and above all, the "three days of darkness" in the Exodus, which would correspond to a sky filled with volcanic ash. The problem is that this date does not coincide with the date of 9000 BC given by Plato. Galanopoulos then imagined the possibility of an error in transcription: if the year were 900 instead of 9000. But the identification with Santorini is just one of the hundreds of hypotheses on which researchers from all nations have been working, sometimes even dedicating their whole lives to this. The hunt for the Lost Continent continues.

_ (78-79 and 80-81) The view of the caldera, the depression left after the volcano's explosion, appears in all its circular perfection. And it leaves us to imagine the firepower that could have upset the Mediterranean Sea, redesigning its geography and plunging the legendary island of Atlantis into the depths.

_ (79) Athanasius Kircher was one of the greatest scholars of the 17th century, an expert in science, volcanoes, the Orient, and Egyptian hieroglyphics. In 1665, he published a mysterious map that situated the mythical island of Atlantis in the Atlantic Ocean.

GREECE

The Palace of Knossos

(35°17'52"N - 25°9'46"E)

THESEUS, ARIADNE, DAEDALUS, AND THE MONSTROUS MINOTAUR: THE GREATEST MYTHS OF GREECE "DANCE" AROUND THE RUINS OF THE PALACE IN THE HEART OF CRETE.

Crete is the largest island of Greece, situated in the heart of the Mediterranean Sea. A few kilometers from the capital Heraklion stands a place shrouded in legend: the Palace of Knossos. It is the ancient prison of the mythical Minotaur, the gigantic semi-human creature with the head of a bull.

The Palace of Knossos is a superb testimony of the Minoan civilization that dominated the island of Crete from the third millennium BC. The city-palace dating from the beginning of the 16th century BC was unearthed in 1900 owing to excavations by English archaeologist Arthur Evans, who also organized restorations and reconstructions of its ruined structures, even reproducing their original paintings.

The ancient complex consisted of 1400 rooms spread over an area of 22,000 sq m (5.4 acres). Today one can visit the processional hall, the storerooms with their antique jars, the sanctuary, the royal apartments, and the throne room with its marble seat.

The city-palace of Knossos has given rise to one of the themes in Western culture, one that has led to many reflections in art and literature: the labyrinth.

Perhaps the construction of this palace, corresponds to the work conceived by Daedalus, the architect passed down through myth.

There are countless myths connected with the labyrinth, to be found in every culture, in every corner of the planet: it is an archetype that has forever obsessed mankind.

According to some, Knossos Palace could be the labyrinth fashioned to enclose the Minotaur. For others, it might be an enormous temple.

The myth of the Minotaur is closely connected with the history of Crete. The theme of the bull recurs in the frescoes at Knossos and in archaeological finds. It is often represented in scenes where young men and women are shown flipping over the animal's back. Coins found at Knossos depict a labyrinth, at whose center are signs that some have interpreted as the horns of the bull, while others have called them a quarter moon. According to one version of the myth that has many variants, Zeus transformed himself into a bull to abduct Europa, the very beautiful young earthly lady, to take her to Crete; with her he sired three children, one of whom was Minos.

Minos was adopted by the king of Crete and succeeded him upon his death with the help of Poseidon, who caused him to win the competition for the succession by causing a white bull to issue forth from the foam of the sea.

Minos, was overcome by the bull's beauty and refused to sacrifice it as he had promised Poseidon. The God of the Sea took his revenge by causing Minos's wife to fall in love with the bull. The union of the two generated Asterion, known as the Minotaur, with the body of a man and the head of the bull, a bloodthirsty beast that fed upon human flesh. The king charged Daedalus to build a prison suitable for holding the monster; the labyrinth, a maze of twisty narrow spaces from which, once one had entered, it was impossible to find a way out.

_ (82) THE VICTORY OF THESEUS OVER THE MINOTAUR IS ONE OF THE OLDEST GREEK MYTHS. THE CRETAN KINGDOM OF MINOS AND THE LABYRINTH BUILT BY DAEDALUS ARE CITED BY THE EARLIEST OF WRITTEN GREEK SOURCES: HOMER. THE ICONIC VICTORY OF MAN OVER BEAST WOULD BE RECORDED FOR CENTURIES THROUGHOUT HELLENIC CULTURE.

_ (82-83) AS WE ENTER THE CENTRAL COURTYARD OF THE PALACE THROUGH THE NORTH ACCESS, WE CAN ADMIRE THE FRESCO OF A BULL LAUNCHED IN A WILD RUN. TO REALIZE THE FRESCO WITH VIVID RESULTS, THE WET PLASTER WAS MODELED AND PAINTED BEFORE IT COULD DRY.

_ (84 top and bottom) THE AREA ON THE SOUTH SIDE OF THE PALACE OF KNOSSOS PRESENTS A STRIKING PROPYLAEUM, THE ACCESS PORCH TO THE COMPLEX. MONUMENTAL PORTICOED ENTRANCES MARKED THE FOUR CARDINAL POINTS, AND THOSE TO THE SOUTH ALLOWED ACCESS TO THE NOBLE LEVEL OF THE PALACE, REACHED THROUGH A STAIRWAY TO THE SIDE. IN THE RESTRUCTURING CARRIED OUT BY ARTHUR EVANS, THE ONLY WOODEN COLUMN WAS SUBSTITUTED BY ONE IN REINFORCED CEMENT, STILL VISIBLE TODAY.

_ (85) THE RUINS UNEARTHED AT KNOSSOS TELL THE STORY OF THE BUILDING DATING BACK TO 1900 BC, DESTROYED BY AN EARTHQUAKE TWO CENTURIES LATER. THE SECOND BUILDING COLLAPSED AFTER THE DEVASTATING ERUPTION OF THE SANTORINI VOLCANO, WHICH OCCURRED AROUND 1550 BC. IN ADDITION TO THE FAMOUS PALACE OF MINOS, THE SITE INCLUDES THE HOUSES OF THE PRIESTS AND THE HOMES OF THE PEOPLE.

The imprisoned Minotaur was fed with young human victims sent from Athens every nine years. But on the third tribute, among the seven youths and seven maidens sent from Athens as predestined victims was the young hero Theseus, who had already defeated the white bull of Poseidon, a source of devastation for Greece. Theseus conquered Ariadne, the daughter of Minos, and with her help (the stratagem of the magic thread allowing him to find the exit to the maze) he entered the labyrinth, killing the Minotaur and freeing the hostages before emerging victorious.

There are some who would read in these myths a reference to the ritual fights the Cretan king performed with animals: a struggle symbolizing the victory of the royal power over nature. On the other hand, the tribute of human sacrifices imposed by Minos upon Athens recalls the historical period of Crete's domination of the Mediterranean. The structure of the palace, testifies to the absolute tranquility of a king who had no fears of attacks or sea invasions. Dangers could arrive only from within: possibly, from the legendary underground crypt, identified as the prison of the Minotaur, the fearsome monster, imaginary or real as it may have been.

_ (86-87) THE ROOM OF FRESCOES ON THE NOBLE LEVEL AT KNOSSOS PALACE IS HOME TO EXCEPTIONAL WORKS. THE DESIGNS SUGGEST AN EGYPTIAN INFLUENCE, ATTRIBUTABLE TO INTENSE TRADE WITH THE CRETAN CIVILIZATION. BUT UNLIKE EGYPTIAN ART, THE FRESCOES AT KNOSSOS PAID HOMAGE TO THE ANIMALS CONSIDERED DIVINE, SUCH AS THE SNAKE AND THE BULL.

_ (87 top and bottom) ONE OF THE BEST CONSERVED SPACES IN KNOSSOS PALACE, THE THRONE ROOM IS HOME TO AN ALABASTER SEAT ON THE NORTH WALL, IDENTIFIED AS THE THRONE WHICH GIVES ITS NAME TO THE HALL. THERE ARE PLASTER BENCHES ON THREE SIDES OF THE ROOM, WHILE BEFORE THE THRONE IS A TANK THAT SERVED AS A LUSTRAL BASIN FOR PURIFICATION CEREMONIES. ALL THIS SUGGESTS THE PRESENCE OF A PRIEST-KING.

_ (88-89) THE MAJESTIC PYRAMID OF KHUFU (CHEOPS) HAS ITS FOUR FACES PERFECTLY ALIGNED WITH THE CARDINAL POINTS. THE ERROR IS ONLY 2 MINUTES OF A DEGREE, EQUIVALENT TO LESS THAN 1/100 OF A SECOND ON A CLOCK WITH HANDS. AN INCREDIBLE RESULT FOR PEOPLE WHO, ACCORDING TO OFFICIAL HISTORY, WERE NOT ACQUAINTED WITH THE WHEEL OR WITH IRON AND WHO HAD ONLY RUDIMENTARY KNOWLEDGE OF ARITHMETIC.

_ (89) KHUFU IS THE TRUE NAME OF THE PHARAOH REFERRED TO AS CHEOPS, A NAME THAT CAME LATER, FROM HERODOTUS, FOR THE PRESUMED BUILDER OF THE GREAT PYRAMID, AKHET KHUFU, LITERALLY "SHINING IS KHUFU." THE REIGN OF THIS SON OF SNEFRU, AGAIN ACCORDING TO HERODOTUS, WAS CHARACTERIZED BY DISSOLUTION AND CRUEL ABUSE OF POWER. HIS MORTAL REMAINS HAVE NEVER BEEN FOUND.

The Pyramid of Khufu

(29°58'45"N - 31°8'4"E)

"MAN FEARS TIME. BUT TIME FEARS THE PYRAMIDS."
ANCIENT ARAB PROVERB.

The pyramid of Khufu (Cheops) is the world's most known and visited monument. It is the only one of the legendary seven wonders of the ancient world that has succeeded in crossing through the centuries to arrive intact to our own time. The monument lies in the outskirts of the modern metropolis of Cairo, on the Giza plateau, right beside the mysterious Sphinx and near two other pyramids of smaller dimensions: those of Khafra (Chephren) and of Menkaure (Mycerinus). Official archaeology sustains that it was constructed as a funereal monument for Pharaoh Khufu of the Fourth Dynasty. But there are many who have imagined and proposed other hypothesis. The fact that the pyramids attributed to the Fourth Dynasty demonstrate a technical level that is incredibly higher with respect to the preceding and, above all, with respect to those following, has aroused numerous debates and more than one suspicion. It is as though in just a few years, technology had passed from that of the printing press to that of the laptop, then reverted to the printing press and movable type: an evolution and involution that are difficult to explain. Supposedly more than 100,000 people worked to build the pyramid, placing 2.5 million blocks of stone in about 30 years. What were the means used and who were the men that the successive pharaohs of the Fourth Dynasty used to construct their pyramids. Originally, the Pyramid of Khufu was greater than 145 m (475 ft) in height. Today it stands 139 m (455 ft) high and is 230 m (755 ft) wide at the base of each side. The proportions of the monument also denote an incredible level of precision. The lengths of the individual parts differ from one another by only 0.1 percent, and the four faces of the pyramid are aligned with the cardinal points.

Even the position of the pyramid does not seem to have been chosen at random; it rises from the point of intersection between one particular meridian and one particular parallel sharing the same characteristic, that is, they are the lines of their sort covering the greatest amount of dry land, making this point, in fact, the center of the world, at least from the point of view of land mass. There are those who have calculated that its weight (5273 million tonnes) multiplied by a billion billions is equivalent to the weight of the planet. Others have calculated that its dimensions are connected with the value of π (pi), which, however, was discovered many centuries after its construction.

The questions and mysteries surrounding the Pyramid of Khufu did not relate only to who constructed it and to what technique was used. Doubt has been raised about whether it actually was a tomb because no remains of any pharaoh have ever been found inside it. But does it have an operational function? What link does it have to the stars? What secrets does it still conceal within itself?

Inside the monument there are only two rooms: one is bare and unadorned, while the other is called "the king's chamber," which houses the presumed sarcophagus and an inscription based on which archaeologists have attributed the pyramid to Khufu. But that which is believed to be the sarcophagus is empty. And not only that: it was realized and worked from a single block of granite, and it is larger than the access door into the room. Its external volume is exactly twice the internal volume: a precision truly difficult to obtain using the instruments available 5000 years ago.

_ (90 left) IT IS STILL UNCLEAR WHETHER THE ACCESS CORRIDORS WERE ACTUALLY USED TO REACH THE KING'S AND QUEEN'S CHAMBERS. THEIR DIMENSIONS AND THE UNUSUAL STRUCTURE OF THE WALLS, FORMED BY A DOUBLE ROW OF STONES, DO IN FACT SUGGEST THAT THEY WERE DESTINED TO BE FILLED AND SEALED.

_ (90 right) THE KING'S CHAMBER INSIDE THE PYRAMID HOUSES A GRANITE SARCOPHAGUS WITHOUT A LID THAT MAY HAVE BELONGED TO THE PHARAOH KHUFU. THE CHAMBER, 10 M WIDE, 5 M LONG, AND NEARLY 6 M HIGH (32.8 x 16.4 x 19.7 FT), ALSO CONTAINS TWO CONDUITS WHOSE FUNCTION IS YET UNCLEAR. SOME CONSIDER THEM TO BE VENTILATION DUCTS, WHILE OTHERS SAY THEY ARE "WINDOWS" POINTING AT TWO PRECISE POINTS IN THE SKY.

_ (90-91) THE GRAND GALLERY INSIDE THE PYRAMID OF KHUFU IS 46 M LONG. BUT WHILE IT IS ABOUT 2 M (6.7 FT) WIDE AT THE BASE, IT BECOMES INCREASINGLY NARROW IN ASCENDING ALONG THE INTERIOR OF THE PYRAMID, SO THAT AT THE PEAK IT IS BARELY 1 M (3.3 FT) IN WIDE. ITS FUNCTION WAS PROBABLY THAT OF SCAFFOLDING, TO BE USED UNTIL THE WORK WAS COMPLETED.

Archaeologist Flinders Petrie maintains that a similar result could only have been obtained using a circular saw of bronze and diamonds. Engineer Christopher Dunn, an expert in working granite, sustains that in order to realize this sarcophagus today without breaking the block of stone, it would take a drill 500 times faster than those commercially available. The ancient Egyptians must have possessed incredible utensils, of which no trace has been conserved.

Then there are the connections with the sky and the stars. There are some who maintain that the three pyramids of pizza reproduce on earth the three stars of the belt of Orion and their respective arrangement within the sky. According to a fantastical but fascinating hypothesis, the Sphinx would then complete the astral picture, by fixing the position of the constellation Leo in the sky and thus dating the entire archaeological area to 10,500 BC. In the epoch of its maximum splendor, when the Great Pyramid was entirely covered over with white limestone from Tura, it shone for great distances. It has been calculated that it even would have been visible from the moon, in all its unfathomable mystery.

EGYPT

The Sphinx

(29°58'31"N - 31°8'16"E)

A HUMAN HEAD ON THE BODY OF A LION,
GUARDING EGYPT'S OLDEST MYSTERY.

The Sphinx at Giza is one of the symbols of Egypt, the enigmatic colossal statue with the body of a lion and the head of man. The interpretation of the mysterious monument right in front of the pyramids of Khufu (Cheops), Khafre (Chephren) and Menkaure (Mycerinus) is controversial. Set at the bottom of a wide and deep pit, the Sphinx is 73 m (240 ft) long, 6 m (19.7 ft) wide, and 20 m (65.6 ft) high. It is the largest statue in the world; majestic and imposing, it has for centuries fascinated travelers, explorers, and archaeologists. Many times the desert sands have tried to bury it, but each time it has reemerged from oblivion. According to official archaeology, its face is the likeness of the Pharaoh Khafre and it was realized around 2500 BC, by liberating its form from the stone that surrounded it. But still no satisfactory explanation has been provided for how the enormous blocks composing it were transported and cut. And there are some who support the theory that the Sphinx actually dates from a much older time, as far back as 10,500 BC.

This hypothesis is linked to the stars. Carved into the limestone rock and perfectly oriented toward the east, the Sphinx faces the rising sun on the days of the vernal and autumnal equinoxes. In 10,500 BC, the constellation of Leo was exactly on the horizon of Egypt. The Sphinx would thus have been "looking at itself" (its leonine body) being reflected in the firmament. Just as the three pyramids of Giza would have been reflected in the three stars shining in Orion's belt.

But what basis could such a fanciful hypothesis have? Is it really possible that the Sphinx could have been produced many millennia earlier than what the Egyptologists believe? Normally it is believed that the Sphinx was built around 2500 BC, considering that the ancient Egyptians would not have had the technology, the social organization, or perhaps even the capability of constructing such a monument thousands of years earlier than the reign of Khafre. But if the official dating is correct, we need to hypothesize that the visible signs of erosion on the Sphinx and on the rocky walls surrounding it were due only to the action of the wind and perhaps a few extraordinary floods of the Nile. For many researchers, the signs of erosion could be the signs of strong and prolonged rains. And this could only have happened before these areas became desert, when the land of Egypt was green and temperate. The last wet and rainy period of northern Africa dates back to the centuries between 13,000 BC and 10,000 BC, which explains the possibility of dating the Sphinx to a very ancient era.

But the Sphinx also conceals another mystery: does its face actually depict Khafre, or did the pharaoh simply modify the existing head? Furthermore, the head appears to have been made of a stone different from that used for the rest of the body, and above all, it is disproportionate. The ancient Egyptians had an outright obsession for symmetry and proportion: is it possible that they would no longer apply this characteristic of theirs in such an important monument?

_ (92) THE FACE OF THE SPHINX IS IDENTIFIED OFFICIALLY WITH THAT OF THE PHARAOH KHAFRE, ALSO KNOWN AS CHEPHREN, THE FOURTH PHARAOH OF THE IV DYNASTY. CHRONICLES DEPICT HIM AS A SEVERE TYRANT OBSESSED WITH EXPANSIONIST AIMS, PARTICULARLY TOWARD THE REGION CURRENTLY KNOWN AS PALESTINE.

_ (92-93) THE SPHINX'S PROFILE FUELS DOUBTS AND CONTROVERSY: IN FACT, NOT EVERYONE AGREES WITH THE OFFICIAL VERSION THAT THE FACE IS THAT OF PHARAOH KHAFRE. ACCORDING TO DETECTIVE FRANK DOMINGO OF THE NEW YORK POLICE DEPARTMENT, AN EXPERT IN FACIAL COMPOSITES, THE FACES OF THE TWO STATUES DO NOT REPRESENT THE SAME PERSON.

_ (94 and 96-97) THE SPHINX OF GIZA IS THE WORLD'S LARGEST MONOLITHIC STATUE: OVER 70 M LONG, MORE THAN 20 M HIGH, AND 6 M WIDE (230 x 66 x 20 FT). THE IMPOSING HEAD IS 4 M (13 FT) HIGH, AND YET THERE ARE SOME WHO NOTE THAT IT IS DISPROPORTIONATE: WHY DOES IT APPEAR SMALL IN RELATION TO THE REST OF THE BODY? ONE HYPOTHESIS IS THAT THE PHARAOH KHAFRE ONLY RESTORED THE ANCIENT ORIGINAL STATUE, IMPRESSING HIS OWN LIKENESS UPON IT.

Egyptologists attribute the construction of the Sphinx to Khafre, because they maintain that the face resembles the one on a famous black diorite statue portraying the pharaoh. This theory, however, was refuted in the 1990s by Frank Domingo, the forensic science expert of New York, who excluded the possibility of their representing the same face. According to analyses performed and facial composites produced, the two faces would even belong to different races.

Another legend regards the existence of a secret underground chamber beneath the Sphinx, containing extremely old archives. According to the prophetic visions of psychic Edgar Cayce, these would correspond to the legendary "Hall of Documents" of the civilization of Atlantis, which also disappeared, according to the myth, 11,000 years ago.

The only thing certain is that the Sphinx has been maintaining its secrets and fascinating researchers and lovers of mystery for millennia. The truth is probably hidden in its face, which has forever been synonymous with mystery itself.

_ (94-95) THE "STELE OF THE DREAM" WAS ERECTED BETWEEN THE PAWS OF THE SPHINX BY PHARAOH THUTMOSE IV. THE PLAQUE COMMEMORATES THE DREAM THAT CAME TO THE YOUNG FUTURE PHARAOH, WHO HAD FALLEN ASLEEP AT THAT POINT: THE SPHINX BEGGED HIM TO FREE HER FROM THE SAND AND PROPHESIED HIS ASCENT TO THE THRONE. ONE CURIOSITY: THERE ARE TWO SPHINXES SHOWN IN MIRROR IMAGE ENGRAVED ON THE STELE; FOR THIS REASON, THERE ARE SOME WHO BELIEVE THERE MIGHT BE A SECOND, IDENTICAL STATUE UNDER THE SANDS OF GIZA.

ETHIOPIA

Axum

(14°7'N - 38°44'E)

THE LARGE STONE STELES RISE INTO THE SKY OF ETHIOPIA'S SPIRITUAL CAPITAL, THE PLACE SAID TO BE GUARDING THE LEGENDARY ARK OF THE COVENANT.

Ethiopia, on the Horn of Africa, is a land of noble peoples, unique animals, and torrid deserts of lava and salt. Some of the most incomprehensible kingdoms in history have sprung from its red soil. Very wealthy kingdoms that have disappeared into nothingness. Legendary civilizations, like that of the Axumites, who left a series of mysterious traces in their ancient capital of Axum.

The first mention of this mysterious realm appears on an ancient document known as *Periplus Maris Erythraei*: in this travel log, the author describes the kingdom of the *Aksumites* as a rich land governed by the king Zoscales, a cultured dictator who was also an expert in literature, but with expansionist aims. The Axumite civilization reached such a level of sophistication that its people produced gold coins of great value, with images representing likenesses of at least 20 different sovereigns. Rare and precious coins that hint at the history and allure of this ancient African kingdom. According to recent studies, the Axumite civilization dates back at least to the 4th century BC, but its origins have not yet been clarified. To add to the confusion, the ancient official Axumite language of Ge'ez, used by the imperial court of Ethiopia in certain documents up until 1974 and still in use by the Ethiopian Orthodox Church as a liturgical language, dates back as far as 2000 BC.

But there is one characteristic that renders this African civilization truly unique and impressive: the monumental steles constructed from single blocks of granite, which can still be seen by the dozens today in modern Axum: some damaged and on the ground, others standing out with their nearly 30 m (98.4 ft) of height. But their significance still remains a mystery. Among those still standing there is the one known as the stele of King Ezana, 24 m (78.7 ft) high, which since 2008 has been standing side by side with its twin stele, returned by Italy to Ethiopia. But the great stele of Axum, whose collapse, according to legend, marked the end of the Axumite empire, was no less than 33 m (108 ft) high; it still lies today at the point where the gods supposedly caused it to fall. The Axumite steles have only one style: the decorations that embellish it seem to represent doors and windows, at times with ornamentations like handles; they are always concave realizations within the steles themselves, as though they were to host plates or precious images, which, however, no one has ever found.

One wonders about the nature of the steles: it would seem strange for them simply to be funereal monuments because there are no graves around their location. And their style, which is more like that of a home than that of a monument, is a mystery, as is also the existence of what may have been the metal plaques, now vanished.

_ (98) THE COLOSSAL STELES OF AXUM ARE MADE FROM SINGLE BLOCKS OF GRANITE. THE MOST FAMOUS IS THE STELE OF KING EZANA, 24 M (79 FT) HIGH.

_ (99) THE APEX OF EACH STELE, LIKE THE ONE FOR KING EZANA, IS MODELED ON THE GEOMETRIC FORM OF A HALF CIRCLE, REPRESENTING PARADISE. ACCORDING TO SCHOLARS, A METAL PLAQUE WAS AFFIXED TO THE FRONT PART OF THE VERTEX AND BORE AN ENGRAVING OF THE SUN AND THE CRESCENT MOON.

_ (100) THE STELE OF AXUM WAS REMOVED BY THE ITALIAN ARMY DURING THE ETHIOPIAN WAR OF 1935, AND TRANSPORTED TO ROME. AFTER THE WAR, ITALY DECIDED TO RETURN THE STELE, BUT THE UNDERTAKING WAS POSTPONED OWING TO EXCESSIVE TRANSPORTATION COSTS. THE STELE WAS FINALLY RETURNED IN 2005.

According to certain calculations, the block of stone constituting the Great Stele ought to weigh about 520 tonnes (573 tons). Modern architects and archaeologists still do not clearly understand how it was possible for them to move it for over 4 km (2.5 mi) — the distance from the quarries — and then position it upright.

But the steles are not the only mystery of the ancient Axumite civilization. According to testimonies of several travelers, it would appear that one can feel the ground resonate under one's feet, owing to the incredible numbers of tombs and caves that pierce the area. Certain legends affirm that the dense network of underground vaults, the majority of which are yet unexplored, conceals a passage leading as far as Arabia.

There remains also the mystery of what caused the downfall of the mythical Axumite civilization, the reason for which a people capable of such cultural sophistication and imposing monuments would fall into oblivion.

The legends reported in certain texts, jealously guarded by local monks, speak of a warrior queen named Judith, perhaps a pagan or perhaps of Hebrew origin, who in a single night destroyed the city by fire. Judith killed the last Axumite sovereign and knocked down a great number of steles. The only thing that is certain is that the last remaining obelisks, the smallest, without inscriptions, are now conserved in a park dedicated to her. The last intangible traces of a majestic, secret people, buried by the sands of time.

Axum today is a destination of great pilgrimages: it is considered the holiest city in Ethiopia. The Ethiopian Orthodox Church affirms that the Church of Our Lady Mary of Zion conserves the legendary Ark of the Covenant, the tabernacle with supernatural powers containing Moses' Ten Commandments. It is too bad that no one can observe it or touch it other than the guardian of the church – the sole person elected to have this privilege – who guards it day and night for his entire life.

But this is just another of the thousand secrets of enigmatic Axum.

_ (100-101 and 101) According to legend, the collapse of the Great Stele coincided with the end of the Axumite empire. Certainly, the spectacle of the colossal monument lying on the ground and broken into four parts instills a sense of sadness and ruin. Along its length of over 33 m (108 ft), the engravings on it reproduce the façade of a 13-story house. Built in honor of the negus Ramhai, the Great Stele supposedly fell during the raising ceremony owing to unstable foundations. According to another version, it was Queen Judith who had it knocked down.

_ (102-103 and 102 bottom) ON A SMALL HILL, 2 KM (1.2 MI) FROM THE PARK NORTH OF THE STELE, STANDS THE 6TH CENTURY MAUSOLEUM THAT BELONGS, ACCORDING TO TRADITION, TO KING KALEB AND HIS SON GEBRE MESKEL. THEY ARE TWIN TOMBS, ALTHOUGH THE SECOND IS MORE REFINED; MOST ASTONISHING IS THE INCREDIBLE PRECISION WITH WHICH THE CONSTITUENT STONES WERE ASSEMBLED. THE TOMB IS CHARACTERIZED BY A LARGE ENTRANCE HALL AND FIVE ROOMS: A MASSIVE ELABORATED PORTAL GIVES ACCESS TO ONE OF THESE CONTAINING THREE SARCOPHAGI, ONE OF WHICH IS ORNAMENTED WITH CHRISTIAN CROSSES. THE TOMB OF KING KALEB IS ACCESSED FROM A LONG STAIRWAY. THE STONES ARE LARGER AND ROUGHER. ACCORDING TO LEGEND, IF YOU PASS A WET BLADE OF GRASS BETWEEN THE CRACKS IN THE WALLS, YOU MAY BE LUCKY ENOUGH TO FIND A PEARL UPON IT WHEN YOU RETRACT IT. LOCAL LEGEND HAS IT THAT A SECRET DOOR CONCEALS A PRECIOUS TREASURE.

ETHIOPIA

Lalibela

(12°2'N - 39°2'E)

SPLENDID CHURCHES CARVED INTO THE ROCK. LEGENDS APPEARING TO INDICATE THAT THE ARK OF THE COVENANT PASSED BY HERE CENTURIES AGO.

Ethiopia is a mythical land, traversed by a thousand mysteries and legends. At 2600 m (8530 ft) elevation, we find what is called the "Petra of Africa": Lalibela. This is the most sacred city after Axum, and it is famous for its incredible churches excavated into the sides of the mountain, or even into the depths of the earth. There are 10 churches and a small prison; nobody knows how or when they were built. The founding of Lalibela is generally dated to the 12th century, but its origin is probably even older. All the churches were built without any masonry elements or wooden structural parts, but only by excavating and working the tufa rock. Making it all even more mysterious is the fact that, except for the churches, there is no other construction from the same era anywhere in the area.

Legend has it that the shrines were built on the orders of King Lalibela, following a mystical vision that came to him. According to some scholars, 40,000 workmen were needed to build the entire complex by excavating it from the rock; that number, however, is incompatible with the actual population of the area during that historical period. According to another version, the construction of the Christian churches was supervised by knights of the Crusades who took refuge in Ethiopia.

The churches of Lalibela are divided into two distinct areas, with the sole exception of the church dedicated to St. George. The most important group is the one to the northwest, which includes Bet Medhane Alem, "the Church of the Savior," considered the largest monolithic rock-hewn church in the world. In its interior are carved stone niches that are identified – in a totally anachronistic manner – with the tombs of Abraham, Isaac, and Jacob; this is also where Lalibela's most precious treasure, a gigantic cross of gold weighing more than 7 kg (18.75 troy lbs), is conserved. Bet Maryam, "the Church of Maria," is reached by passing through a small stone arch in a wall of rock. The plan is highly elaborate: the interior is realized on two floors, and there are many frescoes representing Christian symbols, but there is also a strange beast with two heads fighting two bulls, one white and one black. Farther on, a column with a square base is covered with drapes and very thick fabrics; it is said that under these is a forbidden inscription, which cannot be viewed by anyone other than one particular priest. According to local guides, its sacred pages contain the truth about the Ark of the Covenant. Ancient, mysterious manuscripts bound in leather and bark are conserved in the tiny churches of Bet Meskel and Bet Danaghel. However, Bet Golgotha is the holiest church for the Ethiopians: entry is forbidden to women, and on its walls are frescoes of crusader warriors in fighting gear.

_ (104) King Lalibela, considered a saint of the Ethiopian Church, reigned from 1181 to 1221. It was he who ordered the construction of the splendid complex of churches known today by his name.

_ (104-105) Bet Maryam was probably the first church to be built at Lalibela. According to legend, one of the columns of the building was touched by the Virgin Mary herself, and the Ten Commandments are carved into it.

LEGEND
1) Bet Meskel
2) Bet Mikael
3) Bet Golgotha
4) Bet Maryam
5) Bet Ghel
6) Bet Medhane Alem
7) Bet Giyorgis
8) Monolithic cross
9) Bet Gabriel-Rufael
10) Bet Abba Libanos
11) Bet Merkorios
12) Bet Amanuel

_ (106-107) BET MEDHANE ALEM IS THE MOST IMPOSING OF THE CHURCHES OF LALIBELA: ONE SINGLE MASSIVE MONOLITHIC BLOCK.

_ (107) BET GOLGOTHA ALSO WAS REALIZED FROM ONE SINGLE MONOLITH, ON A RECTANGULAR BASE.

The priest also serves as guard for a series of relics, but above all, for a small corner of earth considered holy.

The second group of churches, the one to the southeast, is poorly conserved and difficult to access. Only the tiny prison, with its shackles and chains, raises several questions: who would have been locked up in a site containing only places of worship?

But the most astonishing church at Lalibela is doubtlessly Bet Giyorgis, realized by excavating 15 m (50 ft) deep into the rocky base of the hill. Dedicated to St. George and based on a cruciform plan, it develops over three floors of depth. Today it still hosts mystical hermits, who live half naked in its sacred niches side-by-side with skeletons that have been deposited there over the centuries. An antique chest and other sealed boxes conserved there are never opened before strangers and no one knows what they contain. Other marks in the rocks are attributed to the hooves of St. George's horse, which manifested to reveal to the saint a secret that remains well-guarded in the depths of the earth.

_ (108-109) THE COMPLEX OF BET GABRIEL-RUFAEL, DEDICATED TO THE ARCHANGELS GABRIEL AND RAPHAEL, IS FAMOUS FOR ITS CHARACTERISTIC ENTRANCE, ACCESSED BY MEANS OF THE "STAIRWAY TO HEAVEN."

_ (110-111 and 111 top) BET GIYORGIS, THE CHURCH OF ST. GEORGE, IS THE ONLY SACRED STRUCTURE THAT IS ISOLATED WITH RESPECT TO THE OTHER TWO GROUPS OF SANCTUARIES. IT IS CHARACTERIZED BY A GREEK CROSS PLAN, LIKE THE EXCAVATION THAT SEPARATES IT FROM THE ROCK. THE ENTIRE 12 M (39,4 FT) OF THE CHURCH'S HEIGHT DEVELOPS BENEATH THE LEVEL OF THE GROUND. THE MARKS LEFT IN ITS ROCK ARE VENERATED: ACCORDING TO LEGEND THEY WERE PRODUCED BY ST. GEORGE'S HORSE, WHICH MANIFESTED AT THIS VERY POINT TO KING LALIBELA.

(111 bottom) During the Timkat, the Coptic feast of the Epiphany, which takes place on 19 January, a copy of the Ark of the Covenant (called the Tabot) is borne to Bet Giyorgis, the rock-hewn church of St. George. The ceremony is one of the most important: all of Ethiopia participates in it, and the entire complex of Lalibela is filled with the faithful.

KENYA

The Ruins of Gedi

(3°19'S - 39°59'E)

A CITY FORGOTTEN IN THE FOREST OF KENYA SEEMS TO BE SHROUDED
BY AN ANCIENT CURSE AND A FASCINATING HISTORY.

Malindi, in Kenya, today is considered one of the paradises of Africa. Its dreamlike coast along eastern Africa is a destination for the most sophisticated tourism. And yet, at a few kilometers (miles) from its exclusive dwellings, there is a mysterious little village, a ghost town with an uncertain past: the Gedi Ruins, the lost village. *Gede* means "precious" in the Oromo language. Embedded within the heart of the forest of Arabuko Sokoke, and distributed over 200,000 sq m (50 ac), the ruins of Gedi represent a yet unsolved mystery: nobody knows the earliest history of the village, that of its inhabitants, or the reasons leading to their sudden abandonment. No sign of battle or epidemic has been discovered: the ruins appear, rather, to suggest a rapid flight of the inhabitants. Locals seem to avoid these impenetrable ruins, perhaps because they fear what happened in this ancient and mysterious place.

The crux of the entire enigma surrounding the city lost in the forest is that there are no written traces of its existence: there is no record of it in the Swahili culture; the Portuguese who came to this area and settled just a few kilometers away did not know about it; the Arab libraries hold no key for deciphering its mystery. The ruins of Gedi appear to have escaped centuries of history with a sort of well-guarded secret.

The campaign of excavations conducted between 1948 and 1958 produced surprising results. Hidden among the ruins, archaeologists discovered precious and unexpected valuables: a Chinese vase from the Ming dynasty, precious wrought glass from Venice, an iron lamp of Indian make, scissors from Spain, and coins from the Far East. All these objects have been on display since 2000 in the small museum at the Gedi complex, and appear to relate the story of a place where merchants and travelers from every part of the planet came together in the past. A rich, pulsating, and vital center of Eastern Africa under the Arab rule flourishing between 1300 and 1700 A.D. Archaeologists estimate the city was home to at least 2500 inhabitants.

The simplest hypothesis advanced by scholars is that, during the migrations of the tribes that descended from the north, the great forest of Arabuko Sokoke became a destination to be conquered, and its inhabitants were thus brutally driven out. According to another version, however, the city of Gedi was the subject of a punitive expedition launched by the city of Mombasa against Malindi.

But all this only adds to the great mystery of the silence that has surrounded the ruins for centuries: how was it possible for such a rich center of commerce, such an extensive city, where great and powerful merchants of the past converged, not to have left any written trace in any travel log? We would almost have to imagine a pact of silence required to be kept by anyone venturing into the ancient Gedi village. Furthermore, its distance from the sea and its position within the forest are not ideal conditions for a center of commerce. And what further deepens the mystery are questions about *what* the inhabitants of Gedi so secretly traded and *who* their actual customers were.

_ (113) THE ENTRANCE TO THE "PALACE OF THE SULTAN" LEADS TO A CLASSICAL EXAMPLE OF SWAHILI ARCHITECTURE. GEDI, A SMALL CITY CONSTRUCTED ENTIRELY OF STONE, WAS INHABITED BY A POPULATION OF SEVERAL THOUSAND SWAHILI AND GOVERNED BY A MYSTERIOUS AND VERY WEALTHY SULTAN. THE RUINS DATE FROM THE 15TH CENTURY AND ARE OPEN TO VISITORS.

What remains to be admired today is the typical medieval Swahili architecture that found its culmination in the construction of the palace, the imposing stone homes, and the great mosque. But the sophisticated toilets, unique of their kind, arouse great interest: the primary material used in the construction comes from the coral reef in the nearby ocean. The plan of the city develops upon right-angled intersections and includes an outstanding network of street drains. According to legend, the ruins are protected by the spirits of their priests. The "Old Ones," as they are called, are said to be capable of cursing anyone who attempts to desecrate the area.

_ (114-115) THE ROOTS OF TREES, INCLUDING SOME MAJESTIC BAOBABS, SWALLOWED UP THE RUINS OF GEDI, AND FOR CENTURIES CONCEALED THEIR ANCIENT SECRET. A GATE LEADS TO THE INTERIOR OF THE MOSQUE OF THE THREE CORRIDORS. THE FIRST SETTLEMENTS IN THIS AREA DATE FROM THE 11TH CENTURY.

_ (115) FROM ABOVE YOU CAN ADMIRE THE PLAN OF THE ARCHAEOLOGICAL SITE AND THE GUIDES WHO LEAD THE TOURISTS THROUGH THE TIMELESS MYSTERIES OF THE RUINS OF GEDI. THE PLAN OF THE ANCIENT CITY, WHICH STRETCHES FOR 200,000 SQ M (50 AC), INCLUDED INTERSECTIONS AT RIGHT ANGLES AND AN INCREDIBLY EFFICIENT SYSTEM OF DRAINAGE CANALS.

ZIMBABWE

Great Zimbabwe

(20°16'23"S - 30°56'3"E)

THE LARGEST MONUMENT IN AFRICA AFTER THE PYRAMIDS OF EGYPT. THE PRIDE OF AN ENTIRE NATION AND THE TRACE OF A DISTANT UNKNOWN PAST.

On the continent of Africa, the second monument in size and importance after the pyramids of Egypt is Great Zimbabwe. And just like the pyramids, it has become the symbol of the land of the pharaohs. Accordingly, this spectacular archaeological site has become the icon of the Republic of Zimbabwe, a state that derives its name from the incredible stone ruins overlooking the endless high-lying plateau of Harare. The symbolic bird of the nation – according to some it would be the Bateleur eagle – is one of the most famous finds discovered in the Great Zimbabwe excavations.

The whole place is shrouded in mystery: it was the capital of an empire, extending over 7 sq km (2.7 sq mi), constructed with 15,000 tonnes of stone, forming a series of majestic buildings and imposing walls. Why was Great Zimbabwe abandoned?

Official archaeological dating indicates human presence in the area beginning from the 4th century AD, but they assert that the construction of the magnificent city began only 1000 years later, toward the end of the 13th century. At the height of its splendor, it must have housed more than 20,000 inhabitants: a true capital, with frenetic traffic and rich with commerce, frequented by Arabs, Indians, and Portuguese. The pulsing heart of the realm of Monomotapa, the legendary Bantu monarch of southeastern Africa.

Great Zimbabwe was inexplicably abandoned and forgotten for centuries, until it was accidentally discovered in 1867 by the explorer Adam Renders. In 1871, German geologist Karl Mauch effected the first reconnaissance and came to establish – erring dramatically – that it was "a copy of the Temple of Solomon and a copy of the palace of the Queen of Sheba." It was not until the early 20th century, with scientific studies not conditioned by racist ideologies, that it was discovered that this spectacular complex was the work of an ancient African people, probably the Shona, even though the Venda and the Lemba claimed to have constructed it: one of the clans of these latter people, in fact, call themselves *Tovakare Muzimbabwe*, "the ones who built Zimbabwe." The name Zimbabwe itself would derive from a contraction of the phrase *dzimba woye*, "the idolized houses." Surrounded by imposing walls, in Great Zimbabwe many stone houses still stand around the city's two great monumental towers (those of mud have been lost), forming narrow passageways among the immense walls of rock. In the highest part of the city (over 2500 m, or 8200 ft, above sea level) we find the Great Enclosure — the largest prehistoric structure south of the Sahara – and the Conical Tower, a masterpiece of design over 9 m (30 ft) high and more than 5 m (16 ft) wide, perhaps the ancient residence of the king. Who were the architects who designed all of this? And after having constructed this enchanting and monumental city of stone, why were the inhabitants constrained to abandon it, leaving it to fall into oblivion for 400 years? The answers seem to remain buried, even today, among its incredibly breathtaking ruins.

_ (116-117) PERHAPS THE BEST-KNOWN NATURAL WONDER OF ZIMBABWE IS VICTORIA FALLS, BUT FOR THE INHABITANTS OF THE REPUBLIC OF ZIMBABWE, THE TRUE NATIONAL PRIDE IS REPRESENTED BY THE MAJESTIC COMPLEX OF GREAT ZIMBABWE: ONE OF THE RARE CASES IN WHICH A MONUMENT HAS GIVEN ITS NAME TO THE STATE WHERE IT IS LOCATED.

_ (117) WHEN THE FIRST WHITE INVADERS REACHED ZIMBABWE, THEY DID NOT BELIEVE THAT GREAT ZIMBABWE COULD HAVE BEEN CONSTRUCTED BY THE LOCAL TRIBES; IN FACT, THE SHONA PEOPLE DID NOT HAVE LARGE STONE CONSTRUCTIONS WITHIN THEIR TRADITIONAL ARCHITECTURE. ARCHAEOLOGICAL STUDIES INVOLVING EXCAVATIONS NEAR THE LARGE ROUND HUTS HAVE DEMONSTRATED THAT THE MOST PLAUSIBLE HYPOTHESIS IS THAT THEY WERE CONSTRUCTED BY THE SHONA PEOPLE.

_ (118 top and 118-119) WHAT IS THE PURPOSE OF THE GREAT ENCLOSURE THAT SURROUNDS GREAT ZIMBABWE? WHY ARE ITS WALLS SO HIGH? WHAT WAS THE FUNCTION OF THE INCREDIBLE PATHS THAT FOLLOW ITS PERIMETER? FROM WHAT ENEMIES DID MONOMOTAPA, THE LEGENDARY BANTU KING OF SOUTHEASTERN AFRICA WHO ESTABLISHED THE HEART OF HIS MYTHICAL KINGDOM HERE, THINK HE NEEDED TO DEFEND HIMSELF? AT 11 M (36 FT) HEIGHT AND 250 M (820 FT) LONG, THIS IS THE MOST MASSIVE STRUCTURE SOUTH OF THE SAHARA DESERT.

_ (118 bottom) THE CONICAL TOWER INSIDE THE GREAT ENCLOSURE IS OVER 9 M (30 FT) HIGH AND MORE THAN 5 M (16 FT) WIDE. ACCORDING TO ARCHAEOLOGISTS, IT COULD BE THE ANCIENT RESIDENCE OF THE KING. IN ANY CASE, ITS FUNCTION IS UNKNOWN. SOME SUGGEST THAT IT WAS AN ENORMOUS GRANARY, WHILE OTHERS IMAGINE IT TO BE A PHALLIC SYMBOL.

119

_ (120-121 and 121) IN ADDITION TO THE ARCHITECTURE, THE MOST FAMOUS ARTWORKS OF ZIMBABWE ARE THE EIGHT STONE BIRDS FOUND AMONG THE EXCAVATIONS OF GREAT ZIMBABWE. THEY ARE MADE OF STEATITE (ALSO KNOWN AS SOAPSTONE) AND THEIR SIGNIFICANCE IS STILL UNKNOWN. STANDING OUT AMONG THESE, HOWEVER, IS ONE DEPICTING THE BATELEUR EAGLE, THE BIRD CHOSEN AS THE ICON FOR THE FORMER RHODESIA AND LATER THE SYMBOL FOR THE REPUBLIC OF ZIMBABWE, APPEARING ON ITS FLAG.

TURKEY

Noah's Ark

(39°42'7"N - 44°17'54"E)

ON THE SUMMIT OF MOUNT ARARAT, IN SEARCH OF EVIDENCE CONFIRMING THE MOST ANCIENT OF LEGENDS.

With its elevation of 5165 m (16,945 ft), Mount Ararat dominates the scenery and culture of the entire region of Kurdistan near Turkey. Its profile appears in the center of the emblem of the Republic of Armenia, for whose people the mountain is sacred. But for the rest of the world, Mount Ararat is simply the mountain at the top of which Noah landed, according to the Bible, after the Great Flood.

In certain photographs, which by now have become famous, one can see a strange, unidentified object called "the Ararat anomaly" at the northwest crest. Many researchers believe this could be the remains of the legendary Ark, but so far the Turkish government has denied scientific expeditions access to the peak, declaring the zone to be a military area.

The myth of Ararat comes from the book of Genesis, where we read: "The Lord then said to Noah, 'Go into the ark, you and your whole family, because I have found you righteous in this generation. Take with you seven pairs of every kind of clean animal, a male and its mate [...] Seven days from now I will send rain on the earth for 40 days and 40 nights; and I will wipe from the face of the earth every living creature I have made.' And Noah did all that the Lord commanded him." (Genesis 7:1).

According to the Bible, the water covered the entire surface of the earth. The highest mountain was covered over by fully 15 cubits – about 7 m (22.9 ft) – and supposedly all this happened around 2370 BC.

The myth of such a global catastrophe is present in the legends of many peoples who are very different and remotely located from one another. The name of Noah is known in many regions of the world: in Amazonia, he is identified as Noa; the Hawaiians call him Nu-u; the Chinese recognize him as Nuwah; and in Mexico, there exists a Nalá. But the legend is even widespread in civilizations that have never come into contact with one another: there are over 150 known stories of the Flood. Even the Mesopotamian epic of Gilgamesh relates a story of the Flood highly similar to that found in the Bible: Tutu is asked to tear down his house in order to build an ark and save himself.

Scholars have attempted to reconstruct Noah's ark. At Dordrecht, in Holland, Joan Huibers built a life-size copy of the ark, following the indications given in Genesis: "So make yourself an ark of cypress wood; make rooms in it and coat it with pitch inside and out. This is how you are to build it: The ark is to be three hundred cubits long, fifty cubits wide, and thirty cubits high. Make a roof for it, leaving below the roof an opening one cubit high all around. Put a door in the side of the ark and make lower, middle and upper decks." (Genesis 6, 14-16).

The result, in fact, is a parallelepiped 156 m (171 yds) long, 26 m (28.4 yds) wide, and over 15 m (50 ft) high. An enormous crate, longer than a soccer field and as high as a four-story building, with neither bow nor stern, nor even a rudder. But he acquitted his task, according to legend: "But God remembered Noah and all the wild animals and the livestock that were with him in the ark, and he sent a wind over the earth, and the waters receded. Now the springs of the deep and the floodgates of the heavens had been closed, and the rain had stopped falling from the sky. The water receded steadily from the earth. At the end of the hundred and fifty days the water had gone down, and on the seventeenth day of the seventh month the ark came

_ (122) ILLUSTRATION FOR A 15TH CENTURY BIBLE DEPICTING NOAH'S ARK.

_ (122-123) THE MOST STRIKING VIEW OF MOUNT ARARAT IS NOT TO BE HAD IN TURKEY, BUT RATHER ON THE ARMENIAN SIDE OF THE BORDER AT THE MONASTERY OF KHOR VIRAP. BUT IT IS ONLY FROM SATELLITE PHOTOGRAPHS THAT WE CAN CAPTURE THE GEOLOGICAL IRREGULARITY IN THE MOUNTAIN'S PROFILE KNOWN AS "THE ARARAT ANOMALY."

to rest on the mountains of Ararat." (Genesis 8, 1-4).

The Bible text speaks of mountains in the plural: in effect the Ararat massif is divided into the Great Ararat and the Little Ararat, two mountains separated about 11 km (6.8 mi). By combining all the information we can establish that Noah ought to have landed at about 800 m (2625 mi) from the summit, at 4365 m (14,320 ft) elevation. In 1840, a massive volcanic explosion involved part of Ararat: at that point the wood of the legendary ark could possibly have slipped downhill. Or it might have been lost forever. At any rate, the research continues.

TURKEY

Göbekli Tepe

(37°13'23"N - 38°55'20"E)

THE OLDEST TEMPLE IN THE WORLD IS LOCATED IN TURKEY, SEEMING TO WANT TO TELL A DIFFERENT STORY ABOUT THE ORIGINS OF CIVILIZATION.

In southern Turkey, a short distance from the Syrian border, there is a hill that is home to what is called "the most ancient temple in the world," Göbekli Tepe. About 11,000 years ago, the local inhabitants scanned lands of the Mesopotamia and erected mysterious and colossal monuments in honor of gods whose names have long since been forgotten.

The discovery of this incredible manmade hill realized 9000 years before Christ, the excavation of which began only in 1994, has constrained us to rewrite the history books: Neolithic men were not, as was believed, merely hunters who lived in caves frescoed by rude graffiti, but instead were capable of constructing places of worship using refined techniques, including the polishing and carving of huge blocks of stone.

At Göbekli Tepe, a series of mysterious columns have been brought to light, produced according to a particular and unusual form, that of a *T*. Some of these reach heights of 6 m (20 ft) and weigh more than 10 tonnes: according to archaeologists' estimates, there are probably 50 throughout the area, and their form could be a stylization of gigantic man.

One wonders how it could have been possible, 3000 years before the invention of writing, for the inhabitants of Göbekli Tepe to conceive, design, and build an entire artificial hill, 15 m (50 ft) high and with a diameter reaching 300 m (984 ft), to render homage to their gods. The purpose for the large terraces and numerous stone circles that have been discovered remains unclear. Not to mention the mystery surrounding the remarkable number of bas-reliefs and sculptures depicting plants and animals of every type (for example, serpents, lions, scorpions, boars and bulls), as well as faceless anthropomorphic figures, and the beings worshipped by the ancient inhabitants of Göbekli Tepe, to whom they dedicated statues representing them as winged men.

Some believe that they were ancient shamans, while others see a relationship to the origin of the myth of angels, and still others hypothesize a link with "the legend of the guardians" cited in the Book of Enoch: according to this ancient apocryphal text, the "guardians," superior beings descended from heaven, gave the people of ancient Mesopotamia the secret knowledge of art and science, before disappearing. Another fantastic hypothesis would identify this as the hill-sanctuary of the biblical Eden: various philological studies seem, in fact, to suggest an exciting parallel between the places described in the Bible and the geographic structure and climate of the Turkish site as it must have appeared thousands of years ago.

But beyond the fantasies, the puzzle of Göbekli Tepe still seems far from a solution. The very existence of the temple is in ill agreement with an epoch in which there existed no other human civilization capable of realizing a megalithic monumental work.

_ (124-125) FROM THE SACRED HILL OF GÖBEKLI TEPE OVER 10,000 YEARS AGO, AN ANCIENT AND MYSTERIOUS CIVILIZATION SET ITS GAZE ON MESOPOTAMIA. THEN THESE PEOPLE DECIDED TO BUILD WHAT TODAY IS CONSIDERED THE MOST ANCIENT SACRED AREA KNOWN ON OUR PLANET. BUT WHICH NO ONE HAS YET BEEN ABLE TO DECIPHER.

_ (125) THE MYSTERIOUS PILLARS CHARACTERIZING GÖBEKLI TEPE MEASURE AS HIGH AS 6 M (20 FT) IN HEIGHT AND WEIGH OVER 10 TONNES. ACCORDING TO SOME THEORIES, THEY COULD BE GIGANTIC ANTHROPOMORPHIC STATUES, WHILE THE CARVINGS ON THEIR SURFACES EVOKE STRANGE FACELESS WINGED BEINGS.

125

(126 and 127) ANIMALS ARE REPRESENTED IN NEARLY ALL THE SCULPTURES AT THE ANCIENT TEMPLE OF GÖBEKLI TEPE. PROBABLY BOARS AND VULTURES, PERHAPS DOGS: THEY WERE FIXED IN THE STONE THOUSANDS OF YEARS AGO BY THE INHABITANTS OF THIS PLACE. BUT THERE ARE ALSO SERPENTS, LIONS, SCORPIONS OR BULLS. IT IS NOT YET CLEAR WHAT THE FUNCTION WAS FOR THE LARGE HOLES APPEARING IN THE WALLS AND BESIDE THE LARGE MONUMENTAL PILLARS.

Jericho, considered the most ancient city in the world, was constructed 1000 years after Göbekli Tepe, while the megalithic site of Stonehenge was constructed fully 5000 years later. For centuries, the knowledge achieved by the founders of Göbekli Tepe seems to have disappeared into nothingness.

Moreover, the sacred hill seems to have been suddenly abandoned around 8000 BC and carefully covered over with a layer of stone and earth, of an estimated volume ranging from 300 to 500 cu m (10,595 to 22,955 cu ft). Was the discovery, millennia later, really just a stroke of fortune, or is it possible that those men from very ancient times, equipped with knowledge superior to those of their own time, had sought to preserve this sacred site so that it would endure to our own days?

All the answers appear still to be buried underground. According to geo-radar and geomagnetic surveys, at least 16 more megalithic rings are buried in the 22 ha (54.4 acres) of surrounding land. And as Klaus Schmidt, the archaeologist directing the works in Turkey, affirms, only 5 percent of the site has thus far been excavated; scholars could excavate for another 50 years and succeed in only barely scratching the surface. The mystery of the world's oldest temple will surely engage more than one generation of archaeologists.

_ (128 and 129) THE VIVID IMAGES OF ANIMALS IN THE STONE SCULPTURES AT GÖBEKLI TEPE RECALL THE WALL PAINTINGS IN PALEOLITHIC CAVES. ACCORDING TO ARCHAEOLOGISTS, THEY ARE RELIGIOUS REPRESENTATIONS LINKED TO THE ANCIENT SYSTEM OF HUNTING AND GATHERING. IT IS LIKELY THAT THE MYSTERIOUS BUILDERS OF GÖBEKLI TEPE BELIEVED IN AN AFTERLIFE FOR ANIMAL SPIRITS, AND VENERATED THEM IN THEIR IMPRESSIVE AND ANCIENT EDIFICES.

(130-131) The site of Megiddo is 30 km (18.6 mi) south of Haifa and occupies a strategic position across the eastern slope of Mount Carmel, along an ancient trade route: the Via Maris, which connected Egypt with Mesopotamia. The architectural structure of the city-state that rose on this hill has remained almost untouched since biblical times.

ISRAEL

Har Megiddo

(32°35'N - 35°11'E)

ACCORDING TO THE SACRED TEXTS, THE LAST BATTLE OF MANKIND WILL BE FOUGHT ON A MOUNTAIN IN ISRAEL. AND IT WILL BE ARMAGEDDON.

If the Carmelo Ridge is peaking to your left, and on your right is the crest of Mount Gilboa, and to your back you have the Samaria region, and before you, the valley leading to Nazareth, you are probably standing on top of one of the most spiritual places on our planet: to be sure, you are right in the middle of Armageddon. The name Armageddon has become popular owing to millennial fears and big Hollywood productions: it is, in fact, synonymous with the end of the world. No one knows how and when it will arrive, but ancient sacred texts indicate its location precisely: it will take place on Mount Megiddo (in ancient Hebrew, *Har Megiddo*, whence derives the modern term Armageddon). This is the place where, according to the New Testament Book of Revelation, the final battle between all the kings of the earth will take place, between the forces of good, guided by Christ, and those of evil, incited by Satan.

But what is so special about this hill in the heart of Israel? The city state of Megiddo is mentioned several times in the Bible, and also in relation to important figures such as Joshua, Solomon, and Josiah. Inhabited for more than 6000 years – from 7000 BC to 500 BC – Megiddo was at the center of the economic and political routes of antiquity, an obligatory stop on the road that linked Egypt to Mesopotamia. As such, the city had great strategic importance.

Mount Megiddo, in particular, is a hill of debris that tells the incredible story of at least 25 civilizations that have succeeded one another over the course of their millennial history. The archaeological layers of Megiddo are a priceless treasure of knowledge: every square meter of earth is a page of a book, yet to be deciphered. A tale steeped in the blood of many armies, who clashed and fought right at Megiddo.

The place that seems destined to be the theater of the final battle of humanity appears already to have known many wars throughout its history. The most recent was during the First World War, when the British and Ottoman armies faced off at Megiddo. The British victory marked the definitive retreat of the Turks from the Middle East after more than five centuries of domination.

Many centuries earlier, in 609 BC, Egyptian soldiers guided by Pharaoh Necho II had the better of the people of Judea, led by King Josiah. The sovereign himself was killed, and ever since that time, in the Jewish culture, the battle of Megiddo has been synonymous with absolute ruin.

But the most famous of the conflicts fought around this hill saw the troops of Pharaoh Thutmose III opposing the people of Canaan in 1478 BC. This is the most ancient battle for which we have historical testimony, documented in the hieroglyphics carved in the temple of Karnak. It was a very long siege, resolved, according to legend, by a mysterious and magical "weapon of light" possessed by the Egyptians.

The immense doors that resisted the pharaoh's fury for months still dominate the city; the higher ones are said to have been constructed by the legendary King Solomon. Another sacred place is the huge round altar for sacrificial offerings. Also suggestive are the 180 steps leading toward the ancient tunnels constructed during the reign of Ahab.

But the complete secrets of Megiddo are yet to be deciphered. Suffice it to say that in this area it was only in 2005 that the remains were found of a mosaic belonging to what may be the oldest Christian church in the world. Excavations continue, delving for the truth about Armageddon. Which here is, fortunately, still only the name of a mountain.

_ (132 top and bottom) ENTRANCE TO THE CITY-STATE OF MEGIDDO WAS FROM THE NORTH SIDE. THE THREE ACCESS GATES ARE STILL VISIBLE. ON EACH SIDE WERE TWO ROOMS FROM WHICH THE SOLDIERS CONTROLLED ENTRY.

_ (133) IT IS UNCERTAIN WHETHER THE LAST CONFLICT OF THE HUMAN RACE WILL ACTUALLY TAKE PLACE AT MEGIDDO, BUT THREE BATTLES HAVE ALREADY OCCURRED ON THIS MOUNT: IN 1478 BC, IN 609 BC, AND IN 1918 AD. BLOODY CLASHES THAT DETERMINED THE OUTCOME OF LONG WARS. IT IS NOT BY CHANCE THAT – FOR THE VERY PURPOSE OF WITHSTANDING SIEGES – THERE IS A LONG TUNNEL REACHING A WELL OF WATER, ESSENTIAL FOR SURVIVAL.

ISRAEL

The Temple of King Solomon

(31°46'40"N - 35°14'8"E)

THE MOST PRECIOUS TREASURE IS PERHAPS HIDDEN IN THE MOST SACRED HEART OF THE HOLY CITY OF JERUSALEM.

The construction of Solomon's first temple began, according to the Bible, in 833 BC, and was completed seven years later. To demonstrate the importance of this building, we need only consider that of the 11 chapters dedicated to the figure of Solomon – third king of Israel, after Saul and David – in the Book of Kings of the Bible, more than three deal with the history of the construction of the legendary temple.

Yahweh revealed to King David, the father of Solomon: "But I have chosen Jerusalem, that my name might be there ..." (II Chronicles 6:6). The sovereign had thus planned to build a temple and Solomon, his son and successor, realized this project. The temple, the earthly seat of Yahweh, conserved within itself the Ark of the Covenant, the fabled chest of acacia wood overlaid with gold that God had caused Moses to build, to conserve "... a golden jar holding the manna, and Aaron's rod which budded, and the tables of the covenant ..." (Hebrews 9:4).

The Ark had already been transported to Jerusalem according to the will of David, with the intention of making Jerusalem the new religious as well as political capital of the new Kingdom of Israel. King Solomon, who had become famous for his wisdom (when Yahweh appeared to him in a dream and promised to fulfill his wish, Solomon did not ask for long life or wealth, but "an understanding heart to judge Your people to discern between good and evil." I Kings 3:9). During his very long reign (970 to 930 BC), he strengthened the process of unification and built the temple that would serve as national shrine. Inside would be hidden the greatest treasure of all time.

Based on the indications of the biblical texts, the structure of the temple was tripartite: a vestibular area, a central hall, and within it the *debir* – the Holy of Holies containing the Ark of the Covenant. The temple was erected on the outskirts of the city of David and dominated the city from above. In the open space before it rose the sacrificial altar. According to the description of the Old Testament (I Kings 6), the temple was about 30 m (98 ft) long, 10 m (33 ft) wide, and 15 m (50 ft) high; it was built of stone, covered entirely with cedar wood, carved with rosettes and flower buds. But the most important part was obviously its sanctuary, filled with treasures and relics: Solomon "prepared the inner sanctuary within the temple to set the Ark of the Covenant of the Lord there. The inner sanctuary was twenty cubits long, twenty wide and twenty high. He overlaid the inside with pure gold, and he also overlaid the altar of cedar. Solomon covered the inside of the temple with pure gold, and he extended gold chains across the front of the inner sanctuary, which was overlaid with gold. So he overlaid the whole interior with gold. He also overlaid with gold the altar that belonged to the inner sanctuary. For the inner sanctuary he made a pair of cherubim out of olive wood, each ten cubits high." (I Kings 3:9).

After the solemn placement of the Ark in the sanctuary, a cloud filled the temple, a sign of the divine presence, and Solomon inaugurated the sacred building with a solemn ceremony and a sacrifice of no fewer than 22,000 oxen and 120,000 sheep. Upon Solomon's death, however, the unity of the kingdom of Israel broke and in 587 BC, King Nebuchadnezzar of the Babylonians had the temple razed. A second temple was constructed 40 years later, but this was definitively destroyed by the Roman emperor Titus in 70 AD.

The only thing remaining from the legendary temple is part of a western retaining wall, what is now known as the famous Wailing Wall. The place where even today, thousands of years later, Solomon's descendants mourn the destruction of the legendary temple.

(134-135) JERUSALEM IS THE RELIGIOUS CENTER SACRED TO THE THREE GREAT MONOTHEISTIC RELIGIONS. THE EAST HILL OF THE ESPLANADE OF THE MOSQUES MAY PERHAPS CONCEAL AN INVIOLABLE SECRET. THE ONLY THING CERTAIN IS THAT THE SOLE VESTIGE REMAINING OF THE LEGENDARY TEMPLE OF KING SOLOMON IS WHAT IS KNOWN AS THE WAILING WALL, WHERE EVEN TODAY JEWS MOURN THE DESTRUCTION OF THE ANCIENT TEMPLE.

MONTIS DOMINI TOTIVSQ. SACRI TEMPLI EXEMPLVM

But perhaps the greatest mystery is that of the disappearance of the Ark of the Covenant. Many think it was hidden by the Knights Templar in some safe place in Europe. According to another legendary version, however, the Ark was given by King Solomon to Menelik, the son born from his relationship with the queen of Sheba, and first Emperor of Ethiopia, where even today the priests of Axum affirm that they are guarding the Ark.

But there also exists a third hypothesis. There are some who maintain, instead, that Solomon had built a hiding place under the shrine, where the Ark was concealed before the Babylonians destroyed the shrine. What is certain is that in the biblical description of the destruction of the Temple and in the detailed report of the plundered booty, the Ark is not mentioned. Some believe it is still located underground, in the area of Jerusalem where the first temple was built, deftly hidden by wise King Solomon. There are two different hypotheses about the actual position of this, the most highly accredited being that it was built on the east hill of the esplanade of the mosques. But in view of the extreme sacredness of the area, holy to three religions, the possibility of excavating there in search of the truth is nothing more than a splendid dream.

_ (136-137) *Many have tried to reconstruct the plan of the ancient temple by following the description in the Bible. To build it, Solomon used 3000 tonnes of gold and 30,000 tonnes of silver: quantities difficult even to imagine. According to the Bible, the original measures were 30 m length by 10 m width by about 15 m height (98.4 x 32.8 x 49.2 ft).*

ANTIQVIS DESCRIPTIONIBVS A BENED. ARIA MONTANO OBSERVATIS,
...RATVS SACRI INSTRVCTIONEM.

The Dead Sea Scrolls

(31°44'27"N - 35°27'31"E)

A SENSATIONAL DISCOVERY THAT OCCURRED WITHIN A SERIES
OF ABANDONED CAVES IN THE DESERT OF ISRAEL.

No place in the world has the same density of history and spirituality as Jerusalem: sacred to three religions, it has forever been the center of conflict. The secrets of its temples are timeless, but about 100 km (60 mi) farther south, in what is now known as the West Bank, in the Valley of Qumran, after centuries of neglect an incredible secret has come to light. A secret that has to do with the origin of Christianity itself.

In 1947, the ancient caves of Qumran were part of Palestine, a territory under British mandate. The caves, abandoned, were used as shelter in the rocky desert scorched by the torrid heat, not far from the salty waters of the Dead Sea. Only a few groups of shepherds or Bedouins trod those inhospitable lands. One of those, the young Mohammed el-Hamed, was playing with his companions, throwing stones, when a muffled sound coming from the depths of a cave revealed a treasure the scale of which he was unable to comprehend: dozens of jars containing scrolls written in ancient languages, words that neither he nor any of his friends were capable of understanding. These were the legendary Dead Sea scrolls, sacred and extremely important texts: the most ancient transcriptions ever found of the Hebrew Bible. The following year, the news was spread to the rest of the world, but the beginning of what was to become the Arab-Israeli war slowed the recovery operation, which lasted until 1956. Eleven caves, over 800 manuscripts, nearly 15,000 fragments: a titanic work to put everything together again.

Experts from every nation worked on it, but the majority of the discoveries were kept secret. What was written there that was not supposed to be known? According to the most fantastical theories, for example, those forming the basis of the bestseller *The Da Vinci Code*, not all of the Gospels have come down to us: those that related the true history of the Holy Grail, instead, were hidden for centuries. And at Qumran they resurfaced.

Today nearly all the Qumran fragments have been published, and they do not include apocryphal Gospels. The most important are visible in the splendid Israel Museum of Jerusalem, where they are conserved at a constant low temperature, shielded from harsh light and atmospheric agents, enclosed within a structure capable of resisting even a nuclear attack, and in a form recalling that of the jars in which the scrolls were found.

The historical and theological disputes about the findings call into question the mysterious sect of the Essenes, who inhabited Qumran between 150 BC and 68 AD: a Jewish community that could have drafted the texts that were found, and could also have possessed initiatory and prophetic knowledge.

_ (138-139 and 138) QUMRAN IS AN ARCHAEOLOGICAL SITE IN THE WEST BANK, AN ARID AND INHOSPITABLE AREA STANDING MORE THAN A KILOMETER (ABOUT A MILE) FROM THE SHORES OF THE DEAD SEA. THE RUINS OF THE SETTLEMENT ARE AS NOTHING COMPARED TO THE INCREDIBLE TREASURE THAT WAS CONSERVED IN ITS CAVES: IN 11 OF THESE, SOME 900 PRICELESS SCROLLS WERE DISCOVERED, THE MAJORITY IN PARCHMENT, BUT ALSO VARIOUS PAPYRI. THE TEMPERATURE INSIDE THE CAVES PROTECTED THE SENSATIONAL DOCUMENTS FROM THE UNSUPPORTABLE HEAT OF THE DESERT AREA: ACCORDING TO CERTAIN SCHOLARS, THE CAVES WERE THE LIBRARIES OF THE MYSTERIOUS COMMUNITY LIVING AT QUMRAN, WHO COULD AVAIL THEMSELVES OF THE PRECIOUS AND SACRED TEXTS. WHO WERE THEY?

_ (140) THE HUGE CLAY JARS DISCOVERED IN THE CAVES OF QUMRAN CONTAINED THE PRECIOUS DEAD SEA SCROLLS: THEIR STRUCTURE ALLOWED THE MANUSCRIPTS TO BE PRESERVED.

_ (140-141) ONE OF THE LONGEST SCROLLS DISCOVERED AT QUMRAN IS THE ONE THAT IS CALLED THE TEMPLE SCROLL. IT CONTAINS THE DESCRIPTION OF AN UNKNOWN JEWISH TEMPLE, ALONG WITH THE DESCRIPTION OF THE PRACTICES FOR SACRIFICES AND OTHER RELIGIOUS FUNCTIONS. IT IS ALL COMMUNICATED WITHIN THE CONTEXT OF A DIALOGUE BETWEEN GOD AND MOSES, TO WHOM THE DIRECTIVES ARE IMPARTED FOR REALIZING IT. THE TEMPLE SCROLL IS COMPOSED OF 65 COLUMNS ON PARCHMENT, AND IT IS ABOUT 9 M (29.5 FT) LONG.

The attention of treasure hunters, however, concentrates on one particular fragment discovered in the Qumran caves, the fragment catalogued as 3Q15. By contrast with all the other Qumran scrolls, this fragment is made of copper, perhaps because it had more value than the others. It is a list of 64 locations in which treasures have been concealed. Today many of the names cited on fragment 3Q15 no longer exist, which makes it difficult to orient oneself and follow this ancient treasure map. The only location that still conserves its ancient name is the mausoleum of Av Solom, located at the foot of the Mount of Olives. The copper fragment reads: "Eight talents of silver can be found by digging under the western side of the mausoleum of Av Solom. Seventeen talents are hidden under the water basin at the base of the baths. Gold and baskets of offerings are in this basin, at its four corners."

The attempt is being made to identify the other 63 hiding places indicated on fragment 3Q15, to try to understand what relics they may conceal. Many think about the legendary treasure of the Temple of King Solomon, razed to the ground by Roman soldiers under Titus in 70 AD: the treasure could have been stolen, scattered, and hidden all around the area of Jerusalem. Could the manuscripts be the key to finding it?

Petra, the lost city

(30°19'43"N - 35°26'31"E)

"MATCH ME SUCH MARVEL SAVE IN EASTERN CLIME,
A ROSE-RED CITY HALF AS OLD AS TIME." JOHN WILLIAM BURGON (1845).

In Jordan, at the edge of the spectacular red desert of Wadi Rum, centuries of time have concealed a thrilling mystery connected to a secret past, to a vanished kingdom and a treasure never found. They call it the City of Tombs, the Pink City, the Lost City, or more simply, Petra.

An entire monumental city carved into the rock, Petra was declared in July 2007 to be one of the Seven Wonders of the Modern World, but its beauty dates back to a very distant time.

In the 6th century BC, a mysterious nomadic people, the Nabataeans, took control of Petra and turned it into a major commercial hub. The Nabataeans were wealthy and cultivated, but almost all of their original documents have been lost. How was it possible for such an advanced people not to want to leave any trace of themselves?

At its maximum splendor, Petra counted a population of over 20,000. Then, inexplicably, in 106 AD, Petra allowed itself to be annexed by the Roman empire. During the first Crusade, Petra was occupied by King Baldwin I of Jerusalem, and it remained in the hands of Christians until 1187, when Saladin definitively defeated the Christian kingdoms. The last reference to the city appears in the chronicles from 1276 of the sultan Baibars al-Bunduqdari, after which the name of this fabulous city fell into oblivion. Such a silence and disappearance from the chronicles is unusual for a capital of the kingdom that at one time was very wealthy.

But if today it is possible for us to visit Petra, we owe this to the courage of the young Swiss adventurer Johann Ludwig Burckhardt. In 1812 he disguised himself as an Arab pilgrim and succeeded in having himself guided to the secret passage that today still marks the entrance to the stone canyon, over 1 km long, leading to Petra.

The first building one encounters on coming out of the canyon is El-Khazneh, "The Treasury": legend has it that a pharaoh at war with the Israelites hid his wealth in the urn that dominates the façade, 43 m (141 ft) high and 30 m (98 ft) wide. The Hollywood film *Indiana Jones and the Last Crusade* gives the impression that the Holy Grail was concealed in this very edifice carved into the rock. But beyond the fantasy, in the 12th century the Crusaders built fully five castles (one of which has yet to be found). Many believe that it was not by chance that Petra fell into oblivion after the fall of the Crusades. Was it simply destiny? Or was there something that needed to remain secret and well-guarded at Petra?

Whether or not a hidden treasure ever existed, the forgotten city certainly was unmatched in wealth.

_ (142 and 143) FEW EMOTIONS CAN EQUAL WHAT YOU FEEL UPON ENTERING PETRA FOR THE FIRST TIME. AFTER WALKING A KILOMETER (A LITTLE OVER HALF A MILE) ALONG THE NARROW CANYON THAT CONCEALED IT FROM THE WORLD FOR CENTURIES, SUDDENLY AND UNEXPECTEDLY YOU GLIMPSE THE MAJESTIC PROFILE OF EL-KHAZNEH, "THE TREASURY," THE SYMBOL OF PETRA ITSELF. AN IMPRESSIVE FACADE, 43 M (141 FT) HIGH AND 30 M (98.4 FT) WIDE, SCULPTED ENTIRELY INTO THE PINK ROCK OF THE MOUNTAIN. THE INTERIOR IS COMPOSED OF TWO BARE AND UNADORNED ROOMS: FOR THIS REASON, SOME BELIEVE THE COLOSSAL EDIFICE WAS ONLY A PRESTIGIOUS MAUSOLEUM.

_ (144-145) THE AVENUE OF THE FAÇADES DISPLAYS AN INCREDIBLE SERIES OF EDIFICES SCULPTED INTO THE ROCK, KNOWN AS THE ROYAL TOMBS, A NAME THAT REFERS TO THE MAGNIFICENCE OF THE CONSTRUCTION. THE SPECTATOR AT AN ELEVATED VIEWPOINT IS REGALED WITH A SPECTACLE UNIQUE IN THE WORLD, ALLOWING THE GAZE TO RUN OVER THE SIDE-BY-SIDE TOMBS: THE URN TOMB, THE SILK TOMB, THE CORINTHIAN TOMB AND THE PALACE TOMB, ON TO THAT OF SEXTUS FLORENTINUS.

_ (146-147) THE URN TOMB, ALSO KNOWN AS "THE COURT," IS PETRA'S SECOND LARGEST MONUMENT. BUILT IN 70 AD, IT HAS AN EXTERNAL COLONNADE LEADING INTO A COURTYARD SUSPENDED ON A SERIES OF ARCHES, REACHED VIA STAIRWAY.

_ (147) BECAUSE OF THE MAMMOTH PROPORTIONS OF PETRA'S EDIFICES, THE BEST WAY TO APPRECIATE THEM IS FROM AN ELEVATED VIEWPOINT.

The Avenue of the Façades is home to the monumental, breathtaking Royal Tombs and the Roman Theater (constructed by the Nabataeans) that seated nearly 3000 persons, arranged in three sections over 45 rows. What spectacles these public crowds may have viewed there is still unknown.

Dominating the whole area there is also a fascinating and frightening place, called "the Altar of Sacrifices": its polished platform and the channels for allowing the blood to run off make this the world's best conserved sacrificial site. The two obelisks, 7 m (23 ft) tall, represent the totems sacred to Dushara and Al-'Uzza, the divinities worshipped by the Nabataeans, who required blood tributes. Here access was forbidden to ordinary mortals.

But even more impressive is the place called "the Monastery." To reach it, one must face 800 long steps over a steep drop. After arriving to the top, one is in the presence of a colossal edifice carved into the rock, 50 m (164 ft) wide and 45 m (148 ft) high. Possibly the tomb of the Nabataean King Obodas I originally, the Monastery owes its name to the crosses sculpted in its interior, and to a miracle. The conversion of the people of Petra to Christianity was marked by a supernatural event: in the year 423 AD, the Syrian monk Barsauma arrived in Petra and found a people afflicted by four years of drought. The monk kneeled and prayed: immediately a torrential tempest emptied itself upon Petra, resulting in the conversion of the inhabitants to the faith of Christ. According to archaeologists working at Petra, the enchanting pink city represents barely 15 percent of what might be found still underground. An essay performed right beneath El-Khazneh, in fact, shows an entire underground level of magnitude equal to that which is already apparent. It is as though there were another Petra underneath Petra. Still waiting to be discovered.

(148 and 148-149) EL-DEIR – "THE MONASTERY" – IS PETRA'S LARGEST BUILDING, REACHED ONLY BY MEANS OF A LONG STEEP CLIMB THROUGH THE ROCK. BUT ONCE IN ITS PRESENCE, THE EXPERIENCE PROVES WORTH THE EFFORT: 50 M (164 FT) WIDE AND 45 M (148 FT) HIGH, IT DOMINATES THE ENTIRE CITY OF PETRA FROM ABOVE. LEGEND HAS IT THAT THE CROSSES INSIDE ARE TRIBUTES TO THE MIRACLE OF BARSAUMA, THE SYRIAN MONK WHO ARRIVED IN PETRA IN 423 AD, INVOKING A TORRENTIAL RAIN TO BATHE THE CITY AFTER FOUR YEARS OF DROUGHT.

PAKISTAN

Mohenjo-daro

(27°19'35"N - 68°8'15"E)

ON THE BORDER BETWEEN INDIA AND PAKISTAN, THE RUINS OF AN ANCIENT CITY SEEM TO TESTIFY TO AN INCREDIBLE BATTLE THAT TOOK PLACE IN THE SKIES.

In 1922 near the current border between India and Pakistan, an exceptional archaeological discovery brought to light the remains of an evolved and unknown civilization, which was given the name "Indus Valley civilization" after the great river flowing nearby. But it is also known as the Harappan civilization in reference to another ancient archaeological site discovered in the region. The city unearthed in 1922 was well-conserved and guarded an incredible secret, still waiting to be discovered. Its name is Mohenjo-daro, "the Mountain of the Dead."

According to archaeologists, the city was built around 3000 BC upon an area of 1 sq km (0.4 sq mi), and could accommodate at least 70,000 persons – a true metropolis for the time. The plan of the city reveals a clear urban design: those who built Mohenjo-daro equipped it with a wonderful water system, a perfect drainage system, and a system for heating and ventilation.

The upper part houses the famous Great Bath, two temples, and a granary, while the lower part is dense with dwellings nestled in the series of city blocks that were traced out with geometric precision within the grid of streets. Also found were shops, workshops, and products bearing inscriptions composed of over 400 different characters, which no one has yet been able to decipher. This evolved and unknown civilization was perhaps the one referred to by the Vedas, the ancient sacred texts of the Hindu religion, when they described a magnificent, advanced, nonviolent society living on the shores of the River Sarasvati.

Around 1500 BC, however, the Harappan civilization disappeared. Mohenjo-daro itself was abandoned. Academic hypotheses about why this occurred point to the changing of the courses of water that supplied the city. Other scholars have considered it possibly related to excessive overpopulation: upon reaching 400,000 inhabitants, the city would have collapsed. Still others consider the possibility of an invasion by the Ari in their destructive campaign of conquest made in honor of the god Indra, "the destroyer of forts."

But there is also another fantastical and incredible hypothesis, one that smacks of science fiction. In 1979, the Sanskrit scholar David Davenport published the book *Atomic Destruction in 2000 BC*. According to the theory proposed in the volume, Mohenjo-daro was destroyed with incredible violence. Analyses performed by experts from the University of Rome show how the bracelets, amphorae, and vitrified stones were all exposed in the past by a wave of heat having a temperature equal to about 1500 °C (2372 °F). The exhibited type of fusion with crystallization is compatible with a nuclear explosion or the impact of a meteor. Furthermore, few skeletons were found after what must have been a dramatic end. And yet laboratory analysis has shown that these, like the stones of the area, are radioactive: the levels of uranium and plutonium registered are absolutely beyond normal. According to Davenport, thousands of years ago, an atomic war was fought in the skies over the Indus Valley; perhaps it was actually fought using the famous "Vimana" cited in sacred Indian texts such as the Vedas and the Puranas. In these texts, it is written that the gods used the Vimana, meaning flying chariots, in combat.

_ (150-151) THE RESIDENTIAL AREA OF MOHENJO-DARO LED TO A CITADEL WHERE THERE WERE BATHS FOR MYSTERIOUS CEREMONIES AND RITES. ITS NAME, HOWEVER, SIGNIFIES "THE MOUNTAIN OF THE DEAD." WHAT WAS THE REASON FOR THIS? AND WHEN WAS THE LARGE STRUCTURE RECALLING A BUDDHIST STUPA BUILT?

_ (151) MANY HAVE MISTAKEN THE CYLINDRICAL CONSTRUCTIONS OF MOHENJO-DARO FOR A SERIES OF ENIGMATIC TOWERS. IN REALITY, IT IS MOST LIKELY THAT THEY WERE ENORMOUS CONDUITS TO REACH THE WELLS OF WATER BELOW.

_ (152) THE BEAUTIFUL STONE TABLETS DISCOVERED IN THE EXCAVATIONS AT MOHENJO-DARO SHOW PICTOGRAPHIC WRITING. THEY HAVE BEEN DATED TO THE PERIOD OF THE HARAPPAN CIVILIZATION, BETWEEN 2500 BC AND 1700 BC. THESE STONE SEALS DEPICT ANCIENT ANIMALS, INCLUDING EVEN THE LEGENDARY UNICORN. THE ACCOMPANYING INSCRIPTION, HOWEVER, HAS NOT YET BEEN DECIPHERED.

_ (153) THE KARACHI MUSEUM IN PAKISTAN HOUSES A MAJORITY OF THE INCREDIBLE AND UNDECIPHERABLE DISCOVERIES FOUND IN THE EXCAVATIONS AT MOHENJO-DARO. ONE OF THE MOST ENIGMATIC IS THE SCULPTURE DEPICTING A HUMAN FIGURE, PROUD AND STERN, WHICH SCHOLARS HAVE IDENTIFIED AS POSSIBLY BEING A PRIEST OF THE INDUS VALLEY CIVILIZATION.

In the epic poem *Ramayana*, we can read the following descriptions: "That chariot moves by itself, all shining and painted ... as it flies it emits a melodious sound that seems like a murmur." Or further: "Suddenly there came a great wind that caused the mountains to shake, and one could see a flame of fire that navigated through the air." In another great Hindu poem, the *Mahabharata*, it is written: "We saw in the sky ... an enormously dark Vimana, which launched flaming projectiles. It approached the ground at an incredible velocity, hurling wheels of fire." The text also speaks of a ray that could incinerate entire armies and provoke, among the survivors, the falling of fingernails and hair, as well as describing the weapon of Agneya: "An arrow that had the dazzling splendor of smokeless fire was launched. ... The world, burned by the heat of that weapon, seemed gripped by a fever. Even the waters became hot, and the creatures that lived in the waters seemed to burn. The enemies fell like trees burned by a devastating fire." The descriptions cannot fail to recall the tragedy of Hiroshima and Nagasaki. What happened at Mohenjo-daro thousands of years ago and why today it still seems radioactive is a yet unsolved mystery.

(154) The ancient inhabitants of Mohenjo-daro seem to have disappeared suddenly and without any obvious reason. And yet their level of development was on the cutting edge for a civilization of 5000 years ago. As an example, the bathrooms in their dwellings were even equipped with a system for discharging through a plumbing tube.

(154-155) Various skeletons have been found among the ruins at Mohenjo-daro, but in particular, the excavation conducted by archaeologist John Marshall identified 13 human cadavers that were overcome by sudden death. Their burials are not normal, and they display no combat wounds, but rather only evidence of calcination, suggesting a sudden and terrifying blast of heat.

INDIA

The Pillar of Ashoka

(28°31'28"N - 77°11'6"E)

IN THE HEART OF MOST SPIRITUAL INDIA, A COLOSSAL IRON PILLAR HAS CHALLENGED THE RAINS WITHOUT EVER RUSTING FOR OVER 1500 YEARS. HOW IS THIS POSSIBLE?

In New Delhi, the sprawling metropolitan capital of India, we find one of the greatest enigmas of the past: a mysterious iron column, also known as the Ashokan pillar. Not everyone among the thousands of tourists who crowd the Quwwat-ul-Islam complex every year knows the importance of the manmade object found in the courtyard of the ancient mosque.

The mosque and the gigantic 74 m (243 ft) minaret were built in the 12th century during the Muslim domination of India. The iron pillar of Delhi, however, is a "standard of Vishnu" at least 1600 years old, an object of worship that must have been part of a Hindu temple, not a mosque. We do not know where it came from, or who produced it, and above all, we do not know how an iron pillar could have resisted 16 centuries out in the open without having been destroyed by rust.

Made of solid iron, the column is over 7 m (23 ft) tall and weighs nearly 7 tonnes: the pillar must have been made of wrought iron. How it could have been possible to create a work like this without modern technology remains an unsolved riddle. The most impressive part of the column is the capital: the eight pieces that compose it were designed, forged, and assembled with absolute precision. On the top, there is also a rectangular hole that probably housed a circular disk of metal, a chakra. Among the different significances of the chakra, one was that of a weapon of the god Vishnu: a deadly, tapered disk. Vishnu hurled the chakra, and when the disk reached his enemies, it decapitated them before returning into his hands like a boomerang.

Laboratory analyses conducted in 2010 demonstrated that the pillar's exceptional resistance to corrosion is due to a thin film of oxide and the high phosphorus content of the iron. The secret, according to scientists, is the type of iron that was used. But 1600 years ago, who could have been capable of producing a substance of this sort? In the Madhya Pradesh, a region in central India, there was an ancient tribe, the Agaria, who by tradition had always extracted and worked the iron. Their secret consisted in selecting a particular type of iron ore that did not rust because it was rich in phosphorus.

One of the major puzzles concerning the pillar of iron was where it was originally located. An inscription on the monument affirms that the column was erected at *Vishnu-pada-giri*, a hill with a footprint of Vishnu. And in the zone of Vidisha, in Madhya Pradesh, one can find a hill with a very unusual form: seen from above, it shows, in fact, the outline of a gigantic footprint. The hill of Udaygiri is located along the line of the Tropic of Cancer, an ideal site for astronomical observers, who flourished in this very zone. The incredible column of Delhi might thus be what remains of a very ancient, forgotten observatory. And its shadow would have aided ancient priests in understanding the sky above them. A plausible hypothesis, at least until the precious metal disk, now lost, that once adorned it is found again.

_ (156) The complex of Quwwat-ul-Islam in New Delhi presents a suggestive series of monuments, buildings, and tombs, among which is India's oldest mosque.

_ (157) The iron pillar of Ashoka is considered a standard of Vishnu. The eight constituent parts of the capital were forged and welded together with an impressive degree of precision.

158

Mogui Cheng

(45°30'N - 85°55'E)

THE "CITY OF DEMONS" SEEMS TO TAKE ON A SINISTER LIFE DURING THE NIGHTS OF THE INHOSPITABLE CHINESE DESERT.

In the Chinese autonomous province of Xinjiang, we can find the lowest point (in the Taklamakan Desert, 155 m or 509 ft below sea level) as well as the highest point (the peak of K2, with its 8611 m or 28, 251 ft) in all the People's Republic of China. Also in Xinjiang, we find the point of land most distant from any sea on the entire planet: this point in the Dzoosotoyn Elisen Desert is 2648 km (1645.4 mi) distant from the closest seashore. It is a region of the world where nature appears extreme and at times unwelcoming. It is a meeting place for the stories and legends of many different peoples all bordering together: Mongolia, Russia, Kazakhstan, Kyrgyzstan, Tajikistan, Afghanistan, Pakistan and India. The famous Silk Road passes through this area, and there is still a vivid suggestion of the echoes of ancient armies crossing it, recounted by Marco Polo or by whoever recounted the exploits of Genghis Khan. Legend has it that one of these armies disappeared into nothingness, swallowed up by a demonic song and a sinister sandy wind. It happened in the Urho District, 100 km (60 mi) north of the city of Karamay, in the unsettling ghost town of Mogui Cheng. They also call it "the Nuomin Wind (or Ghost) City," while the Mongols refer to it as Sulumuhak, "the Castle of Specters."

Mogui Cheng is not really a city; it is an amazing desert area covering 30 sq km (11.6 sq mi), where gusts of wind and tumultuous rain have eroded and shaped the terrain, resulting in imposing and disturbing structures that actually recall the abandoned ancient castles, towers, and dwellings of a ghostly city. But there are also human and nonhuman faces, terrifying profiles of unknown demons, as were masterfully immortalized in the film *Crouching Tiger, Hidden Dragon*, the 2001 Oscar-winner.

Here the wind blows relentlessly 24 hours a day, reaching speeds difficult to find recorded on dry land, but which can be found on the open sea, such as winds of storm force 10. By night, sands fly, stones bump together, and terrifying sounds chase one another around the curves of the structures of the "ghost town."

According to local tradition, these would be the voices of demons that torment Mogui Cheng, or the diabolical ranks of Yen-lo-wang, the Taoist divinity known as guardian and judge of hell.

In stepping through the crackling pebbles of Mogui Cheng, those who are more fortunate find gems of red carnelian, also known as the "crystal of the oracle," owing to its presumed magical properties allowing seers to look into the past. And for this city, the past means a boundless loneliness and desolation, but also an entirely different story: that of lakes where dinosaurs came to drink hundreds of millions of years ago, to the south of Dinosaur Valley, before the great cataclysm that swept them away forever. But this is truly another history, one that also transited through the valleys and peaks of this enigmatic and fascinating region of China.

_ (158-159) DURING THE DAY THE HILLS SHAPED BY THE WIND AT MOGUI CHENG APPEAR AS SUGGESTIVE, AESTHETICALLY INTERESTING FORMATIONS. BUT IT IS AS THE SUN SETS THAT THE CURVES AND ANGLES OF THE GEOLOGICAL RELIEFS SEEM TO TRANSFORM INTO ARCHAIC CONSTRUCTIONS, AND THE WIND PASSING THROUGH THEM ANIMATES THEM WITH VOICES AND BLOODCURDLING SCREAMS.

_ (158) GAOCHANG IS AN ANCIENT CITY DATING BACK TO THE 1ST CENTURY BC, BUILT NEAR AN OASIS IN THE INHOSPITABLE TAKLAMAKAN DESERT IN THE XINJIANG PROVINCE OF CHINA. FOR CENTURIES IT WAS AN OBLIGATORY STOP FOR MERCHANTS TRAVELING ALONG THE SILK ROAD, UNTIL IT WAS DESTROYED BY LOCAL WARS DURING THE 14TH CENTURY UNDER THE MING DYNASTY.

_ (160-161 and 161) CROUCHING TIGER, HIDDEN DRAGON IS ANG LEE'S FILM MASTERPIECE, WINNER OF FOUR OSCARS IN 2001, INCLUDING BEST FOREIGN FILM. BUT THE ENIGMATIC STRUCTURES OF THE GHOST TOWN OF MOGUI CHENG, CHOSEN BY THE TAIWANESE DIRECTOR TO EVOKE THE "UNNATURAL" WONDER OF THE REGION OF XINJIANG, PROBABLY PLAYED A CRUCIAL ROLE CONTRIBUTING TO ITS RECOGNITION FOR BEST ART DIRECTION AND BEST CINEMATOGRAPHY.

CHINA
The Pyramid of Xi'an

(34°22'53"N - 109°15'14"E)

THE LARGEST TOMB IN THE WORLD WAS TO CONTAIN EVERYTHING CONQUERED IN LIFE BY QIN SHI HUANG, THE MAN WHO UNIFIED CHINA.

At 2 km (1.2 mi) from the city of Xi'an, in the Chinese province of Shaanxi, exists an extraordinary world: hundreds of mounds of earth that rise among the farms, some of medium size, others gigantic. What is contained inside them is still a mystery, but we know who was buried there: emperors, generals, nobles, some of whom were the richest and most powerful persons ever to live on earth.

Some 2000 years ago, these lands were the theater of bloody wars; massive armies clashed and dynasties rose and fell. All around echoed the sounds of thousands of workers engaged in building tombs. Monuments of a fantasy world, which was to continue even after death: symbols of power and wealth, status symbols that were to last for eternity.

The most important of these tombs is also connected to the most powerful of curses. In 246 BC, a united China still did not exist. A series of small kingdoms fought among one another for supremacy. In the region of Qin, a very young sovereign, who had just inherited the throne, ordered the construction of his own tomb. The tombs of important people were supposed to be built upon higher ground, and that of the king was supposed to be the highest of all, so the builders chose a site on the slopes of Mount Li. What they could not have known at that point was that the mausoleum they were building was to become one of the greatest works ever created on earth. The child-king of Qin succeeded in later years to unify the kingdoms into a single empire under his command: thus was born the empire of Qin, or China.

The architects were now called upon to create a monument for the most powerful man in all of Chinese history: an entire royal palace, reproduced underground, in the interior of a mountain created for the occasion. An artificial mountain that measures about 350 m (1150 ft) per side and 70 m (230 ft) in height. It was realized using over 3.5 million tonnes of earth, carefully pressed. It was much more than a tomb; it covered nearly 6000 ha (23 sq mi) of terrain and constituted one of the largest funerary complexes ever built in the world.

Ancient accounts describe the burial place in these terms: "On the ceiling shone the heavenly constellations. The floor reconstituted the realm of the Emperor, with rivers and oceans made of mercury and replicas of all his royal palaces, ready to welcome his soul. The entirety was surrounded by everything he would need for governing in the beyond, just as he had done in life." The grave goods must have been impressive. One need only think that there was not even any mention of the entire army of 8000 terra-cotta soldiers, the spectacular "Army of Xi'an" that was interred near the tomb.

_ (162) ONE OF THE MONUMENTAL COMPLEXES OF SHAANXI, NEARBY XI'AN, IS THE MAOLING, A MAUSOLEUM INCLUDING THE TOMBS OF EMPEROR WUDI OF THE HAN AND THAT OF EMPRESS LI AND PRINCESS YANG XIN.

_ (163) THE FIRST EMPEROR'S TERRA-COTTA ARMY, ALSO KNOWN AS "THE ETERNAL ARMY," IS JUST ONE OF THE INCREDIBLE TREASURES INSIDE THE MAUSOLEUM OF QIN SHI HUANG. DEPLOYED FOR MORE THAN 2000 YEARS, THE ARMY CLOSES ITS RANKS TO ACCOMPANY THE EMPEROR IN THE JOURNEY TO ETERNITY AND TO FIGHT UNDER HIS ORDERS IN THE AFTERLIFE.

(164) QIN SHI HUANG WAS THE FIRST CHINESE EMPEROR, THE MAN WHO UNIFIED CHINA, THE NAME FOR WHICH, IN FACT, IS OWED TO HIM. HE IS ONE OF THE MOST CONTROVERSIAL PERSONALITIES IN HISTORY, AND HIS MAD DREAM OF REPRODUCING THE EMPIRE WITHIN HIS OWN MAUSOLEUM PROBABLY FOUNDERED OWING TO ITS FEROCITY AND TO THE INCREDIBLE TRIBUTE OF LIVES FOR THE CONSTRUCTION OF THE TOMB AND ITS ORNAMENTS.

The entire world of the Emperor was replicated by forging bronze and terra-cotta, but also by offering blood tributes. Beyond the hundreds of propitiatory human sacrifices, in fact, the lives of thousands of workers were consumed: they worked from dawn until sunset, until the exhaustion of their energy, deprived of food and sleep, until death. All the Emperor's citizens had to spend one year of their life in service of the construction of the tomb. Many, however, remained there much longer and never returned home.

Then there is another question: according to historical records, at the end of the building process, the tomb supposedly measured 150 m (492 ft) in height, much higher than it is today. A pyramid of that height would have to have a base of 500 m (1640 ft) per side, which means a dimension five times greater than it currently is, and four times larger than the Egyptian pyramids. Experts believe that the reduced dimensions we see today are owing to the prolonged action of winds and rains, which have eroded the enormous mound of earth. But another theory suggests that the tomb is lower because it was never completed. In 210 BC, when the Emperor died, the people rebelled against the atrocities they had endured and put an end to his dynasty forever. Perhaps Qin's mad dream to re-create an underground empire, so that he could be accompanied in the afterlife, failed. But what remains alive instead, after more than 2000 years, is the most incredible of his undertakings: the unification of China. A nation traveling full kilter toward a leading role in the near future.

(164-165) THE "ETERNAL ARMY" OF THE FIRST EMPEROR IS ONLY A SMALL PART OF HIS INCREDIBLE TREASURE. THE MORE THAN 8000 WARRIORS, READY TO FOLLOW QIN SHI HUANG INTO THE AFTERLIFE, ARE NOT EVEN MENTIONED IN REPORTS OF WHAT COULD BE FOUND INSIDE THE MAUSOLEUM. THEY OCCUPY A SECLUDED LOCATION, ALMOST AS THOUGH CRAMMED INTO A LATERAL AREA OF THE STRUCTURE, ALMOST AS IF TO INDICATE THAT THERE WAS QUITE A BIT MORE TO LOOK AT WITHIN THE MARVELOUS TOMB OF XI'AN.

JAPAN

The Ruins of Yonaguni

(24°26'58"N - 122°56'1"E)

AN INCREDIBLE UNDERWATER FORTRESS SEEMS TO HAVE SUNK OFF THE COAST OF OKINAWA. THEY CALL IT "THE SEA PALACE."

In the ocean abysses of the westernmost point of all of Japan, the archipelago of Ryukyu, lies an ancient mystery. Off the shore of the small island of Yonaguni, underwater explorer Kikachiro Aratake made a sensational discovery in 1985: a majestic rock formation, a sort of underwater pyramid, shaped and sculpted, apparently by human hands. The exceptional discovery immediately raised questions about the dating of the unusual structure, as well as the identity of the unknown builders who thousands of years ago erected this temple forgotten on the sea floor.

After years of research coordinated by Masaaki Kimura, professor of oceanography at the University of Ryukyu, the data regarding the incredible underwater discovery seem to identify a single block of carved stone, 20 m (66 ft) high, 200 m (656 ft) deep, and 100 m (328 ft) wide. The structure is pyramidal, with huge terraces, stairways, and genuine avenues within it.

Some geologists maintain that the structure could only be the work of nature, a combination of natural underwater events that could have brought about a spectacular and geometric erosion of the submerged pyramid. According to Professor Tamora, however, there are two possible scenarios, which correspond to two possible datings. In the first scenario, the entire area would have been submerged by the melting of glaciers from the last glaciation, with the consequent rising of sea levels, some 10,000 years ago. According to this hypothesis, a very ancient, unknown civilization would have been annihilated during the climatic upheaval. In the second scenario, the archaeological complex of Yonaguni would date back to a more recent epoch: between 4000 BC and 400 BC. In this case, it would have ended up at the bottom of the sea as a result of one of the devastating earthquakes and tsunamis that cyclically affect this region of the planet.

Many inhabitants of the island cite an ancient local legend that tells of the exploits of Taro Urashima, the hero who was borne on the back of a turtle to "the underwater palace of the god of the sea." This is the very animal that appears to be sculpted within the Yonaguni structure. One section of the pyramid, in fact, is called the "Sacred Area" owing to certain curious discoveries found inside it: a bird of stone, a triangular basin, and a block sculpted in the form of a turtle, very similar to the *kamekobaka*, the turtle-shell tombs typical of the Okinawa tradition.

Around the central body of Yonaguni, a terraced structure, runs a circular route between 6 m (20 ft) and 50 m (164 ft) wide, bordered by a low wall that opens only at an arched gate. Outside this ring, which defines the perimeter of the principal pyramid, five other, smaller edifices rise.

The façade of the construction is oriented toward the south, and it is from here that the stairs begin that lead to the two areas called the "Sacred Area" (to the east) and the "Terrace" (to the west), the latter being characterized by suggestive rock sections perpendicular to one another and perfectly cut at right angles.

At the highest level of the structure are three large cylindrical holes that can accommodate large pillars, which perhaps collapsed, and a trap door leading to a room below, inside which a dolmen is housed. Another structure, called *Goshintai*, contains a fascinating stone that, according to certain researchers, could have functioned as an ancient sundial.

_ (166-167) THE MAIN BODY OF THE UNDERGROUND STRUCTURE OF YONAGUNI IS AN ENORMOUS PYRAMID 20 M HIGH, 150 M WIDE, AND 200 M LONG (65.6 x 492 x 656 FT). ALL AROUND, A CIRCULAR AVENUE CALLED THE RING ROAD RUNS, FROM 6 M (19.7 FT) TO 15 M (49.2 FT) WIDE, AND BOUNDED BY A LOW WALL OPENING OUT AT A SUGGESTIVE ARCHED GATE. OUTSIDE THIS, FIVE MORE SMALLER BUILDINGS SURROUND THE INCREDIBLE FORTRESS.

_ (168) Two places at Yonaguni are referred to as "terraces": the main one and the upper one. The rocks composing them are perpendicular and perfectly cut, with the entire structure facing south. Even if the entire structure is a work of nature, as the skeptics argue, the spectacle still is unique in the world.

_ (169) There are two ways to admire the underwater ruins of Yonaguni: the first is diving to the seabed, located about half an hour by boat from the small port of Yonaguni, while watching out for the hammerhead sharks that profusely populate the area. The alternative is a glass bottom boat tour, organized over the ruins on a weekly basis.

Outside the main complex, the other buildings are all connected by walkways, such as the one leading to the fascinating megalith similar to one of the Moai on Easter Island. It is 7 m (23 ft) high, and at its upper part, has some engravings that seem to suggest the features of the face; there are two horizontal fissures called "the eyes of Jacques," in honor of the deceased Jacques Mayol, the great French diver who was enamored of the pyramid of Yonaguni.

Could the enigmatic underwater structure of Yonaguni be the work of nature? Or must we rather think of a civilization that disappeared thousands of years ago without leaving any other traces of itself besides this underwater pyramid? Among the supporters of the human hypothesis, there are many who call into question the legend of Mu, the hypothetical continent that supposedly existed in the distant and forgotten past, before disappearing right into the Pacific between Japan and South America.

The only thing certain is that, for the dates indicated by scientists as possible periods for the realization of the underwater structures of Yonaguni, no known evolved civilization inhabited the Japanese island. The truth about the Yonaguni pyramid seems to be well-guarded on the ocean floor.

CAMBODIA

Angkor

(13°24'45"N - 103°52'0"E)

IN THE HEART OF CAMBODIA, FORGOTTEN FOR CENTURIES IN THE FOREST, AN ANCIENT AND WONDERFUL SECRET IS SCULPTED IN STONE

Angkor, in Cambodia, is an impressive place, shrouded in mystery. An ancient city, today it is considered one of the great marvels of our planet. Angkor Wat is the most famous temple and its name derives from the ancient Sanskrit; in the Khmer language, it means "the temple of the capital." It is a magical place, enveloping, with extremely suggestive architecture: it is not by chance that it has become Cambodia's major attraction or that an image of it now appears on the Asian country's national flag. But within it, many yet unresolved mysteries are concealed. The walls of the sacred temples of Angkor, in fact, enclose a very ancient history: its stones and its bas-reliefs recount an incredible legend, suspended between sky, stars, and prophecies.

Viewed from above, the entire Angkor Wat complex appears like a map. Its principal building is an *equinoctial structure*, that is, oriented according to the east-west axis, and arranged in such a manner that at the spring equinox, the sun rises over its central tower. Then, the number 72 plays an important role: apparently the ancient builders wanted to emphasize this number in a very obvious way within the architectural complex. Perhaps it is only a coincidence, but there are also 72 architectural structures of Angkor Wat, and 72 is the number of degrees of longitude that separate it from the legendary Pyramid of Cheops to the west, and 144 (72 x 2), the number of degrees from the Moai of the Easter Island to the east.

And nothing at Angkor Wat seems to have been left to chance. We need only think that there are four epochs of Hindu mythology – the Krita Yuga (which lasts 1,728,000 years), the Treta Yuga (1,296,000 years), the Davpara Yuga (864,000 years), and the Kali Yuga (432,000 years) – and the sections at Angkor register exactly the same values if measured in *hat* (the local unit of measure, equal to about half a meter). Whoever built this architectural jewel knew exactly what the numbers of this place were supposed to represent.

If we were to think about a link between the great mythical places of our planet, this could probably be represented by the stars. This fantastical hypothesis has sparked some of the most incredible theories: the design of the buildings of Angkor, for example, would appear to reproduce the constellation of Draco, in the same manner in which the Pyramids of Giza appear to reproduce the belt of Orion. Draco the Dragon, however, was visible during the spring equinox at the latitudes of Angkor for the last time in 10,500 BC. This was the same era when the Sphinx of Giza was reflected on the horizon with the constellation of Leo, which the Sphinx would represent, according to certain views. It is a fanciful theory that would overturn everything we know about the history of ancient civilizations of our planet. As far as we know, 12,000 years ago there were no civilizations well enough developed to be able to produce works of this magnitude and complexity.

_ (170-171) ACCORDING TO A RECENT STUDY, ANGKOR WAS THE LARGEST METROPOLIS IN THE MIDDLE AGES: AROUND ITS SACRED BUILDINGS, A SETTLEMENT STRETCHED OVER 1000 SQ KM (386 SQ MI), CHARACTERIZED BY A COMPLEX CANAL SYSTEM. AN AREA COMPARABLE TO THAT OF MODERN LOS ANGELES. AT THE HEIGHT OF ITS DEVELOPMENT, IT HAD NEARLY 1 MILLION INHABITANTS.

_ (171) FOR EACH CARDINAL POINT THERE IS AN ENTRANCE TO ANGKOR WAT. THE LARGEST IS THE WESTERN ONE, OVER WHICH THE RUINS OF THREE TOWERS LOOM. THE ENTIRE TEMPLE REPRESENTS THE OLYMPUS OF THE KHMER, MOUNT MERU: FIVE TOWERS FOR ITS FIVE PEAKS, AND THE WATER LIKE THE OCEAN SURROUNDING IT. ACCESS TO HIGHER LEVELS WAS GRADUALLY MADE MORE EXCLUSIVE: PERSONS OF LOWER RANK HAD TO STOP AT THE OUTERMOST, LOWEST LEVEL.

171

Official archaeology, however, establishes that the construction of Angkor Wat took place between the years 1113 and 1150, by order of Suryavarman II.

But among the 1200 sq m of spectacular and detailed bas-relief carvings that adorn the buildings of Angkor Wat, there exists an interesting clue: sculpted in the stone is a tale from Hindu mythology called the "churning of the ocean of milk." According to some, this would be a metaphor describing a specific scientific theory: the precession of the equinoxes, a fundamental astronomical phenomenon for those observing the skies. In the relief, the Asura (gods) and the Deva (angels) pull on the coils of the serpent —which would represent the constellation of Draco — wrapped about Mount Mandara, to facilitate the transition from one astrological age to the next. And thus explaining why the sky we observe changes slowly through the centuries.

One final curiosity: in the temple of Ta Prohm, one of the few temples have not been restored, another curious engraving ignites tourists' fantasies: the "dinosaur bas-relief." It's an animal figure that bears a strong resemblance to the prehistoric stegosaurus, a creature that became extinct 140 million years ago, when humans did not yet live on this planet.

_ (172 top and bottom) THE PERIMETER OF ANGKOR WAT'S CENTRAL TEMPLE IS LINED BY A BREATHTAKING GALLERY, WHOSE INTERIOR WALL ON EACH SIDE HOSTS A LONG SEQUENCE OF BAS-RELIEFS: ALTOGETHER THEY COVER ABOUT 800 M (0.5 MI) OF WALL. BUT THE MOST AMAZING PANEL IS THE ONE REPRESENTING THE FAMOUS "CHURNING OF THE OCEAN OF MILK": A HINDU MYTH RELATED TO THE ASTRONOMICAL PHENOMENON OF THE PROCESSION OF THE EQUINOXES.

_ (172-173) THE RELIEF OF "THE HEAVENS AND THE HELLS" REPRESENTS 32 HELLS AND 37 HEAVENS OF HINDU MYTHOLOGY. THE PURPOSE WAS TO REPRESENT THE ATROCIOUS AGONY RESERVED FOR THOSE WHO VIOLATE THE LAWS OF THE COMMUNITY, CHARACTERIZED BY DISPROPORTIONATE PENALTIES: GATHERING FLOWERS IN THE GARDEN OF SHIVA, FOR EXAMPLE, WAS PUNISHED BY HAVING ONE'S HEAD PIERCED BY NAILS THROUGHOUT ETERNITY.

_ (174 top) THE NAME OF THE TEMPLE OF TA PROHM SIGNIFIES "OLD BRAHMA": IT WAS ONE OF THE FIRST TO BE BUILT BY JAYAVARMAN VII. A STELE INDICATES THE SITE THAT WAS INHABITED BY MORE THAN 12,000 PEOPLE. WITH THE END OF THE KHMER EMPIRE, HOWEVER, IT FELL INTO RUINS AND WAS SWALLOWED UP BY THE FOREST, PARTICULARLY BY STRANGLER FIGS.

_ (174 bottom) THE DENSE DECORATIONS ADORNING THE TEMPLE OF TA PROHM REPRESENT VARIOUS TYPES OF ANIMALS: MONKEYS, DEER, WATER BUFFALO, PARROTS, LIZARDS. ONE OF THESE, HOWEVER, HAS SPARKED DEBATES AND FANTASIES: IT WOULD APPEAR TO REPRESENT A STEGOSAURUS STENOPS, A DINOSAUR EXTINCT 140 MILLION YEARS AGO.

_ (175) THE BAYON TEMPLE IS THE LATEST ONE TO BE BUILT AT ANGKOR. THE TEMPLE TOWERS ARE CHARACTERIZED BY HUGE STONE FACES. ACCORDING TO SOME HYPOTHESES, THESE WOULD BE REPRESENTATIONS OF KING JAYAVARMAN VII; OTHERS BELIEVE THEY REPRESENT THE BODHISATTVA LOKESVARA, THE SACRED BEING WHO, ACCORDING TO BUDDHISM, IS THE MASTER OF COMPASSION, CHARACTERIZED BY A BENEVOLENT SMILE.

AUSTRALIA

Uluru

(25°20'42"S - 131°2'10"E)

THE PULSATING AND MYSTERIOUS HEART OF AUSTRALIA IS AN ENORMOUS ROCK, AT THE CENTER OF THE AUSTRALIAN CONTINENT'S ARID DESERT AND OF THE ANCIENT KNOWLEDGE OF THE ABORIGINES.

Australia is one of the most ancient lands on the planet. It is as mysterious as it is rich in resources, a continent that in some periods of the year becomes arid and inhospitable. Here, in this huge land, more than 50,000 years ago, what is perhaps the most ancient civilization still existing on our planet arrived: men and women who appear to have had mysterious sensory abilities, knowledge now lost for the rest of the world.

The center of Australia – also called its "red heart" on account of the color of its earth – is an arid place, hiding secrets that have not yet been revealed, beginning with the unusual geological forms of certain sites. The most famous is the legendary site of Uluru, but the same enigmas also cross through Mount Conner, with its flat top, and Kata Tjuta, a marvelous place that is sacred for the Anangu.

The English Captain James Cook was the first European to explore the coast of Australia in 1770. At that time, the Aborigines were estimated to number between 300,000 and 1 million. They divided into many tribes or clans, each of which spoke a different language; there were more than 500.

Many scientists have long studied the shamanic powers of the Aborigines: the first anthropologists who visited the Australian tribes told of having seen men who had extraordinary powers, such as being able to climb up a rope suspended in the void, to fly, to appear or disappear at will, to levitate, to see through bodies, to traverse long distances in an instant, as well as telepathic communication and clairvoyance. Many sacred Australian places are forbidden to those who are not Aborigines, because the energy of these sites is considered to be so powerful as to overwhelm those who are not capable of enduring it.

The culture of the Aboriginal people is the oldest in the world, older even than the Assyrian-Babylonians or the Egyptians. But how long have the Aborigines lived in Australia? The most ancient archaeological sites date back to about 40,000 years ago. One of the most important Aborigine areas is that of the Northern Territories, a region as large as Italy, France, and Spain put together. Here a major part has been found of the testimony of the millennial presence of the Aborigines.

At 460 km (286 mi) from Alice Springs, the city standing at the center of the continent of Australia, we find one of the most mysterious places in the world: its name in the Aborigine language is Uluru; the English call it Ayers Rock. It is the largest monolith on our planet, the most ancient rock in Australia. Its perimeter is 10 km (6 mi) and it rises 348 m (1142 ft) high: a colossus that is continually changing its color, through the entire range of red, in accordance with the hour of the day and the season. The most exciting moment, however, is doubtlessly twilight, when Uluru shines of its own accord, monumental and magical amid the dark desert surrounding it.

The Aborigines consider it to be the principle of the creation of the world, linked to ancient legends of what they call "the dream time." Uluru is a sacred site, powerful, charged with energy. Here they still celebrate shamanic rites. Some caves still conserve sacred paintings narrating the very ancient history of the earth, which the Aborigines consider to be a dream materialized.

(176-177 and 177) TO UNDERSTAND THE MAGIC OF ULURU, YOU NEED TO VISIT AT SUNSET. THE ANCIENT AND IMPOSING MONOLITH HAS ONE UNIQUE CHARACTERISTIC: THE STONE IT IS MADE OF, ARKOSE, CHANGES COLOR VORTICALLY AT TWILIGHT. PASSING THROUGH EVERY SHADE OF RED, WHEN THE DESERT ALL AROUND IS TOTALLY DARK AND BLACK, ULURU TAKES ON A VIVIDLY ORANGE GLOW. ANOTHER CHARACTERISTIC OF THIS INSELBERG – GEOLOGICALLY, A MOUNTAIN ISOLATED FROM OTHER ROCKY FORMATIONS – IS THE COMPACTNESS OF ITS SURFACE.

177

In the Aboriginal view of the world, time is not linear: words do not exist for *past* or *future*. The memory of the fathers, passed down exclusively by word of mouth for thousands of years, recounts the stories of "the dream time," when the first beings emerged from the earth, from the sky and from the sea, taking on the forms of living beings and moving about the territory, giving life, with their bodies, to men, plants, and animals. Although known by many names, today they are commonly referred to as Ancestor Spirits.

Uluru is an important place for the Aborigines because many ancestors passed through here and their traces would still be visible today. They are part of the territory and form part of the dense network of sacred sites, connected to one another by the pathways called "songlines." Some scholars believe these are lines of particular geomagnetic force that the Aborigines can perceive owing to their particular sensitivity and expertise. Certainly, people followed some of these pathways during migrations – just as birds do in flight – that are vital in such an inhospitable land.

By contrast, geology considers the bizarre rock forms that can be seen everywhere as the simple result of the erosive action of atmospheric agents. But also as the result of a meteorite shower that 4700 years ago devastated this area of the planet. In any case, a force from heaven.

_ (178 and 178-179) When water flows down Uluru's majestic flanks, near Mutitjulu, the phenomenon is more than rare. The storm surrounding the unmistakable profile of Ayers Rock on the night of 14 October, 2010, dumped the same quantity of water that falls, on the average, upon this tract of desert in an entire year.

(180 top) The representations of the Wandjina, the mythological gods of the Aborigines who descended to Earth from the Milky Way, are among the most suggestive examples of Aborigine art from the Kimberley region. Painted by the Worrorra people in the Raft Point caves, these pictograms dating back to 6000 BC represent a collective fishing scene.

(180 bottom and 180-181) KAKADU NATIONAL PARK IN AUSTRALIA IS ONE OF THE MANDATORY STOPS FOR ANYONE WANTING TO LEARN ABOUT THE CULTURE OF THE ABORIGINES. THE AREA WHERE IT STANDS WAS ALREADY INHABITED BY THE ABORIGINE POPULATION 40,000 YEARS AGO. ONE OF THE BEST TESTIMONIES OF THE PICTORIAL ART OF THESE MEN FROM ANCIENT TIMES APPEARS AT THE SITE OF NOURLANGIE ROCK. THE MOST FAMOUS WALL OF ALL IS THE ONE REPRESENTING NAMONDJOK – THE PROGENITOR OF THE HUMAN RACE WHO, ACCORDING TO THE MYTHOLOGY, ATE HIS SISTER – BESIDE A MYSTERIOUS FIGURE OF A SKELETON KNOWN AS NAMARRGON, "THE LIGHTNING MAN."

UNITED STATES

Area 51

(37°14'6"N - 115°48'40"W)

THE MOST CONTROVERSIAL MILITARY BASE IN AMERICAN HISTORY SEEMS TO CONCEAL TOP-SECRET MILITARY ACTIVITIES, FUELING THE MOST EXTREME OF SCIENCE-FICTION THEORIES.

Each day from the Las Vegas airport, airplanes take off that belong to an airline company called "Janet." The company does not exist but is indirectly owned by the U.S. Air Force. Each airplane transports more than 100 persons to a top-secret location in the Nevada desert. A military base on which thousands of military personnel are working in strict confidentiality on inconceivable projects. They call it Area 51, and for over 60 years it has been a mystery with which journalists, historians, ufologists, and conspiracy theorists have been testing themselves.

Extending for 26,000 sq km (10,038 sq mi), the area is entirely militarized and under strict surveillance. In order to reach its borders, you need to take the special exit off State Highway 375, the one that the state of Nevada has officially rechristened "Extraterrestrial Highway," a name that refers directly to legends involving this military base and the numerous sightings of unidentified flying objects reported by motorists traveling along it.

The entire area is wedged between the desert, the skyline of the mountains, which seem to want to protect it from prying eyes, and the dry bed of the salt flat Groom Lake: they call it Dreamland. Inside the area one can make out dozens of hangars, the most famous of which is Hangar 18: a structure about 100 m (328 ft) in width and length, and over 30 m (98.4 ft) high. One wonders what sort of aircraft a structure of such dimensions is designed to contain. Thanks, again, to satellite imagery (the airspace, in fact, is strictly off-limits, even to pilots of the nearby Nellis Air Force Base) we can make out the very long runways, huge strips of asphalt in the middle of the desert. Some exceed 3 km (1.9 mi) and the longest reaches 7 km (4.3 mi), an unusual size for a common landing.

But what you can see from above is only a small part compared to what appears to be hidden from curious eyes. Witnesses speak of a structure extending underground for more than 50 stories, with increasingly restricted levels of access, and of mile-long tunnels branching off all throughout the underground.

The extremely high levels of secrecy surrounding Area 51 – just consider that for decades the U.S. government has denied the very existence of the base – have given rise to all sorts of assumptions about what is happening inside: from top-secret technology projects to military tests to the presence of traces of extraterrestrials.

All the hypotheses revolve around the words of people who claim – without having incontrovertible evidence, however – to have entered within the confines of Area 51. Among these, the most famous is doubtlessly Bob Lazar, a self-styled physicist who claims to have worked near the base and seen tests of spaceships made out of nonterrestrial materials.

But the most incredible legend is the one known under the name of the "Roswell Incident." On 2 July 1947, a mysterious object fell from the sky at Roswell, New Mexico. The remains were rapidly hidden away by the military, and the incident was shrouded in secrecy. Although government sources deny the event, ufologists believe that what fell at Roswell was a spaceship with extraterrestrial pilots inside. Many believe that the mechanical components of the vehicle and the biological remains of the aliens were brought directly to Area 51. Supposedly an autopsy was performed on the aliens, similar to the one represented in the famous Santilli film, which the English producer himself admitted to having falsified. But Santilli also swore that he had been inspired by an original film that he had seen with his own eyes.

Beyond the science-fictional theories, it is within the confines of area 51 – patrolled by Jeeps armed with assault rifles, monitored by latest-generation radar, under surveillance by military helicopters flying over, and surrounded by motion sensors hidden on the ground – that the American government has supposedly tested some of its most incredible prototypes over the course of the years.

_ (182-183) ACCESS THROUGH THE NEVADA DESERT TO THE LEGENDARY AREA 51 IS FORBIDDEN TO THE PUBLIC, AS WELL AS TO NUMEROUS EXPEDITIONS OF THE CURIOUS SEEKING TO SNEAK A LOOK AT THEIR TOP-SECRET ACTIVITIES. AN ENDLESS FENCE PATROLLED BY ARMED VANS. THE GROUND SCATTERED WITH UNDERGROUND MOTION SENSORS. AND THE SKIES UNDER CONSTANT SURVEILLANCE BY RADAR AND HELICOPTERS IN FLIGHT. WHATEVER IS INSIDE THERE IS NOT SUPPOSED TO BE SEEN.

Yungay, Peru, March 1967

Yungay, Peru, March 1967

June 1978. Sra.Montserrat Batllori-Housewife.

Portland, Oregon, Spring 1992. Photografer Unknown.

-Unterbacthel, Switzerland.
76. By Edward Meier.

Ochre Point, Maslin beach, south Australia
March 10th 1993 by Eric Thomason

Hasseldorf
Germany. M

_ (184-185) The history of sightings of UFOs is rich with images and videos giving rise to science-fiction hypotheses. The only official study on the subject, Project Blue Book, was conducted by the U.S. Air Force. Out of the 12,618 cases recorded between 1947 in 1969, 95 percent have an explanation. However, 701 cases were officially classified as unidentified.

_ (185) According to many ufologists, Area 51 holds proofs of the existence of extraterrestrial aircraft Some clues in support of this science-fiction hypothesis are represented by the network of enormous landing runways and the presence of dozens of hangars, including the most famous — for long the largest — the one known as Hangar 18. What aircraft could it shelter, with each of its sides extending to 100 m (328 ft)?

Yungay, Peru, March 1967

Summer 1976 Fyffe, Alabama. Photographer unknown

Marsh, SW of Brokedorf, near Hamburg
7th 1977. By Herr Walter Schilling.

In 1955, the Lockheed Corporation, in agreement with the CIA, chose the area to test the legendary U2 spy plane, constructing the first nucleus of what would later become the legendary Area 51. Then came the CIA's Project Oxcart: ultrafast aircraft for high altitude reconnaissance, from the first Blackbirds of the 1960s, to the F-117s of the 1980s, on to the latest top-secret prototypes for drones and aircraft supposedly capable of reaching extremely high speeds, such as Mach 6, or of making an entire circuit around the planet in less than five hours. The truth about Area 51 lies under the sun in the Nevada desert, but still remains invisible to the eye.

UNITED STATES

The Sailing Stones

(36°40'53"N - 117°33'43"W)

IN THE CALIFORNIA DESERT OF DEATH VALLEY, HEAVY STONES MOVE ABOUT FOR
NO APPARENT REASON, LEAVING BEHIND MYSTERIOUS TRACKS IN THE SOIL.

Death Valley, in California, is an infernal desert. This lowest point in America has been measured at its center, where the highest temperature of the continent, 56.7°C (134.1 F°), was recorded. Something unexplainable occurs at Death Valley, a phenomenon that agitates those who come upon it and challenges scientists. In the area called Racetrack Playa, boulders, even the enormous ones, move by themselves through the desert, leaving a mysterious track on the ground. The phenomenon is known as the *sailing stones*.

The rocks, which come primarily from a nearby dolomite hill, move several meters (yards) every two or three years, leaving different trails, which are very straight if the stone has a rough surface, but more erratic if the surfaces of the rock are well polished. Sometimes one single trail presents two distinct types of paths, a sign that the mass has suddenly been overturned during its mysterious shifting. Other times the trajectories veer abruptly, forming surprising angles. The depth of the trails never exceeds 3 cm (1.2 in).

Scholars seek to understand how these rocks, abandoned in the desert, some weighing hundreds of pounds, can move without any apparent force. Is it a natural phenomenon, or in the heart of Death Valley is there a yet unknown force that causes them to move?

Racetrack is a perfect name for what goes on at Racetrack Playa. It is the bed of an exceptionally scenic dry lake, extending more than 4 km (2.5 mi) in length and 2 km (1.2 mi) in width, at an elevation below sea level. Its surface is incredibly flat; there is a difference in elevation of only 4 cm between the northern edge and the southern.

The history of the sailing stones began in 1948 when geologists McAllister and Agnew began systematically mapping the area. *Life* magazine produced an unforgettable photo shoot on the topic. In 1972, 30 of the boulders that had moved during that year were identified, and each one of these was assigned a name so as to follow its shifts throughout the following seven years. The results were interesting: no rock ever moved during the summer; they only moved during the winter (even though in some winters there was no movement). The longest single itinerary was registered for a rock named Nancy, which traced a groove of 201 m (660 ft). Karen, the heaviest, with its 318 kg (700 lbs.), by contrast, never moved during the seven years of the test.

Possible explanations of the phenomenon all point to the role of ice, which freezes a part of Death Valley during the winter. Various experiments were performed in laboratories of several universities, but not all were fully convincing. The latest occurred in 2011, and the results were published in the prestigious *American Journal of Physics*. According to the scientists, the phenomena could be explained by a combination of light winds and small formations of ice called "rafts."

Yet even the most satisfactory scientific explanation fails to minimize the emotion of encountering a rock that, during the night, in the inhospitable Death Valley, has embarked upon a journey with no apparent destination, even though its solemn advancement has left a visible trace for the telling. For some, this would be a surprising metaphor of our own existence.

_ (187) NONE OF THE SAILING STONES HAS EVER MOVED DURING THE SUMMER: WINTER IS THE SEASON FOR THE CURIOUS ROCKY "MIGRATIONS" IN DEATH VALLEY. THE ROCKS MOVE EVERY TWO OR THREE YEARS, AND IT TAKES AT LEAST FOUR YEARS TO LEAVE A DECENT TRACK. THE ROUGH STONES LEAVE STRAIGHT FURROWS, WHILE THE SMOOTH ONES TRACE OUT CURVED TRAJECTORIES.

_ (188-189) A SCIENTIFIC EXPERIMENT MONITORED 30 SAILING STONES OVER SEVEN YEARS. THE LONGEST RECORDED TRACK WAS DUG INTO THE SOIL BY A ROCK CALLED NANCY: AN IMPRESSIVE CHANNEL OVER 200 M (656 FT) LONG. THE SHORTEST PATH WAS MADE BY THE VERY HEAVY ROCK NAMED KAREN, WHICH DID NOT MOVE EVEN AS FAR AS 1 M (3.3 FT).

UNITED STATES

The Disappearance of the Anasazi

(36°3'30"N — 107°57'32"W)

WHAT HAPPENED TO THE ANCIENT INDIAN PEOPLE WHO LIVED IN THE SUGGESTIVE CHACO CANYON OF NEW MEXICO?

Pueblo Bonito is considered the greatest archaeological mystery of the United States. About 800 years ago in the New Mexico desert, an entire tribe consisting of over 8000 persons suddenly disappeared, leaving a series of traces, all to be deciphered. This population was known as the Anasazi, *the People of the Eagle*, and their name in the Navajo language signifies "the Ancient Ones."

Chaco Canyon in New Mexico is 19 km (11.8 mi) long and 1500 m (0.9 mi) wide, and it is here that the Anasazi people lived peacefully before disappearing.

It all began in 1888 when, almost by chance, two cowboys arrived at Chaco Canyon. At the base of the canyon, they found an imposing construction consisting of 800 dwellings: Pueblo Bonito, the home of the Anasazi. Some think this was their capital, while others believe it was a spiritual center. One thing certain is that at the time of its construction, sometime around the year 1000, nothing of the sort existed in this arid zone of North America. It was an absolutely pharaonic complex for the epoch. Round, underground and circular, the kivas are the compound's most famous architectural element. The largest of this kind is the *Casa Rinconada*, just outside Bonito, 20 m (65.6 ft) wide and 5 m (16.4 ft) high. The kivas were probably used for sacred ceremonies: they were constructed with holes in their roofs through which spirits could enter or exit, according to the liturgy of the vanished ancient tribes.

The Anasazi had a devotional relationship with nature, especially with the Earth and the Sun. In many kivas, the ray of sunlight coming through the windows at dawn at the summer solstice went to strike a specific niche found within the construction. This phenomenon has yet to be interpreted, but it becomes even more obvious at the site of *Fajada Butte*: the rock engraving of the "sun dagger" represents two spirals; owing to the formation of the cracks in the rocks at the entrance to the cave, the larger spiral is crossed by a veritable blade of light at the summer solstice. At the winter solstice, however, the sun penetrates into two cracks delimiting the outer borders of the spiral. It is a sort of calendar from a very ancient era engraved in stone.

In addition to being oriented in accordance with the surprising astronomical knowledge of the Anasazi, the kivas themselves were also built upon precise points on the ground. These sites, chosen by the shamans, manifested what they interpreted as a strong Earth-energy, represented by a spiral.

Another obsession for the Anasazi people was represented by their network of major roadways. They constructed over 300 km (186 mi) of roads, a majestic example of which is the Great Road of the North overlooking Pueblo Bonito: 33 km (20.5 mi), traced out with an astonishing precision. It would be difficult to realize such an alignment even with a compass, an instrument the Anasazi did not possess. This demonstrates that their knowledge was much more advanced than what traditional archaeology is capable of imagining.

(191) THE MOST CHARACTERISTIC FEATURE OF PUEBLO BONITO FROM THE POINT OF VIEW OF ITS CONSTRUCTION IS DOUBTLESSLY A SERIES OF KIVAS, ROOMS OF CIRCULAR SHAPE THAT DEVELOP WITHIN THE EARTH. THEIR FUNCTION IS NOT ENTIRELY CLEAR. THE LARGEST HAS A DIAMETER OF 20 M (66 FT), AND SOME CONSIDER THAT THEY WERE PLACES UTILIZED FOR THE SACRED CEREMONIES OF THE ANASAZI.

_ (192) THE EVERYDAY LIFE OF THE ANASAZI TRIBE HAS BEEN IMPRESSED UPON THE WALLS OF CANYONLANDS NATIONAL PARK IN UTAH. ONE STONE IN PARTICULAR, CALLED THE NEWSPAPER ROCK, CONSERVES STIRRING GRAFFITI IN THE STONES, IMMORTALIZING MEN, ANIMALS, HUNTING SCENES, AND ANCIENT IMPRINTS.

But there exists another disturbing aspect of this culture. Scientific studies conducted on human remains found in Chaco Canyon appear to demonstrate that the Anasazi were a people dedicated to cannibalism. There are numerous indications: fractured skulls, bones drained of their marrow, organic proofs in the fossil excrement, and even traces of myoglobin (a protein found in muscle) found among the deposits in a pot. Also present in the midst of this desert is a significant tomb, that of Richard Wetherill, one of the first explorers to arrive in Chaco Canyon. He was murdered by the very people he wanted to study.

His testimony, however, is significant. Wetherill writes: "When we entered Navajo Canyon and discovered the ruins, we went back into our own world an unknown number of centuries. Everything was intact, exactly as it had been left by the original inhabitants. The objects were arranged in the rooms as though the persons had just left to make a visit to their neighbors. Perfect examples of crockery were lying on the ground, while iron utensils and other household items had been left in the places where the Anasazi women had used them for the last time."

A striking scene, the one described by Wetherill: an advanced civilization forced suddenly to abandon its center, with no signs of battle or epidemics. The mysterious destiny of the Anasazi, the tribe of the Ancient Ones, remains an enigma.

_ (192-193 and 193) PUEBLO BONITO IS CONSIDERED THE ENIGMATIC ARCHAEOLOGICAL PEARL OF ALL OF CHACO CANYON. A WALL PERFECTLY ALIGNED ALONG THE NORTH-SOUTH AXIS DIVIDES THE CITY INTO TWO DISTRICTS, EACH OF WHICH PRESENTS A LARGE KIVA NEXT TO THE SEPARATING WALL. DOZENS OF THE OTHER KIVAS ARE SCATTERED ABOUT THE CITY, TOGETHER WITH OTHER PLACES PROBABLY UTILIZED FOR RELIGIOUS CEREMONIES. THE HUNDREDS OF DWELLINGS PRESENT DIFFER FROM THOSE FROM THE SAME PERIOD: THE INTERIOR SPACES ARE, IN FACT, MUCH LARGER WITH RESPECT TO THOSE OF OTHER LOCAL CULTURES, AND SOME OF THE WALLS REACH A THICKNESS OF 1 M (3.3 FT).

(194 and 194-195) IT IS NOT EASY TO GIVE A PRECISE DEFINITION FOR THE BOUNDARIES OF THE BERMUDA TRIANGLE. BUT IF WE PUT TOGETHER THE DATA SHOWING ALL THE FINAL POSITIONS OF THE SHIPS AND AIRPLANES BEFORE THEY DISAPPEARED THERE, THESE INDICATE A TRIANGULAR PORTION OF THE ATLANTIC OCEAN WITH VERTICES IN MIAMI, FLORIDA, THE ISLAND OF BERMUDA IN THE HOMONYMOUS ARCHIPELAGO, AND SAN JUAN, PUERTO RICO.

The Bermuda Triangle

(26°37'N - 70°53'1"W)

ONE OF THE PLANET'S GREATEST MYSTERIES, A SEA AFFLICTED BY AN INCREDIBLE SERIES OF NAVAL AND AIR CALAMITIES.

A stretch of the Atlantic Ocean is known as the sinister theater of one of the most famous legends in the world: that of the curse of the Bermuda Triangle. An unsettling portion of sea, bordered by Puerto Rico to the south, Florida to the west and the Bermuda archipelago to the north. Enormous ships, entire air squadrons, and above all, hundreds of human lives, have literally disappeared – without apparent cause – into these waters.

The unexplainable events that appear to occur cyclically in this triangle of ocean date back to ancient times. Already at the time of the pirates, ancient mariners cursed the pitfalls of what they called the Sargasso Sea, populated by mysterious ghost ships and troubled by difficult navigation. But there is one day on which the legend of the Bermuda Triangle was truly born: on 5 December, 1945, a beautifully sunny day, the entire Squadron 19 of the U.S. Air Force mysteriously disappeared. Five military aircraft, with five officers and nine soldiers aboard, were participating in a simple exercise not far off the coast of Florida. Suddenly they began sending confused messages to the control tower: they indicated that they were lost, their words were confused, and the instruments of all the planes were out of order. There was no further news from them.

To bring relief to the squadron, a Martin Mariner even took off from the coast, a hydroplane with a crew of 13. This also disappeared into nothingness. In the days following the mysterious event, not even more than 4000 hours of flight resulted in finding a single wreck of one of the six airplanes that disappeared into the sea. All this is even more disturbing if we think about the fact that the planes of the squadron where capable of landing gently in the sea and staying afloat for 90 seconds, while their crews were trained to leave the aircraft in 60 seconds, and they even had life rafts available.

But the tragic list of airplanes that vanished into thin air in the Bermuda triangle is very long. Even if we consider only the most sensational disappearances, we come up with this bewildering list: in 1947, a Skymaster C-54 airplane of the U.S. Army disappeared with six soldiers on board; in 1948, a four-engine Tudor IV with 31 persons on board; also in 1948, a DC-3 with 32 passengers; in 1952, a British York Transport with a crew of 33; in 1954, a U.S. Navy Super Constellation with 42 seamen on board; in 1963, two Boeing KC-135s; in 1965, a C-119 with 10 passengers; in 1972, an Eastern Airlines flight with more than 100 victims.

But even merchant ships and military ships, genuine giants of the sea, have disappeared into the Bermuda Triangle without a trace. In this case as well, the list is only partial: in 1800, the *USS Insurgent* with 340 passengers aboard; in 1814, the *USS Wasp* with a crew of 140; in 1880, the British frigate *Atalanta* with 290 men on board; in 1918, the *Cyclops* with 306 persons on board; in 1931, the *Stavenger* and her 43 men; in 1938, the *Anglo-Australian* with 39 men; in 1951, the battleship *Sao Paulo* with eight men; in 1963, the *Marine Sulphur Queen* with 39 persons; and in 1973, the *Anita* with 32 men aboard.

Moreover, even in Christopher Columbus's ship's log, strange phenomena were indicated as having occurred in this area, especially during the historic crossing of 1492.

On Thursday, 13 September, 1492, the Genoese navigator wrote: "On this day, at nightfall, the compass needles moved to northwest, and in the morning, they moved rather toward the northeast (...)."

Two days later, the diary pages reported: "As night was falling, they saw a marvelous streak of fire falling from the sky, at four or five leagues from the ships." And on Monday, 17 September, 1492: "The pilots took stock of the situation and acknowledged that the compasses did not indicate the proper direction; and the seamen were fearful and distraught, though they did not say about what."

Many hypotheses have been advanced to explain the mystery of the Bermuda Triangle: from water spouts to seiche waves; from alien abductions to lethal CAT (clear air turbulence). The most recent scientific theory, however, calls methane hydrate into question: colossal gas bubbles that periodically detach from the bottom and would be capable of swallowing up entire ships and setting low-flying airplanes afire.

MEXICO

Chichén Itzá

(20°40'N ✺ 88°34'W)

BETWEEN APOCALYPTIC PROPHECY AND ENCHANTING ARCHITECTURE, THE MOST RESPLENDENT HEART OF THE MAYAN EMPIRE HAS YET TO REVEAL THE LAST OF ITS SECRETS.

While Europe was living in the Dark Ages, the Mayan civilization was flourishing on the Yucatán Peninsula of Mexico: immense cities were built in the middle of the tropical forest, rich with marvelous pyramids and magnificent temples. There is one location, however, which, more than others, links religion with astronomy. Chichén Itzá, rising upon an area of 3 sq km (1.2 sq mi), was one of the most important Mayan cities. The site includes many buildings, each different and incredibly fascinating. The most mysterious, however, are the legendary pyramids of Kukulkán, the El Caracol astronomical observatory, and the famous Pelota ball court, besides, obviously, the Cenote of Sacrifices, to which an entire chapter of this book is dedicated.

Caracol means spiral staircase and refers to the interior stairway of the ancient astronomical observatory. Its entrances are aligned with the vernal equinox, while other elements recall astronomical events regarding the moon and the legend of the Serpent God, the bringer of knowledge. During the day, the Mayans studied the movements of the sun, analyzing shadows cast inside the building, while at night, they observed the reflections of the stars within the great stone receptacles filled with water. The Mayans were profound observers of the night sky; they knew the movements of the universe, the stars, and the planets, and in this manner established their legendary calendar. Their scientific knowledge was based on religious beliefs. The Mayans appeared to be aware that our galaxy, the Milky Way, is a spiral, and that a black hole can be found at its center. In fact, for the Mayans, the god of creation was Hunab Ku, represented in the form of a spiral from the center of which it created life by means of powerful explosions. For some, this would be a clear religious metaphor describing the Milky Way.

The principal monument of Chichén Itzá is a marvelous pyramid, which also is closely connected to astronomy: Kukulkán, according to myth, was the Serpent God from whom the Mayans obtained their knowledge and whose return they awaited. The pyramid dedicated to the god is constructed in such a manner that, on the day of the equinox, the sun illuminates the northwest stairway, creating a shadow that appears just like an enormous serpent. Moreover, the pyramid is built so that on 21 December, 2012, the well-known date concluding the cycle of the threefold Mayan calendar, the northwestern edge will project a play of lights on the steps. This will join with the head of the serpent sculpted at the base of the stairway, illuminating it. For some, this will be the sign of the return of the Serpent God.

But at Chichén Itzá, there is also an imposing playing field designed for playing the game of Pelota: 170 m (558 ft) long and 50 m (164 ft) wide, it is surrounded by perimeter walls reaching nearly 8 m (26 ft) in height. Pelota was a very violent game, but it was greatly loved by the Mayans, a sacred game.

_ (196) ONE OF THE MANY ENIGMAS OF CHICHÉN ITZÁ IS REPRESENTED BY THE SO-CALLED CHAC MOOL: STATUES DISCOVERED IN VARIOUS PLACES, REPRODUCING AN ANTHROPOMORPHIC FIGURE IN PRONE POSITION, WITH HEAD TURNED HARD TO THE RIGHT AND WITH A SORT OF HORIZONTAL OBJECT RESTING ON ITS BELLY. WHAT DID THIS UNNATURAL POSITION SIGNIFY? WHY REPRODUCE IT IN DOZENS OF SCULPTURES?

_ (196-197) THE MAYAN NAME FOR QUETZALCOATL IS KUKULKÁN, THE GOD TO WHOM THE IMPOSING STEP PYRAMID DOMINATING THE CHICHÉN ITZÁ COMPLEX IS DEDICATED. ALSO CALLED EL CASTILLO ("THE CASTLE"), IT IS THE ICON OF THE ENTIRE YUCATÁN AND IS, LIKE NEARLY EVERYTHING AT CHICHÉN ITZÁ, AN EDIFICE INTIMATELY LINKED WITH THE STARS: AT EVERY EQUINOX ITS CORNERS PROJECT THE SHADOW OF KUKULKÁN ONTO THE NORTHWEST STAIRWAY.

_ (198 and 198-199) EL CARACOL ("THE SNAIL") IS PERHAPS THE MOST INTRIGUING BUILDING AT CHICHÉN ITZÁ: A ROUND CONSTRUCTION HOUSING A SPIRAL STAIRCASE FOR ACCESSING THE OBSERVATION POINT. ALL OF EL CARACOL, IN FACT, IS A REFINED ASTRONOMICAL OBSERVATORY: THE OPENINGS TOWARD THE OUTSIDE ALLOWED STUDY OF THE SHADOWS CAST INSIDE BY THE SUN DURING ITS APPARENT MOTION THROUGH THE SKY, WHILE THE TRAJECTORIES OF STARS AND PLANETS WERE VIEWED VIA THEIR REFLECTIONS IN THE STONE BASINS FILLED WITH WATER. IT IS HERE, IN SHORT, THAT THE CALCULATIONS WERE BORN FOR THE LEGENDARY MAYAN CALENDAR.

_ (199 top and bottom) THE WORLD'S BEST PRESERVED PELOTA BALLFIELD IS DOUBTLESSLY ONE AT CHICHÉN ITZÁ (ALTHOUGH IT ALSO HAS SIX OTHERS). THE PLAYING FIELD – 166 M X 68 M (545 X 223 FT) – AND STANDS ARE IN PRACTICALLY PERFECT CONDITION. EVEN THE RINGS THROUGH WHICH THE PELOTA WAS TO PASS ARE INTACT. IT IS NOT YET CLEAR WHETHER IT WAS THE CAPTAIN OF THE LOSING TEAM WHO WAS TO BE DECAPITATED AT THE END OF THE MATCH OR WHETHER, INSTEAD, THIS WAS AN HONOR AWAITING THE CAPTAIN OF THE WINNING TEAM.

The aim of the game was to cause the ball to pass through a ring of stone fixed at about 7 m (23 ft) above ground: the first team that managed to score was the winner. A macabre panel in the central courtyard of Chichén Itzá, however, depicts the beheading of a Pelota player; some argue that this was the fate of the defeated. A more recent interpretation maintains instead that it was the captain of the winning team who was to be decapitated. The glory consisted in the honor of being sacrificed to the gods: a victory that led to death, a way to be considered on the level of a god. But there are also some who believe that the entire game of Pelota was nothing more than an elaborate metaphor for representing the astronomical phenomenon of the procession of the equinoxes: extremely important information for someone who was obsessed with the movements of the stars and with calendars.

There remains the mystery of how it could have been possible for the Mayans to gain such highly developed astronomical and architectural knowledge, and, above all, from whom did they learn it? The depressing response is reported in the diaries of John Lloyd Stephens, the explorer who in 1841 told of his discovery of Chichén Itzá: "We were sitting on the edge of the wall and we tried in vain to penetrate the mystery surrounding us. Who were the people who had built these cities? When one finds oneself among the ruins of the Egyptian cities, or even in those of Petra, the foreigner knows the history of the persons to whom those ruins belonged. But when we asked the Indians about it, their monotonous response was always the same: *quien sabe?, who knows?*"

(200 and 200-201) *The Mayan calendar demonstrates this people's great attention to the relation between astronomical events and terrestrial happenings. A ritual calendar of 260 days, composed of cycles of 20 days and 13 figures, was crossed with a solar calendar of 365 days. The combination of the two calendars was engraved on a wheel with glyphs and numerical signs. The wheel completed one full turn in 52 solar years, and was to be compared with the Long Count, a cycle of days that began on 13 August, 3114 BC. All three calendars complete their current cycle on 21 December, 2012.*

202

MEXICO

The Magic of the Cenotes

(20°41'15"N - 88°34'4"W)

THE MOST UNATTAINABLE TREASURE CHEST OF THE MAYA IS HIDDEN UNDER WATER, IN AN INCREDIBLE NETWORK OF UNDERGROUND TUNNELS.

All the most flourishing civilizations of antiquity developed around great rivers: the Nile for the Egyptians, the Euphrates for the Babylonians and the Indus for the Harappan civilization. For the Mayans, however, there were no rivers. The Yucatán is a peninsula with no mountains and no surface watercourses. The terrain is calcareous and porous, so that any water that falls becomes rapidly swallowed into the depths of the earth, creating freshwater wells and abundant underground sources, which, however, would have been inaccessible if a meteorite had not fallen some 65 million years ago into the Caribbean Sea, ripping open, with an apocalyptic rain of rocks, the surface of the earth in a jagged series of points. Those points are what today we call the cenotes, enormous natural wells. For the Mayans, the cenotes represented the possibility of survival in an otherwise inhospitable land, and for this reason they were considered sacred. The cenotes provided for life, and through them one could enter into contact with the ancient gods who, according to the Mayans, lived in the underwater depths of Mother Earth.

Today it is estimated that on the Yucatán Peninsula alone exist some 30,000 cenotes: some of them are easily accessible, others are reserved for archaeologists, while still others are unexplored. Many of them connect to one another by an amazing network of underground caves, channels, and lakes, some of which are majestic. Stalactites and stalagmites unite to form spires or entire welded columns, making these underground environments seem like underwater cathedrals.

The Mayans had strong ties with these caves, and they celebrated important ceremonies in their sacred waters. The first reports in this regard are from the diaries of Bishop Diego de Landa. If he was responsible, on the one hand, for the destruction of the writings of the Mayans, causing the cancellation of a major part of history that we might have known, on the other hand, he did leave us an account of what he observed directly: the bloody Maya rituals. For the Mayans, physical pain was one of the means by which it was possible to make contact with the divine: for this reason, they inflicted upon themselves terrible injuries and, after having fallen into a trance, threw themselves into the cenotes, ready to communicate with the gods. Also into the cenotes they threw priceless treasures as well as young children and babies to be drowned in sacrifice.

On the basis of these stories, in 1904, American explorer Edward Herbert Thompson decided to set off in search of the underwater treasures of the Mayans. He searched among the ruins of Chichén Itzá, one of the most representative centers of the Mayan Empire. Its name means "on the edge of the well of the Itza." Thompson found the two cenotes of Chichén Itzá and decided to dive in, making use of a rudimentary diving suit, a tube for breathing, and weights tied to his shoes. In the attempt, he almost lost his hearing, but at over 40 m (131 ft) deep, he found everything that was told by the legends: precious

_ (202) THE SACRED CENOTE LOCATED IN CHICHÉN ITZÁ IS LESS SUGGESTIVE THAN THE OTHERS, BUT IT WAS REVERED BY THE MAYA PEOPLE. ITS DIAMETER MEASURES 65 M (213 FT) AND IT REACHES 35 M (115 FT) DEEP: IT WAS HERE THAT THE PRINCIPAL MAYAN CELEBRATIONS OF THE AREA TOOK PLACE: GOLD, PRECIOUS STONES, ANIMALS, AND HUMAN LIVES WERE OFFERED TO THE SACRED CENOTE.

_ (202-203) LOCATED NEAR CHICHÉN ITZÁ, THE IK-KIL CENOTE, ALSO CALLED THE BLUE CENOTE, IS CHARACTERIZED BY THE BRILLIANT BLUE OF ITS WATERS. THE WATER FOUND INSIDE IT IS NOT COLLECTED RAINWATER BUT RATHER SUBTERRANEAN WATER OWING TO KARST PHENOMENA. UNLIKE OTHER CENOTES, HERE A STAIRWAY HAS BEEN CARVED INTO THE ROCK ALLOWING ONE TO REACH THE LEVEL OF THE WATER WITHOUT HAVING TO DIVE.

_ (204) INSIDE THE GRAN CENOTE AT TULUM – A LUSH CENOTE IMMERSED IN THE GREEN AND NOW A RECREATIONAL SITE FOR FAMILIES AND CHILDREN – 120 HUMAN SKULLS WERE DISCOVERED, PROOF OF THE SACRIFICES CHARACTERIZING THE MAYA CEREMONIES. THE GRAN CENOTE IS PART OF THE SAK AKTUN, THE WHITE CAVE, AN IMMENSE KARST NETWORK RUNNING BENEATH THE YUCATÁN.

_ (205) THE CENOTES OF MEXICO ARE CONNECTED BY A COMPLEX NETWORK OF CAVES AND TUNNELS, STILL LARGELY UNEXPLORED. VENTURING INSIDE THEM CAN BE LETHAL EVEN FOR THE MOST EXPERT FROGMEN. AND YET THERE ARE MANY WHO DEFY THE DANGERS OF THE KARST CAVES TO HUNT FOR THE LEGENDARY TREASURES OF THE MAYAN EMPIRE.

treasures and fearsome skeletons, including those of children. Thompson discovered what would be called the "Sacred Cenote" or the "Cenote of Sacrifice." Not far away, he identified another cenote, called Xtoloc, which was used for the population's water supply. The Cenote of Sacrifice measures 60 m (197 ft) in diameter and is over 80 m (262 ft) deep, but in order to access it, you need to make a dive from the ground of about 20 m (66 ft). Beside the cenote stands an ancient building, probably utilized for purification ceremonies for the sacrificial victims. Today, more than a century after Thompson's first daring dive, the cenotes still represent a challenge even for the most experienced divers. The network of caves and galleries connecting them spreads over at least 133 km (83 mi): an entire underground region, and mostly unknown. These inaccessible caverns still conceal many treasures. Bones and offerings have been conserved here for many centuries, discouraging even the most daring plunderers. The cenotes are veritable "time capsules" that have remained intact. Soon, perhaps, using technologies still inconceivable to us, we shall succeed in deciphering them. And they may reveal to us the secrets of the Mayan people and their knowledge that was lost in the blaze along with their manuscripts.

_ (206 and 206-207) The "Room of Tears" is reached by entering into the cenote Aktun Ha, also known as Carwash Cenote, located 8 km from Tulum. The cenote is only a few meters (yards) deep, but from its submerged walls, an intricate and dangerous system of canals and caves unravels, allowing one to reach the spectacular Room of Tears, which owes its name to the discoverer, who burst into tears, overwhelmed by its beauty, upon seeing it for the first time. According to many divers, it is one of nature's most impressive masterpieces.

_ (208-209) THE SPECTACULAR VIEW FROM ABOVE THE ARCHAEOLOGICAL SITE OF UXMAL ALLOWS US TO APPRECIATE THE RELATIONSHIP BETWEEN THE PYRAMID OF THE MAGICIAN AND THE NUNNERY QUADRANGLE. THE LATTER OWES ITS NAME TO AN ERROR BY THE CONQUISTADORS, WHO THOUGHT IT WAS A CONVENT. A DECORATION OF TWO VERY LONG STYLIZED SERPENTS SURROUNDS THE PERIMETER OF ITS 74 ROOMS.

_ (209) THE GOVERNOR'S PALACE IS A STRUCTURE TYPICAL OF THE PUUC ARCHITECTURE: 18 M (59 FT) HIGH, IT IS COMPOSED OF THREE BUILDINGS THAT ARE IMPRESSIVE FOR THEIR EXCELLENT DEGREE OF CONSERVATION. THE UPPER PART OF THE FAÇADE IS STUDDED, OBSESSIVELY, WITH MASKS OF THE LEGENDARY CHAAC, THE RAIN GOD.

Uxmal

(20°22'N - 89°46'W)

ONE OF THE JEWELS OF THE YUCATÁN CONTAINS ITS INCREDIBLE HISTORY WITHIN ITS NAME, MEANING "REBUILT THREE TIMES."

Uxmal is an ancient city of the classical period of the Mayan civilization, a UNESCO World Heritage Site. It is located in Mexico, about 80 km (50 mi) from the sea, in a hilly region of the Yucatán. It is characterized by a particular architectural style called Puuc, marked by rich tiles decorated with sacred figures, which cover the rough stone, and rich ornaments of exquisitely carved stone reliefs.

In the Mayan language, the word *uxmal* means "constructed three times." The area was inhabited in ancient times, but the actual city was founded only in the 7th century AD, by the Xiuh family, which continued on until the 10th century, when it was occupied by the Toltecs. As throughout the Yucatán, water resources were scarce, and for this reason the most highly venerated of all the divinities was Chac, the god of rain. In 1200, the city was completely abandoned – possibly owing to the malevolence of Chac – and the jungle soon swallowed it up. Not before the passing of seven centuries did Uxmal once again, in 1943, see the light.

The area extends over 1 km (0.6 mi) north to south and over 500 m (0.3 mi) east to west. Inside are eight groups of sacred buildings and buildings of power: the Adivino (Pyramid of the Magician), the Nunnery Quadrangle, the Governor's Palace (with a marvelous throne in the form of a two-headed jaguar), the House of the Turtles, the Pelota Ballcourt, the House of the Witch, the Cemetery Group, the Temple of the Phallus, and the House of the Pigeons.

In front of the governor's palace is a broken monolith, a sort of cylinder with a conical tip that has provoked much discussion: there are some who consider it to be a tribute to fertility and others who hypothesize that it is a mysterious object that came from the sky and drove itself into the ground.

However, the most imposing and suggestive building is doubtlessly the Adivino (also known as the Pyramid of the Dwarf or of the Magician), which dominates the area with its 35 m (115 ft) of height. What make it so unique are its rounded edges (a characteristic found only here) and its elliptical base. On its summit stands a temple entirely decorated with ominous masks, which would represent the jaws of the powerful god Chac. According to local legend, the entire edifice was constructed in one single night by a dwarf with the aid of his mother's magical practices. Probably it was the temple of an oracular divinity that manifested through a priest-prophet. The virtual line joining the pyramid with the center of the Nunnery Quadrangle marks the point on the horizon where the sun sets on the day that it passes through its zenith.

According to Stansbury Hagar, an ethnographer who wrote in the first half of the 20th century, the skulls and bones decorating the façade suggest that the temple is dedicated to the god of death. The wide access road toward the western façade, according to the scholar, forms an open mouth: the jaws of a human face. It is the symbolic depiction of the death one must pass through in order to enter into contact with the magician who issues the prophecy. The pyramid also represents the constellation Scorpio, which is connected with the god of death. Stansbury Hagar performed extensive research on Uxmal, and in 1921 he published a paper on the correspondences between the zodiac and the temples there. His hypothesis is that all the cities sacred to the Mayans were designed to reproduce a celestial pattern. This is because the Mayans believed that the microcosm corresponded to the macrocosm, and that everything on earth was an imitation or reflection of the perfect reality existing in the universe. The sacred city that imitated the heavenly vault would thus attract to itself a portion of that perfection.

In studying the positions and iconographic characteristics of the individual architectural elements found on the map of Uxmal, Hagar succeeded in identifying each one of these as referring to one of the 12 constellations of the zodiac, on the basis of correspondences he found (except in the case of Aquarius, for which nothing more than a small collapsed temple remained). Moreover, it is certain that the Mayans had astounding levels of knowledge regarding the sky and time, as is demonstrated by their complex and very precise calendars, and their ability to predict eclipses. How they could have developed their knowledge, however, and how much of their prophecy is true, remains to be discovered.

_ (210 top) THE HOUSE OF TURTLES IS LOCATED AT THE NORTHEAST CORNER OF THE COMPLEX. IT IS SMALLER THAN THE OTHER BUILDINGS, AT 10 M WIDE BY 30 M LONG (33 x 98 FT): A SERIES OF TURTLES ADORN ITS CORNICE. THE TURTLE, IN MAYAN MYTHOLOGY, WAS LINKED NOT ONLY WITH CHAAC, THE GOD OF RAIN, BUT ALSO WITH YUM KAAX, THE GOD OF CORN.

_ (210 bottom) THE PELOTA BALLFIELD AT UXMAL IS NESTLED BETWEEN THE GOVERNOR'S PALACE AND THE NUNNERY QUADRANGLE. THE STONE RINGS THROUGH WHICH THE TWO TEAMS ATTEMPTED TO PASS THE PLAYING BALL ARE STILL PRESENT, ALONG THE STANDS TO THE SIDE. BY MEANS OF THE INSCRIPTIONS, THE STRUCTURE HAS BEEN DATED TO THE 7TH CENTURY AD.

_ (210-211) AT THE HEART OF THE GOVERNOR'S PALACE STANDS THE MYTHICAL THRONE OF THE TWO JAGUARS. THE TWO ANIMALS ARE FUSED AT THE TRUNK, AND IT IS HIGHLY LIKELY THAT THE PLATFORM WAS USED AS A CEREMONIAL ALTAR, CONSIDERING THAT IT IS PERFECTLY ALIGNED FROM NORTH TO SOUTH.

MEXICO

Teotihuacán

(19°41'33"N - 98°50'37"W)

THE CITY WHERE THE GODS ARE BORN. ONE OF MEXICO'S GREATEST MYSTERIES. WHO BUILT IT? AND WHY WAS IT ABANDONED?

For many centuries, Teotihuacán has been the largest metropolis of Central America, the heart of a civilization that dominated ancient Mexico for over 500 years. It was the cradle of a civilization, and even today it is wrapped in mystery. It has, however, left us an immense treasure: hundreds of surprising artifacts and masterpieces that recount the history and culture of one of the most fascinating peoples of pre-Columbian America.

Founded 200 years before Christ, Teotihuacán today is still the vastest archaeological site of Central America. A broad boulevard, 2.5 km (1.6 mi) long, crosses the city, dominated by two imposing pyramids: the Pyramids of the Moon and of the Sun. The latter, with a perimeter of 900 m (2953 ft) and a height of 71 m (233 ft), is the third largest pyramid in the world. But after years of study and archaeological investigations, many questions remain unanswered: What people founded this great city? What was their story? And why did they suddenly abandon their city?

Temples, pyramids, statues, masks: the legacy of Teotihuacán is carved in stone, but no written document has come down to us. It is hard to believe that such an advanced civilization could be unacquainted with writing – unless someone had wanted their memory to be canceled forever. What is most striking about Teotihuacán is its city plan: 22 sq km (8.5 sq mi) of streets rich with buildings.

The architects of Teotihuacán knew highly advanced constructional techniques, such as the one referred to as *talud-tablero*, which consisted of alternating a horizontal platform (the *tablero*) with an inclined wall (the *talud*). This architectural style, first used here, was later employed by the Mayans and by many other peoples of Central America in building their own pyramids. And yet no subsequent civilization was able to build a structure as imposing as those of Teotihuacán.

Among their most incredible edifices, beside the two great pyramids dedicated to the sun and the moon, there is the Temple of the Feathered Serpent. It is a smaller pyramid, but rich with bas-reliefs and impressive decorations. As an example, the finely sculpted head of the serpent could weigh as much as one tonne. And originally, the temple had more than 360.

Teotihuacán was a very important spiritual center: many of the divinities worshipped here continued to be venerated by many other peoples until the arrival of the Spanish conquistadores. The capital of a genuine empire, Teotihuacán was a cosmopolitan city as well as being situated at the center of important commercial routes. Its culture profoundly influenced all the peoples of Central America, including the Mayans and the Aztecs. It was long believed that the people of Teotihuacán were pacific, but more recent excavations have brought to light murals and statues of warriors. Furthermore, just like in many pre-Columbian cities, in Teotihuacán as well, bloody rituals were practiced, including human sacrifices.

_ (212-213) THE PYRAMID OF THE SUN IS THE DOMINANT STRUCTURE OF THE COMPLEX AT TEOTIHUACÁN: ITS SIDE MEASURES ABOUT 223 M (733 FT), WHILE ITS HEIGHT EXCEEDS 71 M (233 FT). IT IS THE THIRD-LARGEST PYRAMID IN THE WORLD (AFTER CHOLULA AND CHEOPS). THE CAVE, NOT ACCESSIBLE TO THE PUBLIC, IS THE PLACE WHERE THE ANCIENT INHABITANTS OF TEOTIHUACÁN BELIEVED THE GODS CREATED THE WORLD.

_ (213) THE AVENUE OF THE DEAD, CONNECTING THE CITADEL TO THE PYRAMID OF THE MOON: 2 KM LONG AND PERFECTLY STRAIGHT ALONG THE NORTH-SOUTH AXIS. ALONG THE WAY, A SERIES OF TERRACES FOLLOW THE SLOPE OF THE LAND: IN ANCIENT TIMES THESE WERE SQUARES WHERE THE INHABITANTS OF TEOTIHUACÁN GOT TOGETHER; THESE PRECEDED THE ENTRYWAY TO THE INCREDIBLE NUMBER OF TEMPLES PROLIFERATING IN THIS SACRED AREA.

213

(214) THE SKELETONS RECENTLY DISCOVERED AT THE BASES OF THE PYRAMIDS OF THE MOON AND OF THE FEATHERED SERPENT — THOSE OF DECAPITATED MEN WITH THEIR HANDS BOUND BEHIND THEIR BACKS, EXHIBITED TODAY AT THE MUSEO NACIONAL DE ANTROPOLOGÍA IN MEXICO CITY — MAKE ONE THINK OF THE SACRIFICIAL CEREMONIES THAT MUST HAVE TAKEN PLACE AT TEOTIHUACÁN. THIS POSSIBILITY IS ALSO SUGGESTED BY THE LARGE RITUAL KNIVES OF OBSIDIAN DISCOVERED IN THE AREA.

In recent years, archaeologists have found, at the bases of the Pyramids of the Sun and of the Feathered Serpent, some skeletons of decapitated humans, with the hands bound behind the back. An impressive image, to be added to the various depictions of bleeding hearts pierced by large daggers. And these very daggers are still intact: elaborated in disturbing forms with sharp black obsidian, they were used during sacrificial ceremonies.

During its period of greatest expansion, Teotihuacán had about 200,000 people who lived in more than 1000 residential complexes. Still visible are the large architectural structures and the immense artistic treasures, including mural pictures, decorated ceramics, statues, and hypnotic masks. The human faces are represented in a stylized manner, with precise geometric proportions and inscrutable expressions. Theirs is a highly symbolic art that transmits great composure and solemnity.

Teotihuacán reached the peak of its splendor around the 5th century AD, but it was entirely abandoned just two centuries later. The reasons for its decline remain a mystery. Just as the origins of this incredible city, and of the people that built and governed it without leaving any written testimony, remain mysterious. And lastly: what was the true name of that which the Aztecs called "the city of the gods"? What gods actually lived there?

(214-215) THE PYRAMID OF THE MOON IS THE SECOND LARGEST MONUMENT OF THE SITE, AFTER THAT OF THE SUN, WHICH IS ABOUT TWICE ITS VOLUME. ITS PROFILE SEEMS TO REPRODUCE THAT OF THE MOUNTAIN OF CERRO GORDO (LITERALLY, "FAT HILL"), AND ITS CORE IS MORE ANCIENT THAN THAT OF THE PYRAMID OF THE SUN. AT ITS SUMMIT, CEREMONIES TOOK PLACE IN HONOR OF THE GREAT GODDESS OF TEOTIHUACÁN.

_ (216-217 and 217) THE STRUCTURE THAT INCLUDES THE TEMPLE OF QUETZALCOATL AND THE PYRAMID OF THE FEATHERED SERPENT IS THE THIRD LARGEST EDIFICE OF TEOTIHUACÁN. MORE THAN 200 SACRIFICIAL VICTIMS ARE BURIED AT ITS FEET, MEN WHO LIVED BETWEEN 150 AND 200 AD. THE SIX-LEVEL PYRAMID IS COVERED WITH RELIEF REPRESENTATIONS OF THE FEATHERED SERPENT, ESTIMATED TO BE 260 IN TOTAL, AND BELOW EACH ROW OF HEADS, THE LEGENDARY REPTILE APPEARS IN BAS-RELIEF, IN ITS ENTIRETY.

MEXICO

The Olmecs

(18°6'12"N - 94°2'25"W)

HUGE STONE FACES THAT SEEM TO REVEAL AN ANCIENT HISTORY, ONE THAT HAS NEVER BEEN TOLD.

Through centuries of domination and occupation of the Mesoamerica region, the Spanish conquistadores never heard of them. They knew the Incas, the Aztecs, the Mayas, without understanding all their secrets, but they never imagined that all these peoples descended from one single mysterious civilization: the legendary Olmecs, an enigmatic people and very powerful, forgotten for entire generations.

The term Olmec derives from the Nahuatl language spoken by the Aztecs and means "rubber people," referring to the many rubber trees within their territories. The Olmec civilization seems to have manifested around 1200 BC, principally in three large centers of Mexico: San Lorenzo Tenochtitlán, La Venta, and Tres Zapotes. But their influence went well beyond these boundaries and arrived to contaminate entire areas in Guatemala, Belize, El Salvador, Honduras, Nicaragua, and Costa Rica.

An ancient Mayan poem narrates how the Olmecs arrived from a land of rain and fog "in a certain era/that no one can calculate/that no one can remember." Why they then suddenly disappeared around 400 BC remains an unsolved mystery.

The discovery of the Olmecs is owed primarily to archaeologist Matthew Stirling. While on a mission for the Smithsonian Institution, he succeeded in bringing to light the remains of this incredible vanished civilization, and in dating it as preceding all the other civilizations known at that time.

The most famous discovery is doubtlessly that of the enormous stone faces that, since that time, have become the very icon of the forgotten Olmec people: 17 colossal sculpted heads, distributed among the sites at San Lorenzo, La Venta, and Tres Zapotes. What raises doubts and fantasies about these exciting works in basalt is the set of facial features represented: they are not Amerindian. Rather, they have Asiatic characteristics (at San Lorenzo) or African ones (at La Venta). Certain Olmec engravings on steles, moreover, seem even to portray European features. It is difficult to believe that these would be errors owing to imprecisions of the ancient artists, seeing that in their other sculptural representations, the Olmec demonstrated almost an obsession for anatomical details of perfectly represented men and animals. And on the other hand, it is difficult to conceive that this is simply fortuitous, that characteristics of men actually existing on this planet were reproduced accidentally, even while they were completely unknown to the ancient inhabitants of Mesoamerica, at least according to the history we know.

Throughout the eight centuries during which the Olmec culture developed, although their history is still largely unknown, certain concepts were elaborated that left a mark on all successive cultures.

(218 and 218-219) LA VENTA, THE PARK-MUSEUM AT VILLAHERMOSA IN MEXICO, HOUSES THE LARGEST COLLECTION OF OLMEC DISCOVERIES. FINDINGS THAT COME FROM THE FAMOUS LA VENTA ARCHAEOLOGICAL SITE IN THE MUNICIPALITY OF HUIMANGUILLO. THE MOST FAMOUS AND SUGGESTIVE ARE THE GIGANTIC HEADS, MADE OF BASALT SOME 3000 YEARS AGO AND LOST FOR CENTURIES AMID THE MEXICAN JUNGLE. IN ALL, THE NUMBER OF HEADS FOUND THROUGHOUT MEXICO TOTAL 17; FOUR OF THESE WERE FOUND RIGHT AT LA VENTA: THEY ARE ABOUT 3 M (9.8 FT) HIGH AND WEIGH SEVERAL TONS.

(220) INSIDE THE LA VENTA PARK MUSEUM AT VILLAHERMOSA, IN MEXICO, SEVEN ALTARS IN BASALT HAVE BEEN DISCOVERED AT THE SITE; ABOUT 4 M (13.1 FT) WIDE AND 2 M (6.6 FT) HIGH, AT THE CENTER THEY HOST A MYSTERIOUS FIGURE. IN THE ONE KNOWN AS THE ALTAR OF TRIUMPH, A CREATURE IS SEATED IN THE JAWS OF A MONSTER, WHICH IS HOLDING A CORD WRAPPED AROUND THE BASE OF THE ALTAR.

A people that apparently vanished suddenly perhaps held the knowledge that opened to the Mayas the secrets of the heavens and of the calendar. The Olmecs, by contrast with peoples who were their contemporaries, seemed to live in the future and to know objects such as the wheel, the lens and the astrolabe.

The fanciful hypotheses based on these clues have found their confirmation in the bas-relief called *El Rey*, "the king," discovered at Chalcatzingo, an Olmec archaeological site. Carved directly into the mountain wall, the bas-relief represents a curious scene that lends itself to different interpretations. The one verging most nearly on science fiction identifies the carved glyphs as clouds, falling rain, and at the center, a large "ship" sailing through the air, leaving a prodigious wake. Driving it is the king, who holds in his hands an object similar to a gear lever. A sort of photograph "snapped" into the stone, of an event that was unforgettable in the eyes of the sculptor.

The only thing that is certain is that around 400 BC, the Olmecs disappeared suddenly: their cities were destroyed and their imposing statues were knocked down, decapitated, buried. And with them, all the ancient secrets of the most mysterious people of all of Latin America disappeared as well.

_ (220-221) IN FRONT OF THE ALTAR OF TRIUMPH, WE SEE ALTAR 5: THE DIFFERENCE IS IN THE CENTRAL FIGURE, WHICH SEEMS TO HOLD THE CADAVER OF A WERE-JAGUAR (HUMAN-JAGUAR) INFANT IN ITS HANDS. ON ITS LEFT SIDE, THERE APPEAR TO BE SOME LIVING WERE-JAGUAR INFANTS. SOME BELIEVE THAT ALL THIS ALLUDES TO THE SACRIFICE OF CHILDREN.

_ (221) THE ALTAR OF THE JAGUAR IS A TRIBUTE TO THE DIVINE FORM THE SHAMAN COULD ASSUME, TRANSFORMING HIMSELF INTO THE SACRED FELINE. THE ALTARS WERE PROBABLY USED AS THRONES BY THE OLMEC KINGS.

_ (222 left) "La Abuelita" (literally, "little grandmother") is the nickname given to the archaeological find discovered at the site of La Venta and officially known as Statue 5. Among the various hypotheses formulated, one considers that the sculpture depicts a dwarf, since its height is just over 1.4 m (4.6 ft).

_ (222 right) The archaeological find discovered at La Venta and classified as Monument 56 has been renamed Mono que mira al cielo ("monkey looking skyward"). At a height of 124 cm (4.1 ft), its posture, however, is uncertain: it is likely that originally it was positioned horizontally inside one of the surrounding buildings.

_ (223) The archaeological find discovered at La Venta and catalogued as Monument 77 has been called "the Governor." In spite of the fact that it barely exceeds 1 m (3.3 ft) in height, it weighs over 12 tonnes and displays an almost perfect state of conservation, demonstrating the quality of the Olmecs' sculpture. And its symbolism, not yet completely deciphered, is extraordinary: the entire figure is decorated with cross-shaped symbols on the chest and waist.

Palenque

(17°29'3"N - 92°2'47"W)

THE SACRED TOMB CONCEALS A MYSTERIOUS INSCRIPTION IN THE HEART OF THE MAYAS' MOST AMAZING SITE.

Chiapas is one of the poorest states in Mexico, but it is rich with incredible and mysterious archaeological wonders. One of its major attractions is certainly Palenque, one of the main sites of the Mayan civilization. The friar Pedro Lorenzo de la Nada discovered it in 1567, christening it Palenque ("the Fortress"). The most important buildings of the site are the Temple of Inscriptions, the Palace, and the Group of Crosses. The ruins extend over an area of about 3 sq km (1.2 sq mi): according to many, however, this would represent only 10 percent of the original surface, and a good part of the city would still be concealed in the forest.

The palace is an architectural complex connected by a network of courtyards, rising at the center of the archaeological zone. The Group of Crosses is an ensemble of pyramidal temples with bas-reliefs relating the principal events of the local mythology.

The Temple of Inscriptions is a grand funereal monument dedicated to the legendary King Pacal. The name of the temple refers to the incredible hieroglyphic inscription that it bears: the second longest in all the Mayan cities. The building is a pyramid of rectangular base nearly 30 m (98.4 ft) in height, at the top of which an 11 m (36 ft) high temple stands. Some of the stones with which it was built even reach weights of 15 tonnes and are positioned at its top. But it is at the foundation that its most precious treasure was found. While he was examining the temple floor in 1952, Mexican archaeologist Alberto Ruz Lhuillier managed to move the stone that was covering an unexpected secret passage. A long marvelous stairway opened out before his feet: it led to the legendary tomb of King Pacal, the one that would later be defined as "the most important tomb of the entire Mesoamerican zone." Here the archaeologists discovered a precious colossal sculpted sarcophagus, rich with ornaments and bas-reliefs.

The find that most sparked the fantasies of researchers is the stone that covered King Pacal's sarcophagus, the one that has become famous as "the astronaut's stone." On the slab is a depiction of a man who, according to supporters of theories verging on science-fiction, appears to be driving an aircraft with rocket propulsion. The figure appears to have in his fist a sort of gear lever, and at the rear of the presumed aircraft, an engine is identified, from which emanate tongues of fire.

There are also some who have identified a pilot's seat in the bas-relief, as well as a mask for breathing, and in general, an aerodynamic fuselage.

In a famous and highly criticized book from 1968, Erich von Daniken affirms that the sarcophagus stone is definitive proof of the presence of an alien civilization in ancient Mexico. Obviously the scientific community rebelled at this, labeling such texts as ludicrous. Archaeologists believe, rather, that the depictions represent a priest – or perhaps King Pacal himself, who died in 683 AD – captured at the moment of passage between terrestrial life and the beyond: the man was thus not embarking upon interstellar space travel but, more simply, experiencing death. Even if perhaps the two events were, after all, not so distant in the eyes of the Mayans, a people extremely attentive to the movements of the heavens and the perfection of their constellations, which they must have studied and replicated on earth. Perhaps realizing eternal masterpieces, such as the marvelous and enigmatic Palenque.

_ (224-225) THE TEMPLES OF THE CROSS ARCHITECTURAL GROUP AT PALENQUE INCLUDES THE TEMPLE OF THE SUN, THE TEMPLE OF THE CROSS, AND THE TEMPLE OF THE FOLIATED CROSS. ONE OF THE MOST SUGGESTIVE VIEWS OF THE ENTIRE COMPLEX CAN BE ENJOYED RIGHT FROM THE SUMMIT OF THE TEMPLE OF THE CROSS. THE TEMPLES ARE BUILT UPON A STEP PYRAMID, AND THE CROSSES HAVE NOTHING TO DO WITH CHRISTIAN ICONOGRAPHY: RATHER, THEY REPRESENT THE LEGENDARY TREE OF CREATION, WHICH, ACCORDING TO MAYAN MYTHOLOGY, GROWS AT THE CENTER OF THE WORLD.

_ (226 left and right) THE ENTRANCE TO THE SARCOPHAGUS CHAMBER INSIDE THE TEMPLE OF INSCRIPTIONS CAN BE REACHED BY MEANS OF A LONG SECRET STAIRCASE: IN FOLLOWING IT ALONG, YOU CAN RELIVE THE EMOTION FELT IN 1952 BY ARCHAEOLOGIST ALBERTO RUZ LHUILLIER AS HE DESCENDED TO DISCOVER WHAT WOULD BECOME THE MOST IMPORTANT MAYAN TOMB EVER FOUND: THE TOMB OF KING PACAL. ITS ENIGMATIC INSCRIPTIONS REMAIN UNDECIPHERED EVEN TODAY.

_ (226-227) THE TEMPLE OF INSCRIPTIONS IS LOCATED IN THE EASTERNMOST AREA OF THE ENTIRE PALENQUE COMPLEX. BUILT ON A LARGE RECTANGULAR STEP PYRAMID 60 M (197 FT) WIDE AND NEARLY 30 M (98.4 FT) HIGH, THE TEMPLE ITSELF EXTENDS ANOTHER 11 M (36.1 FT) UPWARD. ONE SINGLE FUNEREAL MONUMENT, IT IS THE MAUSOLEUM FOR KING PACAL. INSIDE IT, BESIDES THE SUGGESTIVE SARCOPHAGUS DATING PROBABLY FROM 675 AD, ONE FINDS THE SECOND-LARGEST HIEROGLYPH OF THE ENTIRE MAYAN WORLD.

_ (228) THE MAYAN CIVILIZATION PROBABLY REACHED ITS ARTISTIC ZENITH AT PALENQUE. THE SCULPTURES REALIZED IN JADE OR PAINTED PLASTER ARE COMPARABLE TO THOSE PRODUCED ON THE OTHER SIDE OF THE OCEAN, DURING THE SAME PERIOD, IN ROME. THEY ARE CHARACTERIZED BY A STRONG REALISM THAT MOVES THE VIEWER EVEN AT A DISTANCE OF CENTURIES, SUCH AS, FOR EXAMPLE, THE PLASTER MASK OF A MYSTERIOUS MAN DISCOVERED INSIDE THE TEMPLE OF THE SUN.

_ (229 left and right) THE FAMOUS "ASTRONAUT STONE" AT PALENQUE IS THE SLAB COVERING KING PACAL'S SARCOPHAGUS INSIDE THE SECRET CHAMBER IN THE TEMPLE OF INSCRIPTIONS. ACCORDING TO PALEO-ASTRONOMICAL FANTASIES, THIS WOULD BE AN ENGRAVING DEPICTING A PILOT NAVIGATING A SPACESHIP, WITH INDICATIONS OF COMMANDS IN HIS HANDS AND AN ENGINE EMITTING BURSTS OF PROPULSION. ARCHAEOLOGISTS MAINTAIN, INSTEAD, THAT IT IS A DEPICTION OF THE KING DURING HIS SACRED PASSAGE FROM LIFE INTO DEATH.

COSTA RICA

Las Bolas

(8°42'20"N - 83°52'43"W)

MYSTERIOUS AND PERFECT STONE SPHERES APPEAR IN DIFFERENT PLACES ON THE PLANET. BUT THEIR NATIVE LAND IS COSTA RICA.

Costa Rica is a small country in Central America: 4 million inhabitants who welcome 1 million tourists every year. Most visitors are attracted by the idyllic nature of the country but others come in search of what is considered to be an incredible unresolved enigma: *Las Bolas*, the mysterious stone spheres of Costa Rica.

The story began in 1930 when excavators came across spheres of stone with an impressive frequency, which they were unable to explain: they were too perfect to be manmade, and too incomprehensible to be the work of nature. The spheres were discovered in various areas, but especially along the course of the River Diquis, with an astonishing concentration in the locality of Palmar Sur. The smallest spheres have a diameter of 1.5 m (4.9 ft), while the largest are over 2 m (6.5 ft); they are all of granite and can weigh more than 20 t. In addition to their nature, the site of their discovery raises many questions: the closest granite quarry, in fact, is 50 km (31 mi) away from the river delta. Who could have been capable of transporting spheres of such dimensions over rough and uneven terrain? One of the problems encountered in attempting to understand the spheres is that they are timeless: it is not possible to date them, they have no inscriptions, they are not connected to any known civilization, and it is not possible to intuit their function. And yet there are hundreds of them strewn all around the country. Scholars are unable to formulate definitive hypotheses, by means of indirect dating of deposits, established that the spheres date back 2000 years. But the technique by which they could have been produced remains unimaginable in view of the level of perfection shown by the artifacts: the spheres are perfectly polished and they reproduce the elementary geometric solid precisely.

Other scholars maintain that the original arrangement – altered through the course of the centuries, especially for the lighter spheres, which today adorn many roads and dwellings of various towns and villages – might have reproduced heavenly constellations. Probably they would be all that remains of a mysteriously vanished civilization preceding the Mayans by several thousand years.

Considering the absence of firm scientific references, the field of hypothesis has become populated with fantastical theories: the most famous is the one formulated by Estonian scholar Ivan Zapp, who, in reference to the work of American archaeologist Samuel Lothrop, related the spheres found at Uvita, on the Pacific coast, to the homonymous island in the Atlantic Ocean. According to this interpretation, the line uniting the two places named Uvita would cross through a village by the name of Bolas and the gigantic Cerro Chirripò, dominating Costa Rica from its height of 3820 m (12,533 ft). The spheres would thus constitute the points on a navigational map even though they would only be visible from above.

Regarding Chirripò, one of the trails climbing the mountain is called "the trail of the burial place of the Golden Machine" by locals. Its name recalls the popular belief according to which, a legendary flying object was buried at the top of the mountain. The reflections of light from the perfectly polished *bolas* would have constituted an incredible aerial map for this flying "object." Impossible theories have been advanced, but none seems to satisfy all the questions. All we know is that they are extremely old. And that their secret seems to resist the flow of time unscathed as well as their granite does.

_ (230 and 231) THE STONE SPHERES OF COSTA RICA ARE ON THE VERGE OF BEING RECOGNIZED BY UNESCO AS A WORLD HERITAGE SITE. A SURPRISING RECOGNITION FOR WHAT APPEAR TO BE SIMPLE, NATURAL SPHERES. BUT IT IS PRECISELY THEIR SIMPLICITY, THEIR PERFECT SPHERICAL SHAPE, THAT DEFIES RESEARCHERS: ARE THEY THE WORK OF MAN OR OF NATURE?

BRAZIL

El Dorado

(Coordinates - Unknown)

THE HUNT FOR THE MOST FABULOUS TREASURES OF SOUTH AMERICA,
HIDDEN IN THE AMAZON FOREST, IS NEVER OVER.

The name of El Dorado indicates a lost city, covered in gold. According to legend, it was a world created by the gods to conserve our planet's most ancient knowledge. One wonders whether there is any truth to this myth. Was El Dorado only a dream? Or did this enchanted place truly exist somewhere? Various people have searched for the legendary lost city of gold.

Among these, Percy Fawcett, the British colonel who penetrated into the most unknown territories of the earth, and was probably the inspiration for the film character of Indiana Jones, dedicated his very life to the myth of El Dorado. In 1901, Fawcett was charged by the Royal Geographic Society to draw up maps of South America. In the course of his research, he became aware of a legendary manuscript; among its pages, the road to El Dorado seemed to be concealed.

The legend of El Dorado was born in the 16th century, when King Charles V decided to send legions of treasure-hunting explorers into the South American colonies. In 1536, Gonzalo Jimenes de Quesada and Sebastian de Belalcazar reported the story of a native chief who took pleasure in covering himself with gold before diving into a lagoon. More than 100 official expeditions were organized in an attempt to identify the elusive city of El Dorado, situating it first in Florida, then in Venezuela, but also between Peru and Bolivia, and lastly, in Brazil in the Amazon forest region. Even Hitler supposedly organized secret research expeditions in Amazonia.

In 2001, the Italian anthropologist Mario Polia discovered an extraordinary manuscript in the Jesuit archives in Rome: it tells of a legendary lost city, hidden by a waterfall, inside the Amazon rain forest. In this document dating from 1600, the Jesuit father Andrea Lopez writes about having found the city and requests that the pope be personally notified.

Another document, equally old and fascinating, is conserved at the national library in Rio de Janeiro. Known as "Manuscript 512," it is the diary of a Portuguese soldier dating from 1753: it relates that during a scouting mission, while entering the forest from the Brazilian side, he came upon an incredibly gorgeous city surrounded by jungle. In particular, he describes a circular plaza housing a large statue of black basalt, pointing north. And all around, there were astronomical symbols and depictions of the planets of the solar system.

In 1920, Percy Fawcett had in his hands not only Manuscript 512, but also a basalt statuette which he identified as the miniature of the statue described in the manuscript. Upon the statuette were engraved 22 letters of an unknown alphabet; these same symbols recurred in the manuscript. For Fawcett, this was proof of the existence of El Dorado. Fossett organized two large expeditions in the Amazon region: in the Mato Grosso and in the Northeast. But the Mato Grosso is an impenetrable and boundless region, and it is extremely difficult to discover its secrets. Fawcett sought the support of the indigenous tribes, living with them, gaining their trust and overcoming trials of initiation. Eventually, he managed to obtain the information that El Dorado was to be found in the Serra do Roncador, an immense, unexplored area between the Rivers Xingù and Araguaia. For the Indians, this zone was populated by strange presences: a sacred place, not to be desecrated. Today is a military area, forbidden to the public: we know only of the *Gruta dos pezinhos* ("the cave of the little feet"), an archaeological site dating back thousands of years, where one can admire curious footprints of beings with two, three, four and six toes.

Fawcett was convinced that he would succeed in finding El Dorado, in spite of the fact that the Indians had advised him not to venture into the Serra do Roncador: the explorer's last letter, dated 29 May, 1925, was addressed to his wife, Nina: "We are here, at Dead Horse Camp, the exact point where my horse died in 1920 […]. I hope to be able to resume travel very quickly and finally reach the much-discussed waterfall […] I am well. I compensate for my advancing years with an unwavering enthusiasm […] you must never fear I shall fail."

Nothing more was ever heard about Fawcett and his expedition companions, and their fate remains a mystery. Some believe they were killed by the savage inhabitants of the Serra do Roncador, while others prefer instead to imagine that the explorers actually found El Dorado. And that they are still there, waiting for the rest of the world to join them.

_ (232-233) The Serra do Roncador is an impressive mountain range, rising from within the Amazon forest in the Brazilian state of Mato Grosso.

_ (233) Percy Fawcett, the man who perhaps had within his hands the map for reaching El Dorado, was seen for the last time together with the natives of Serra do Roncador, on a river near "Dead Horse Camp." That was in 1925. Since then, no one ever heard any more news from him, nor about the expedition accompanying him.

PERU

The Nazca Lines

(14°43'S - 75°8'W)

FOR WHOSE EYES WERE THESE COLOSSAL DESIGNS TRACED IN THE ARID PERUVIAN DESERT? WHO COULD HAVE, WHO SHOULD HAVE SEEN THEM FROM SO HIGH UP?

In the middle of the Peruvian desert, which covers about 300 sq km (116 sq mi), the famous Pan-American highway runs, unique in the world, for 27,000 km (16,750 mi). But this zone is also important for other reasons, much more ancient than the famous *carretera*. Dozens of airplanes fly over this area to admire an incredible archaeological site, designated in 1994 as a UNESCO World Heritage Site.

Discovered in 1926 by Peruvian archaeologist Julio Tello, the mysterious Nazca Lines became famous thanks to American geographer Paul Kosok, who flew over the area in 1939 in a small airplane. From the ground, one cannot recognize anything other than a series of small shallow furrows in the soil. From a height of 14 m (a tower has been built on the site for tourists) the reading improves, but only slightly. Only in flight can one clearly see the more than 200 designs and over 13,000 geometric figures that inexplicably fresco the Peruvian desert. The geoglyphs are of cyclopean dimensions: from a minimum of 25 m (82 ft) to a maximum of 275 m (902 ft).

It is not possible to give a certain dating for this highly extravagant manmade work. It is presumed to be very ancient and thought that only the particular arid climate of the region has prevented time from canceling it out. Here the sun shines for about 1200 hours each year over a highly mineralized surface and creates a thermal vacuum reaching up to 1 m (3.3 ft) in height; for this reason winds, which here are called *paracas*, do not touch the soil.

The legendary Nazca Lines are a sort of bas-relief carved into the ground, to a depth of between 7 and 10 cm (2.8 to 3.9 in). Official archaeology attributes these works to the Nazca, a primitive tribe that supposedly disappeared inexplicably centuries earlier than the appearance of the successive Inca culture. The lines were supposedly traced between 200 BC and 700 AD, utilizing rudimentary means and instruments. How the Nazca could have created such large figures with precision is unclear. And no one even understands what their purpose was.

The most traditional hypotheses maintained that these were sacred paths, utilized during ceremonies connected with the cult of water and fertility of the earth, or indicators of the presence of sources.

According to Paul Kosok, the lines were used as indicators of the dawn and sunset and of other stars. German astronomer Maria Reiche, who spent her life at Nazca, is of the same opinion; she believes that the geoglyphs were used to determine solstices and equinoxes, eclipses of the sun and the moon, and suitable moments for sowing and harvest.

But the question remaining at the heart of the mystery of the Nazca Lines is why they produced designs that can be seen and appreciated only from above. There are some who think about the ancient legends speaking of the *Viracochas*, the mysterious visitors who supposedly brought civilization to these areas: men with light skin, beards and reddish hair, endowed with supernatural powers.

_ (234-235) THE GROUP OF LINES KNOWN AS "THE ASTRONAUT" IS ONE OF THE MOST CONTROVERSIAL OF THE ENTIRE NAZCA PLAIN. IT OWES ITS NAME TO THE ANTHROPOMORPHIC IMAGE WITH A DISPROPORTIONATE HEAD: THIS DETAIL HAS SUGGESTED THE REPRESENTATION OF AN ASTRONAUT'S HELMET. ACCORDING TO ARCHAEOLOGIST MARIA REICHE, IT WOULD REPRESENT, RATHER, A SHAMAN OR A PRIEST.

_ (235) THE NAZCA LINES ARE LOCATED IN PERU, ALONG THE PAN-AMERICAN HIGHWAY, A ROAD SYSTEM CROSSING 300 KM (186 MI) OF THE PERUVIAN DESERT AND WELL BEYOND, RUNNING ALONG THE PACIFIC COAST OF THE AMERICAS, FROM ALASKA DOWN TO CHILE.

235

LINEAS Y GEOGLIFOS DE NASCA

PAMPA DE SAN JOSE

SAN PABLO

RIVER INGENIO

LEGEND TO THE MAP

1) PARROT	4) LIZARD	7) HANDS	10) SPIRAL	13) PARROT
2) SEA BIRD	5) ALLIGATOR	8) FLOWER	11) CONDOR	14) SEAWEED
3) HERON	6) TREE	9) SPIDER	12) DOG	15) MONKEY
				16) HUMMINGBIRD

The mysterious mythological figures were able, in fact, the sail the skies.

Beyond the myth, those lines crossing the desert surface leave one truly without words when flying over. The most unusual geoglyphs are those depicting a spider and various types of birds (among them, the condor and the hummingbird) and other animals; moreover, some human figures are represented with strange glowing auras around their heads. Some of the straight lines, all realized with an impressive precision, are more than 8 km (5 mi) long. To increase the sense of mystery, the majority of the animals represented at Nazca are not indigenous to this zone.

The famous Nazca "spider" belongs to a group of arachnids among the rarest in the world: they live only in the most inaccessible areas of the Amazon forest. The spider is characterized by a particular reproductive organ, normally visible only under the microscope. How did the primitive Nazcas come to know about this spider and its unusual reproductive characteristic?

The unsolved mystery of Nazca has fascinated researchers all over the world for decades, evoking science-fiction type theories: according to authors such as Erich von Däniken and Peter Kolosimo, the Nazca figures would be signals and landing strips for extraterrestrial vehicles. Without going to such lengths, we can at least entertain the idea that perhaps what we know about the ancient civilizations of the past is only small part of the truth. The rest seems to have been forgotten – as here at Nazca – under the sands of time.

_ (236-237) THE FIRST GEOGLYPH TO BE DISCOVERED ON THE NAZCA PLAIN WAS THE ONE REPRESENTING THE SPIDER. THE ARACHNID IS SHOWN RUNNING ALONG ONE SIDE OF A GARGANTUAN TRAPEZOID. THE MOST CONTROVERSIAL ELEMENT IS THE TYPE OF SPIDER THAT IS REPRESENTED: ON THE BASIS OF ITS STRUCTURAL FEATURES, IT WOULD APPEAR TO BELONG TO A SPECIES INHABITING A REGION OF THE AMAZON MORE THAN 1500 KM (930 MILES) FROM NAZCA.

_ (238-239) THE HUMMINGBIRD IS ONE OF THE MOST FAMOUS DRAWINGS ON THE NAZCA PLAIN, PROBABLY BECAUSE OF ITS HARMONIOUS BEAUTY. IT HAS A WINGSPAN OF 66 M (217 FT) AND ITS LENGTH APPROACHES 100 M (330 FT). FOR THE ANCIENT PEOPLE OF NAZCA, HUMMINGBIRDS WERE THE MESSENGERS OF THE GODS, BUT ALSO INTERPRETERS OF THE MYTHOLOGICAL SACRED CONDORS.

_ (239 top) THE FIRST GEOGLYPH TO BE DISCOVERED ON THE NAZCA PLAIN WAS THE ONE REPRESENTING THE SPIDER. THE ARACHNID IS SHOWN RUNNING ALONG ONE SIDE OF A GARGANTUAN TRAPEZOID. THE MOST CONTROVERSIAL ELEMENT IS THE TYPE OF SPIDER THAT IS REPRESENTED: ON THE BASIS OF ITS STRUCTURAL FEATURES, IT WOULD APPEAR TO BELONG TO A SPECIES INHABITING A REGION OF THE AMAZON MORE THAN 1500 KM (930 MI) FROM NAZCA.

_ (239 bottom) THE CONDOR IS THE UNDISPUTED LORD OF THE ANDES. ITS HIGH-ALTITUDE FLIGHTS HAVE ALWAYS THRILLED MAN. THE ONE REPRESENTED ON THE NAZCA PLAIN IS 130 M LONG AND OVER 100 M WIDE (427 X 328 FT). IT IS ONE OF THE MOST SACRED ANIMALS OF ALL OF SOUTH AMERICA. FOR MANY PEOPLES IT IS LIKENED TO MOUNTAIN DIVINITIES.

_ (240 top) THE GEOGLYPH OF THE PARROT EVOKES MUCH DEBATE. ACCORDING TO NEW INTERPRETATIONS, IN FACT, IT COULD ACTUALLY REPRESENT A TITANIC ANT: THERE ARE SOME WHO HAVE IDENTIFIED SIX LEGS ALONG THE BODY, OF WHICH TWO HAVE BEEN CANCELED, AND AN ANTENNA ON THE LEFT SIDE. IN SUPPORT OF THIS HYPOTHESIS IS THE FACT THAT NO OTHER BIRD REPRESENTED AT NAZCA HAS THE SAME TYPE OF WINGS AS THOSE OF THIS PRESUMED PARROT.

_ (240 bottom) AT THE EASTERNMOST POINT OF THE ENTIRE NAZCA PLAIN, SUPERPOSED UPON A GREAT RECTANGLE, THE FIGURE OF A WHALE IS INCISED IN THE GROUND. THE COLOSSAL CETACEAN REPRESENTED A MARINE DIVINITY FOR THE NAZCA PEOPLE. THE DESIGN IS NOT ONE OF THE MOST MAJESTIC – IT MEASURES "ONLY" 27 M (89 FT) – BUT IT IS STRIKING FOR ITS DEMONSTRATION OF THE FIGURATIVE ABILITIES OF ITS MYSTERIOUS CREATORS.

_ (240-241) THE SPIRAL-SHAPED TAIL OF THE MONKEY REPRESENTED AT NAZCA HAS BECOME AN ICON OF THE ENTIRE PLAIN ITSELF. IN PERU, MONKEYS WERE VENERATED BECAUSE OFTEN THEY COULD BE FOLLOWED TO FIND PRECIOUS RESERVES OF POTABLE WATER. THE MONKEY AT NAZCA HAS NINE DIGITS INSTEAD OF 10, BUT THIS IS NOT AN ERROR: FOR THE PERUVIAN PEOPLES, MALFORMATIONS WERE A SIGN OF THE DIVINE.

_ (242-243) IT IS FROM ABOVE THAT THE RUINS OF MACHU PICCHU APPEAR IN ALL THEIR FASCINATING MYSTERY, LOST IN THE VALLEY OF THE URUBAMBA: WHO COULD HAVE CLIMBED THESE PEAKS CENTURIES AGO WITH THE INTENTION OF BUILDING A CITY THERE?

_ (243) HIRAM BINGHAM DISCOVERED MACHU PICCHU IN 1911. HE BELIEVED THAT IT WAS ACTUALLY VILCABAMBA, THE CITY WHERE THE INCAS TOOK REFUGE. BORN IN HAWAII, BINGHAM FOUGHT THE FIRST WORLD WAR IN FRANCE. HE LATER BECAME A UNITED STATES SENATOR, AND ACCORDING TO MANY, IT WAS HE WHO INSPIRED THE SUCCESSFUL MOVIE CHARACTER INDIANA JONES.

Machu Picchu

(13°09'47"S - 72°32'44"W)

A JEWEL SET AMONG THE INACCESSIBLE PEAKS OF THE ANDES, AN ANCIENT CIVILIZATION OBSESSED BY THE MOVEMENTS OF THE STARS THROUGH THE SKY.

24 July, 1911: in Peru, a young explorer with a good dose of courage approaches places that until that moment were considered unexplored, discovering, in fact, something important: the lost city of Machu Picchu. The city of a thousand mysteries: Who transported those enormous stones to the top of a mountain so difficult to scale? Who wedged them together so perfectly hundreds, if not thousands, of years ago?

The young explorer was Hiram Bingham, and it was an extraordinary spectacle that presented itself to his eyes. The ruins of Machu Picchu, which in the Quechua language signifies "old peak," are located in a highly inaccessible area of Peru. Perhaps this is why the Spanish conquistadores never discovered it, and why not even the missionaries who settled nearby ever even suspected its existence. According to official archaeology, the area was settled in the 15th century, but according to some scholars, the principal elements of Machu Picchu were oriented in accordance with particular astronomical alignments, from which one could deduce that the original project referred to the period between 4000 and 2000 BC.

The place is enchanting, splendid, especially if appreciated from above while flying. But at the moment of its maximum splendor, it could accommodate only 750 inhabitants. For this reason, some believe it was a place of worship. A curious study performed on the ancient orientation of the plan of the city in relation to the cardinal points would shift its construction to 3172 BC. What is, nonetheless, certain is that whoever did make it up to this remote peak to build a city must have had an important reason for doing so.

In one of the oldest rooms of Machu Picchu, we can recognize two mortars. Some believe they were used to dye clothes, while others think this was actually an astronomical observatory: the tanks filled with water could reflect the movements of the stars so they could be studied. The Incas were the last to inhabit Machu Picchu, but other populations could have lived there before them. The theories on who might have placed the stones at Machu Picchu are numerous. As with the majority of the megalithic ruins found in other parts of the world, some of the constructions at Machu Picchu appear to be veritable "stone computers" for calculating equinoxes and solstices. The "Temple of the Two Windows," for example, is clearly an equinoctial construction: the sun was viewed through the two windows of the building.

Even the "Temple of the Three Windows" was utilized for tracing the movements of the stars and the sun with precision. A staircase carved into the living rock leads to the top of a ridge on which a stone appears like a throne, surmounted by another smaller monolith, called "Intihuatana," the Sunstone.

_ (244) MACHU PICCHU IS DIVIDED INTO TWO LARGE AREAS: THE URBAN AND THE AGRICULTURAL, CHARACTERIZED BY TERRACES FOR CULTIVATION. THE TERRACING GIVES THE APPEARANCE OF A GIGANTIC STAIRCASE CUT INTO THE HILL; IT IS REMARKABLE TO NOTE THAT THE RETAINING WALLS ARE MADE OF MATERIALS ALLOWING THE FLOW OF WATER. A HIGHLY ADVANCED WORK OF ENGINEERING CONSIDERING THE TIME OF ITS CONSTRUCTION.

_ (245 top) THE TEMPLE OF THE CONDOR IS A MARVELOUS EXAMPLE OF THE SCULPTING ABILITY OF THE BUILDERS OF MACHU PICCHU: BY EXPLOITING A PARTICULAR ROCKY FORMATION, THE ARTISTS SUCCEEDED IN RENDERING THE FLIGHT OF THE CONDOR IN A STONE STATUE. ACCORDING TO HISTORIANS, THE BIRD'S HEAD WAS USED AS A SACRIFICIAL ALTAR.

_ (245 bottom) THE URBAN AREA OF MACHU PICCHU IS DIVIDED INTO THREE SECTORS: ONE FOR THE PEOPLE, ONE FOR THE PRIESTS AND NOBLES, AND THE THIRD, A SACRED AREA. IT IS IN THIS LAST THAT WE FIND THE MONUMENTS DEDICATED TO THE GOD INTI: THE TEMPLE OF THE SUN, THE INTIHUATANA, AND THE TEMPLE OF THE THREE WINDOWS, USED FOR FOLLOWING THE MOVEMENTS OF THE STARS THROUGH THE SKY.

Being aligned in accordance with the northeast-southeast axis, this also was used for calculating the solstices and equinoxes.

As in other parts of the world, at Machu Picchu, we find cyclopean walls realized with dozens of enormous blocks. A puzzle of polygonal stones wedged perfectly together with one another, positioned without any sort of cement. One of the largest is a monolith about 3.5 m (11.5 ft) long and 1.5 m (4.9 ft) wide, with an estimated weight of 200 tonnes.

Another mystery surrounding the construction of Machu Picchu: on the mountain, there was no site large enough to realize the entire complex, so 25,000 tonnes of earth were transported from a valley located 400 m (1300 ft) farther down. And this operation was performed with sheer human force or on mule back to an altitude greater than 2500 m, with its lack of oxygen. Who could have produced such perfect inlays or have cut the stone so precisely, with such expenditure of effort? The Incas themselves indicated that their masters were of a civilization that preceded them, that of the Viracocha. A legendary civilization, venerated by all the Peruvian peoples. What remains to be seen is whether Machu Picchu could have been their most sacred place.

_ (246-247) Beginning from 7 July, 2007 (the date was chosen in honor of the number seven: 7-7-7), Machu Picchu has officially been on the list of the "New Seven Wonders of the World." A worldwide survey, also lasting seven years, resulted in this prestigious status, in company with Chichén Itzá, the Colosseum, the Taj Mahal, Petra, Christ the Redeemer at Rio de Janeiro, and the Great Wall of China.

_ (246) Machu Picchu presents an impressive array of temples and shrines. That of the Sun – dedicated, as usual, to the principal Inti divinities – is built in such a way that on the day of the winter solstice the sun enters the central window to strike the large ceremonial stone: the entire curved wall protects the sacred rock.

_ (247) According to the Inca religion, the dead were to be buried outside the city walls. And indeed, archaeologists have unearthed a number of burial places in what is called the Upper Cemetery. Excavations have also uncovered a large funerary tablet of granite, into which three steps have been dug; it was probably used for ritual or sacrificial ceremonies.

PERU

Sacsayhuamán

(13°30'28"S - 71°58'56"W)

AN ENTIRE CITY CONSTRUCTED IN THE FORM OF A PUMA AT THE TOP OF THE ANDES, ONE OF THE MOST SACRED SITES FOR THE LEGENDARY INCA PEOPLE.

There are certain places that appear, more than others, to be veritable treasure troves of unanswered questions, mysteries dating back to eras that official history does not even contemplate. One such place is certainly the famous ancient Inca capital of Cuzco, Peru. The name of the city, in the ancient Quechua language, signifies "navel of the world." Cuzco is located at 3400 m (11,155 ft) above sea level, and according to official archaeology, the first human settlements would date back to about 3000 years ago. The entire city appears to be built upon a pattern of the outline of a puma, the animal sacred to the Incas as the protector of earthly things.

In his famous volume *Comentarios Reales de los Incas*, one of the earliest accounts of the history of the Incas and the Spanish conquest, Garcilaso de la Vega wrote about the area of Cuzco in 1609: "… constructions of such inconceivable proportions as to suggest that some magic has governed their construction, that they are the work of demons rather than human beings [...] made of stones so large and numerous that one wonders how they got the Indians to produce them, because they did not know iron or steel for cutting and polishing the rock, nor had they oxen or carts to transport them."

In the ancient buildings of Cuzco, the stones of green diorite, a mineral that is particularly hard to work, are put in place without any kind of cement. They are worked in such a precise manner that they adhere perfectly to one another: it is not even possible to insert a credit card into the junctures between the stones. It is hard to believe that the Incas, a people who apparently did not possess advanced technology, or even know the wheel, could create such amazing architectural works. And it is even more difficult to imagine how they could have succeeded in shaping the stone as though working with wax, giving them strange forms and developing an ingenious and very sound system of interlocking polygonal blocks. A construction technique that was more refined than those used in Europe during the same period, in spite of the fact that the Old Continent was decidedly more advanced from the cultural, scientific, and technological points of view.

Sacsayhuamán is surely among the most important buildings of Cuzco: a promontory on the outskirts of the city upon which stands an enigmatic construction. The name in Aymara means "place where the hawk is satiated." But if we look at the map of Cuzco as being of the form of a puma, then Sacsayhuamán represents the animal's head, with the zigzag walls recalling the jaws. The entire complex could accommodate tens of thousands of men, and perhaps for this, the conquistadores called it "the fortress," imagining that it had a military purpose.

Many scholars now believe that instead it was a religious complex, a sacred area, or even one single colossal temple. Legends tell that these walls were already ancient when the Incas settled in these places, but official archaeology rejects this hypothesis, attributing the start of construction, which lasted 70 years, to the Inca emperor Pachacútec in 1438.

_ (249) IN LOOKING AT CUZCO FROM ABOVE, WE HAVE A VIEW LIKE NO OTHER ON THE PLANET. THE WHOLE APPEARS TO BE AN ENORMOUS AND COMPLEX DESIGN OF A PUMA, THE ANIMAL SACRED TO THE INCAS. THE CENTRAL SQUARE OF CUZCO CORRESPONDS TO THE FELINE'S BREAST, WHILE THE FORTRESS OF SACSAYHUAMÁN REPRESENTS THE ANIMAL'S HEAD, WITH THE CHARACTERISTIC ZIGZAG WALLS FOR THE JAWS.

_ (250-251) EVERYTHING THAT COULD BE CARRIED AWAY FROM THE FORTRESS WAS PLUNDERED. WHAT REMAINS ARE THE STONES WITNESSING THE INCREDIBLE CONSTRUCTIONAL TECHNIQUE OF THE ANCIENT INHABITANTS OF CUZCO. IT HAS BEEN ESTIMATED THAT THE LOOTED GOODS AMOUNT TO OVER TWICE WHAT IS VISIBLE TODAY AT SACSAYHUAMÁN. WHAT COULD HAVE BEEN LOST?

(252-253) THE MAIN GATEWAY TO THE RUINS OF SACSAYHUAMÁN DOES NOT SIMPLY LEAD TO ONE OF THE MOST THRILLING PLACES IN SOUTH AMERICA. ACCORDING TO SPIRITUAL MASTERS OF THE ANDEAN TRADITION, CROSSING ITS THRESHOLD SIGNIFIES PUTTING ONESELF IN CONTACT WITH THE BELLY OF THE PACHAMAMA, HOLY MOTHER EARTH.

_ (253) BEFORE THE FORTRESS, THERE IS A STRANGE HILL CHARACTERIZED BY A SERIES OF UNDULATIONS IN THE TERRAIN, CREATING PARALLEL FURROWS IN THE STONE. AT ITS VERTEX STANDS THE SO-CALLED THRONE OF THE INCA, AFFORDING A SUGGESTIVE VIEW OF THE ENTIRE COMPLEX, AND WHERE, ACCORDING TO TRADITION, THE INCA HIMSELF SAT DURING THE TRADITIONAL FESTIVAL OF WARAQO, WHERE YOUTHS CHALLENGED ONE ANOTHER IN TESTS OF STRENGTH, DEXTERITY, AND INTELLIGENCE.

At Sacsayhuamán, there are masses as high as 8 m (26 ft), weighing more than 300 tonnes, adhering to one another perfectly in puzzles of different forms. Construction that not even the passing of the millennia has been able to mar. The enigma of the architectural technique used in other buildings at Cuzco – rocks adhering perfectly to one another – develops here on three levels. But the mysteries at Sacsayhuamán do not refer only to the cyclopean walls. In the clearing at the top of the monument, what appear to be ancient foundations have been discovered, characterized by plans based on geometric polygons. To date, no definitive answer has been formulated as to the meaning of these enigmatic ruins or on what these foundations are resting. Further, it is hypothesized that the ruins visible today represent only 30 percent of what once stood at Sacsayhuamán: after looting and plundering prolonged over the centuries, in fact, the only thing left at the "fortress" is that which could not be carried away: the stones. The complex is perfectly aligned with the four cardinal points, and the walls intersecting the three circles at its summit have an ideal orientation for determining the winter and summer solstices.

If Sacsayhuamán truly was an ancient astronomical observatory, we must imagine that the Incas were capable of creating a work of such magnitude. Or does it all date back to an ancient past that we still do not know?

254

Lake Titicaca

(15°54'S - 69°18'W)

THE GEOGRAPHIC HEART OF ONE OF THE OLDEST CIVILIZATIONS ON THE PLANET SEEMS TO GUARD AN INCREDIBLE TRUTH ABOUT ITS UNTOUCHED DEPTHS.

At 3818 m (12,526 ft) elevation, nestled among the Andean peaks on the border between Peru and Bolivia, we find perhaps the most enchanting and mysterious mirror of water in the world: Lake Titicaca. Its hypnotic blue color runs for over 200 km (124 mi) in length and 65 km (40 mi) in width, surrounded by shores of wilderness. It is the world's highest navigable lake and yet in distant times, Lake Titicaca was on the ocean floor. The entire area, in fact, is littered with millions of fossil shells, a sign that the entire plateau was once a seabed, probably thrust upward with the lifting of the earth that formed the entire South American continent. All this would have occurred about 200 million years ago.

Through the course of time, the morphology of the area has undergone other profound changes. In particular, the surface of the lake has undergone significant oscillations, to the point of causing the very bed of the lake to incline, following movements that usually require thousands if not millions of years to unfold. The ancient ruined city of Tiahuanaco, with its colossal docks, must certainly have bordered the water; indeed, recent archaeological discoveries would appear to suggest it may even have been an island within the lake. But today these ruins are located about 30 km (19 mi) from Lake Titicaca. To be able to explain such an anomaly, we would have to hypothesize some devastating cataclysm that occurred in the area, a catastrophe that would have so drastically lowered the level of the lake, a calamity capable of wiping out any civilization might have lived in the region of Lake Titicaca. A series of apocalyptic events that would very much resemble the description of the myth of Atlantis.

Perhaps it is no coincidence that the famous Andean legend, transcribed by the missionary friar José de Acosta – one of the first Europeans to reach the area – narrated thus: "For some unnamed crime, the people living in the most ancient times was destroyed by a flood. After that the Creator appeared in human form from the lake and brought back the sun, the moon, and the stars." The Indians spoke of a flood in which nearly all humankind died, and of the god Viracocha who emerged from the waters of Lake Titicaca and brought back life. The story appears, once again, to touch upon the recurring theme of a civilization destroyed by water, just as was the case for the legendary Atlantis. And yet official history contemplates no evolved civilization during the period in which all this would have occurred, namely around 10,000 BC.

There is also something hidden, however, underneath the surface of Lake Titicaca. Some archaeological expeditions conducted at the beginning of the new millennium have identified the underwater ruins of mysterious settlements: the remains of a temple occupying a surface of more than 3000 sq m (0.74 acres), situated 30 m (98 ft) deep. At 70 m (230 ft) depth, moreover, they have identified a road that appears to connect the coast to Isla del Sol. Furthermore, retaining walls are visible 100 m (328 ft) deep, as well as agricultural terracing and much more. The research team also discovered Inca and pre-Inca amphorae, and vases of Amazonian origin. And the fact that the remains have been found at such different depths would appear to be a further confirmation for the hypothesis that the entire zone may have raised and lowered, then inclined to one side. And a flourishing civilization may have existed on the shores of Lake Titicaca much earlier than previously imagined. Perhaps even during the times of the legendary civilization of Atlantis.

_ (254-255) LAKE TITICACA IS ONE OF THE MOST SUGGESTIVE MIRRORS OF WATER ON OUR PLANET. SHARED BETWEEN BOLIVIA AND PERU, IT EXTENDS OVER MORE THAN 8000 SQ KM (3200 SQ MI).

_ (254) ISLA DEL SOL IS ONE OF THE LARGEST ISLANDS ON LAKE TITICACA: ACCORDING TO THE INCAS, THE SUN GOD WAS BORN HERE. REMAINS OF MORE THAN 180 HUMANS TESTIFY TO THE PRESENCE OF A VERY ANCIENT CIVILIZATION AT A LABYRINTHINE EDIFICE CALLED CHICANA.

BOLIVIA

Tiahuanaco

(16°33'17"S - 68°40'24"W)

MORE THAN A CITY, IT IS AN IMMENSE AND VERY ANCIENT ASTRONOMICAL CALENDAR SCULPTED INTO THE STONE, AT NEARLY 4000 M (13,123 FT) ABOVE SEA LEVEL.

At 3846 m (12,618 ft) elevation, high on top of a barren plateau, nestled between the majesty of the Andes and legendary Lake Titicaca, rises Tiahuanaco: a place shrouded in mystery, one of the most fascinating archaeological sites in the world. Its name means "the city of the gods."

As Pedro Cieza de León reports in his diary in 1549: "The builders of these great foundations and fortifications are unknown, nor do we know how much time has elapsed since their epoch, since today we see only the walls of fine workmanship, erected many centuries ago. Some of these stones are worn and in disrepair, and there are others so imposing that one wonders how human hands could carry them to where they are today. I dare say that these are the oldest antiquities of all of Peru ... I asked the natives if these dated back to the time of the Incas. But the natives, laughing at my question, repeated back to me when I have already said: they were constructed before the reign of the Incas; but they could not indicate or suggest to me who had built them or why."

It is not clear whether Tiahuanaco was the capital of a great empire, but certainly it was a great center of worship where people performed ceremonies and rites of which we know nothing. At the peak of their expansion, the city could accommodate about 20,000 people, distributed over more than 2 sq km (0.77 sq mi). This is the largest pre-Inca megalithic architectural work in South America. The history of the mysterious civilization of Tiahuanaco is divided into five periods: traditionally, it begins around 2000 BC and ends – mysteriously – around 1200 AD. A civilization about which we know very little: no written texts have been discovered at Tiahuanaco. One certainty is that Lake Titicaca played a central role in the development of the site, and the ruins of the former Tiahuanaco stood right on its shores, as the remains of the area called "Puma Punku" would suggest, probably constituting the point of access to the city from the vanished ancient port. Today, Lake Titicaca is located 18 km (11.2 mi) away, and fully 30 m (98 ft) lower, which causes us to consider the possibility that some cataclysm may have fallen upon this area.

The ruins of the Pyramid of Akapana are situated on a hill reaching 16 m (52.5 ft) in height upon a base 200 sq m (2153 sq ft) wide. Its flat top is the site of a mysterious oval basin. Some believe this had the function of collecting water, while others add that the water was used to study the movements of the planets that were reflected therein. Just to the north rises the Kalasasaya, a platform about 3 m (9.8 ft) high on a base measuring 130 x 120 m (427 x 394 ft), for use in performing unknown rites and ceremonies. One of the impressive aspects of the structure is its method of construction: its extremely heavy blocks of andesite and red sandstone fit together perfectly. Inside stands what is considered to be the very icon of the ancient civilization of Tiahuanaco: the Gate of the Sun.

_ (256-257) According to geological and archaeological analyses, in remote times Puma Punku could have been the entry point for Tiahuanaco on the shores of Lake Titicaca; the remaining ruins would thus be those of an ancient vanished port. Today, Lake Titicaca is situated 18 km (11.2 mi) away from Puma Punku and 30 m (98.4 ft) lower: it all makes one suspect that a devastating cataclysm took place in this area.

_ (257) The ruins of the Akapana pyramid are situated on a hill 16 m (52.5 ft) high over a base of 200 sq m (2153 sq ft). Upon its flat summit stands a mysterious oval basin. According to some, its function was to collect water, while others maintain that it was used for studying the movements of the planets from their reflections in the water.

_ (258-259 and 258) JUST TO THE NORTH RISES THE KALASASAYA, A STRUCTURE ABOUT 3 M (9.8 FT) HIGH AND 130 M (426.5 FT) x 120 M (393.7 FT) IN AREA, A PLATFORM WHERE UNKNOWN RITES AND CEREMONIES MUST HAVE TAKEN PLACE. WHAT IS IMPRESSIVE ABOUT THE KALASASAYA IS ITS METHOD OF CONSTRUCTION: THE EXTREMELY HEAVY BLOCKS OF ANDESITE AND RED SANDSTONE FIT TOGETHER PERFECTLY. THE ENTIRE KALASASAYA WOULD APPEAR TO BE A SORT OF CYCLOPEAN CALENDAR, SINCE AT MAJOR ASTRONOMICAL EVENTS, FROM TIME TO TIME, THE SUN LIGHTS UP THE EQUINOCTIAL EDIFICES OR THE MONUMENTS CONNECTED WITH THE SOLSTICES.

_ (259) ANOTHER FASCINATING CONSTRUCTION IS THE SEMI-SUBTERRANEAN QUADRANGULAR TEMPLE, UNEARTHED IN 1960. DOZENS OF STONE HEADS ARE FIXED UPON ITS WALLS, PROBABLY REPRESENTING WAR TROPHIES.

Fashioned from a single block of volcanic rock, it is finely carved with bas-reliefs and features four mysterious niches. The entire gate has an estimated weight of 44 tonnes; it is the largest elaborated monolith ever discovered on our planet. At the center, the gate is surmounted by an enigmatic anthropomorphic figure that seems to be wielding two scepters shaped like serpents. All around, there are 48 winged figures, of which 32 have human faces and 16, heads of condors. The Gate of the Sun owes its name to the day of the vernal equinox, when the rising sun appears exactly at its center. Many believe the 48 figures and four niches are part of an astronomic calendar sculpted into the stone but not yet deciphered. The entire Kalasasaya, at any rate, does seem like a sort of cyclopean calendar, since major astronomical events illuminate its equinoctial edifices, or monuments connected with the solstices, with the light of the sun.

The true origin of this magical place is still a mystery. According to local legend, it was created by the ancient giants who lived there in primordial times. One of the most incredible theories was formulated by Arthur Posnansky, director of the National Museum of Bolivia and founder of the Bolivian Archeological Society. After a life dedicated to studying Tiahuanaco, Posnansky established that it must have been founded as early as 15,000 BC – in the Ice Age – and that it was later devastated by a cataclysm that proved deadly to its population. Such fantastical hypotheses even drew Nazi explorers to Bolivia in the 1940s in search of proof of the existence of the legendary civilization of Atlantis. And of what would be the oldest city on the planet.

_ (260 top and 260-261) ON THE DAY OF THE SPRING EQUINOX, THE SUN RISES AT THE EXACT CENTER OF THE GATE OF THE SUN. THE MONUMENT IS IMPRESSIVE: THE LARGEST ARCHAEOLOGICAL DISCOVERY, WEIGHING MORE THAN 40 TONS, IT WAS CARVED FROM A SINGLE BLOCK OF STONE. THE GATE OF THE SUN'S CONNECTION WITH ASTRONOMICAL PHENOMENA IS NOT LIMITED TO THE EQUINOX: THE ENTIRE ENSEMBLE OF NICHES AND FIGURES ADORNING IT WOULD APPEAR TO BE AN ANCIENT CALENDAR, NOT YET FULLY DECIPHERED.

_ (260 bottom) THE PONCE MONOLITH, ALSO KNOWN AS THE PONCE STELE, IS LOCATED WITHIN THE KALASASAYA ENCLOSURE. REALIZED FROM A SINGLE BLOCK OF ANDESITE AND STANDING 3 M (9.8 FT) HIGH, IT DEPICTS AN ANTHROPOMORPHIC GIANT. IT OWES ITS NAME TO BOLIVIAN ARCHAEOLOGIST CARLOS PONCE, WHO UNEARTHED IT IN 1957. IT PROBABLY REPRESENTS AN IMPORTANT FIGURE DEIFIED BY THE PEOPLE OF TIAHUANACO.

262

Easter Island

(27°7'14"S — 109°21'5"W)

THE MOAI: ENIGMATIC TIMELESS FACES THAT SEEM TO GUARD, IN THE MIDDLE OF THE OCEAN, A FANTASTIC STORY.

Rapa Nui, better known as Easter Island, is perhaps the most mysterious island in the world. It is also the inhabited location on our planet most remote from any other inhabited place: nearly 4000 km (2500 mi) of ocean in all directions separate it from any other dry land. If we look on a globe, the island appears like a small spot in the Pacific Ocean, an error in the blue that fills the geographic map. And yet, on this small undecipherable piece of land stand the most mysterious statues of our planet, the Moai. Colossal stone heads, carved from the basaltic tuff of volcanic craters. Timeless gazes raising questions that today are still unanswered.

Who are the people portrayed in the faces of the Moai? The inhabitants of Rapa Nui in ancient times would have had to be capable, in some manner, to produce and transport these monumental sculptures from one side of the island to the other. But how did they arrive at this enchanted, unreachable place? What watercraft did they use to cross thousands of kilometers of the Pacific Ocean?

Easter Island has a surface area of approximately 160 sq km (62 sq mi) and today numbers about 2000 inhabitants: it is the emerged portion of a volcanic massif, of which two great extinguished mouths are clearly visible. The island was discovered on Easter day (hence its name) in 1722 by the Dutch admiral Jacob Roggeveen. According to his travel logs, the man who was then king of Rapa Nui told Roggeveen that he was the head of the last descendants of a vanished people: only those who had reached the island were saved; the rest of this ancient race no longer existed. Perhaps the sovereign referred to a civilization living on a large island that disappeared into the ocean, and toward which the gazes of the ancient Moai still face.

The imposing statues still present on the island number nearly 600, although originally there must have been nearly twice as many. Despite being of different sizes (from just over 1 m to nearly 22 m, or 3.3 ft to 72.2 ft), they reproduce, obsessively, the same face. They all were fitted with eyes, nearly all of which have disappeared, and with special red head covers. The largest Moai produced – 21.5 m (70.5 ft), called "the Giant" – is still located in the Rano Raraku quarry, lying against the rocky wall from which it was sculpted. Among those standing, the tallest is called "Paro"; at 10 m (32.8 ft), it dominates the coast of Ahu Te Pito Kura. It has been calculated that at least 500 persons must have been required to stand it upright.

According to archaeologists, the first settlements on Easter Island date back to 300 AD, people who succeeded in crossing the incredible oceanic expanses to arrive at the island, using ancient canoes. Scientists still debate whether they were Polynesian or South American, whether they came from the East or the West. Perhaps both hypotheses are true, because local legends tell of bloody feuds between two ethnic groups present on the ancient Rapa Nui, those of the "long ears" of Oriental origin, and

_ (262-263) THE LARGEST AHU OF RAPA NUI IS LOCATED ON THE SOUTHERN COAST OF EASTER ISLAND: AHU TONGARIKI. ERECTED IN THE SHADOW OF THE VOLCANO POIKE, IT IS HOME TO 15 MOAI THAT APPEAR AS GUARDIANS OF THE ISLAND: THEIR GAZE IS FIXED TOWARD THE SEA AND, ON THE DAY OF THE SUMMER SOLSTICE, THEY ALL LOOK DIRECTLY AT THE SUNSET. THE STATUES WERE REPOSITIONED ON THE AHU AFTER THE 1960 TSUNAMI THAT OVERTURNED THEM.

_ (262) THE VOLCANIC CRATER OF RANO RARAKU IS THE FACTORY FOR THE MOAI: THE MONUMENTAL STONE FACES WERE EXCAVATED FROM ITS INTERIOR. MANY WERE ABANDONED ON ITS SLOPES, SURROUNDED BY GRASS, WHILE OTHERS ARE STILL IMPRISONED IN THE INNER WALLS OF THE VOLCANO, AS THOUGH WORK ON THEM HAD STOPPED SUDDENLY.

(264 and 265) THE MONOLITHIC FACES OF EASTER ISLAND WERE CARVED IN VOLCANIC TUFF FROM THE VOLCANO RANO RARAKU. BUT THE VOLCANO'S MOST RECENT ERUPTION, ACCORDING TO MOST RECENT GEOLOGICAL STUDIES, WOULD HAVE OCCURRED NO LATER THAN 2000 YEARS AGO. THIS CONSIDERATION, TOGETHER WITH OTHER SCIENTIFIC EVIDENCE, RESTRICTS THE SCULPTING OF THE MOAI TO A PRECISE PERIOD, BEGINNING IN THE YEAR 1000 AND TERMINATING ABOUT FIVE CENTURIES LATER. MORE THAN 1000 STATUES WERE CREATED IN 500 YEARS, A FURIOUS PRODUCTION FOR THE RESOURCES OF A SMALL ISLAND WITH A FEW HUNDRED INHABITANTS. ANOTHER ONE OF THE MANY QUESTIONS DWELLING AT RAPA NUI.

those of the "short ears" of Occidental origin. A rivalry that degenerated to such a point that the "long ears" were massacred and their bodies dumped into a mass grave. The people of Rapa Nui encountered by Roggeveen believed they were the last survivors. But survivors of what?

There is another question at the center of the various scientific studies on Rapa Nui: how could the inhabitants of ancient times transport the great Moai from the quarries where they were produced all the way to the shores of the island? And yet they managed to hoist tonnes of stone without any knowledge of engineering, any draft animals, and perhaps not even the necessary utensils. According to a recent study performed on the island's fossil pollens, at the time of the construction of the Moai, the trees necessary for building systems of mechanical transport were not there. The wood on the island is said to have been exhausted around 800 AD, before the Moai are thought to have been produced.

Even more mysterious is the writing of the inhabitants of Rapa Nui during ancient times. In fact, archaeological finds known as the Rongo-Rongo tablets were discovered on the island. Unfortunately the majority of these were burned in bonfires ordered by the missionaries who arrived on the island. But it is surprising that none of the inhabitants knew how to read them because the complex symbolic writing on the tablets had been forgotten. And how is it possible that almost identical symbols were found at Mohenjo-daro, in the ancient Indus Valley, practically at the opposite end of the earth from Rapa Nui?

The Rongo-Rongo language has not yet been deciphered, although in 1996, scientist Steven Fisher announced that he had successfully read 22 of the tablets. According to the scholar, the myth of creation was engraved upon them. The only thing certain is that this island, solitary and marvelous, at the center of an immense ocean, contains a puzzle that we have not yet been able to solve.

_ (266) On the north coast of the island lies Anakena, Rapa Nui's only true beach. And it is here that perhaps the most spectacular ahu rises; its conservation can be attributed to the sand, which appears to have protected the seven statues, four of which still have their sacred pukaos, the characteristic headcovers made of red volcanic rock.

_ (267) At ahu Ko te Riku stands the only complete moai on the entire island, still equipped with its red pukao, the hat fashioned of lava rock from the Puna Pau quarry, and its eyes, fashioned from rare white coral, with obsidian for the black of the pupil. According to tradition, when the eyes were inserted, the moai came to life and allowed communication with the afterlife.

AUTHORS

Born in Rome in 1961, **ROBERTO GIACOBBO** received his degree in economics and commerce. A freelance journalist and communications expert, he is docent of "New Media Theory and Technique" at the Faculty of Letters and Philosophy at the University of Ferrara. In 1984 he began his career in radio. He had his television debut in the early 1990s as program writer. Since 1997 he has been writing programs including *Misteri, Numero Zero, L'emozione della Vita* (produced in collaboration with BBC), *La Macchina del Tempo, Cominciamo Bene*, as well as directing *Sportello Italia* on the air for Rai International; he has also hosted the program *Stargate: Linea di confine*, a transmission he has authored for Italian television channel LA7 since 1999. The program became Italy's first "television magazine" style program on the mysteries of archaeology and history, winning for two consecutive years the city of Trieste's international television prize in the research and culture category. He debuted on 20 May 2003 as author and host of the program *Voyager - ai confini della conoscenza*, joined, two years later, by the program *Ragazzi c'è Voyager!* The program has won many national awards in the fields of communications and television production. He has published several books, including *Il segreto di Leonardo (sulle tracce di Maria)* (2005); *Il ragionevole dubbio. Le risposte degli scienziati di fronte al mistero della vita oltre la vita* (2007); and *2012 la fine del mondo?* (2009). "Additionally" he has edited the series *Gli Atlanti di Voyager*.

Born in Rome in the mid-1970s, **GIULIO DI MARTINO** received his degree in theoretical physics at the Sapienza University of Rome. After a period of research at New York University, he returned to Italy to write about science for major popular magazines. At the age of only 25 he began elaborating with RAI as a new media consultant. Since 2003 he has been writing for the program "Voyager – Ai confini della conoscenza," traveling all around the planet making documentaries on the most fascinating mysteries of history, science, and archaeology. One of these — "Isola di Pasqua" — even became a book published by Giunti Editore. He also writes for film and television dramas.

INDEX

c = caption
bold type = dedicated chapter

A
Abraham, 53c, 104
Academy of Applied Sciences, Boston, 20c
Academy of the Lynx-Eyed (Lincean Academy), Rome, 9
Adivino (Pyramid of the Dwarf or Pyramid of the Magician), Uxmal, Mexico, 208c, 209, 210
Agaria, tribe, 156
Agnew, Allen, 186
Agneya, weapon, 152
Ahab, King, 131
Ahu Te Pito Kura, coast of, Easter Island, Chile, 263
Ahu Tongariki, Easter Island, Chile, 263c
Akapana, pyramid of, Tiahuanaco, Bolivia, 256, 256c
Akhet Khufu, see Cheops, pyramid of
Al-'Uzza, divinity, 147
Alatri, Lazio, 50
Alice Springs, Australia, 176
Altar 5, La Venta Park Museum, Villahermosa, Mexico, 221c
Altar of Sacrifices, Petra, Jordan, 147
Altar of the Jaguar, La Venta Park Museum, Villahermosa, Mexico, 221c
Altar of Triumph, La Venta Park Museum, Villahermosa, Mexico, 220c, 221c
Ambras Castle, Innsbruck, 64c
Anakena, beach, Easter Island, Chile, 266c
Anangu, Australian Aborigines, 176
Anasazi, people, **190-193**, 190, 190c, 192, 192c
Andes, 13, 13c, 239c, 248, 256
Angkor Wat, Angkor, Cambodia, 170, 170c, 172, 173c
Angkor, Cambodia, **170-175**, 170, 170c, 174c
Anglo-Australian, ship, 195
Anita, ship, 195
Apollo, god, 73, 74c, 75, 76c
Arabuko Sokoke, forest, Kenya, 112
Araguaia, river, 232
Ararat, Mount, 122, 123, 123c
Aratake, Kikachiro, 166
Area 51, United States, **182-185**, 182, 183c, 184c, 185
Ari, people, 150
Ariadne (daughter of Minos), 82, 84
Ark of the Covenant, 50, 53, 53c, 98, 100, 104, 111c, 134, 136
Armageddon, 131
Arthur, King, 29, 32, 34, 36c
Ashoka, Pillar of, New Delhi, India, **156-157**, 156, 156c
Asterion, see Minotaur
Astronaut Stone, Temple of Inscriptions, Palenque, Mexico, 225, 229c
Atalanta, frigate, 195
Athena Pronaia, sanctuary of, Delphi, Greece, 76c
Atlantis, island of, Greece, **78-81**, 78, 79c, 94, 255, 259
Av Solom, mausoleum of, Israel, 141
Avalon, island, 32, 33, 33c, 34
Avenue of the Dead, Teotihuacán, Mexico, 212c
Avenue of the Façades, Petra, Jordan, 146c, 147
Avon, river, 30
Axum, Ethiopia, **98-103**, 98, 98c, 100, 100c, 101c, 103c, 104, 136
Ayers Rock, see Uluru
Aztecs, 212, 214, 218

B
Baibars al-Bunduqdari, Sultan, 143
Baldwin I of Jerusalem, King, 143
Barsauma, Syrian monk, 147, 148c
Basilica of San Marco, Venice, 57c
Bayon, temple, Angkor, Cambodia, 174c
Benedict XVI, Pope, 56, 57
Bermuda Triangle, Atlantic Ocean, **194-195**, 194c, 195
Bernard of Clairvaux, 50
Bet Danaghel, church, Lalibela, Ethiopia, 104
Bet Gabriel-Rufael, church, Lalibela, Ethiopia, 106c
Bet Giyorgis, church, Lalibela, Ethiopia, 104, 107, 110c, 111c
Bet Golgotha, church, Lalibela, Ethiopia, 104, 106c
Bet Maryam, church, Lalibela, Ethiopia, 104, 105c
Bet Medhane Alem, church, Lalibela, Ethiopia, 104, 106c
Bet Meskel, church, Lalibela, Etihopia, 104
Bingham, Hiram, 242c, 243
Blood Spring, 32
Boeing KC-135, airplane, 195
Bowes-Lyon, Elizabeth, see Queen Mother of England
Bran Castle, Romania, 62c, 64, 64c, 66c
Braşov, Romania, 64, 64c
Burckhardt, Johann Ludwig, 143
Burgon, John William, 143, 199

C
C-119, airplane, 195
Canaan, people of, 131
Canyonlands National Park, Utah, 192c
Carmel, Mount, 130c, 131
Carnac alignments, Brittany, France, **44-49**, 44, 45, 45c, 46c, 47, 47c, 49c
Carwash Cenote, see Cenote Aktun Ha
Casa Rinconada, Pueblo Bonito, United States, 190
Casa Vlad Dràcul, Romania, 62, 68c
Castalia, nymph, 74c
Castalia, spring, Delphi, Greece, 74c
Castel del Monte, Puglia, 50, **58-61**, 59, 59c, 60c, 61c
Cayce, Edgar, 94
Celestine II, Pope, 56
Celestine V (Pietro da Morrone), Pope, 56
Cenote Aktun Ha (Carwash Cenote), Yucatán, 206c
Cenote Ik-Kil (Blue Cenote), Chichén Itzá, Mexico, 203c
Cenote of Sacrifice (Sacred Cenote), Chichén Itzá, Mexico, 196, 203c, 204
Cenote Xtoloc, Chichén Itzá, Mexico, 204
Cenotes, Mexico, 196, **202-207**, 203, 203c, 204, 204c, 206c
Cerne Abbas, Giant of, **38-41**, 38, 40, 40c
Cerro Chirripò, mountain, 230
Cerro Gordo, mountain, 215c
Cesi, Federico, 9
Chaac Mool, Chichén Itzá, Mexico, 197c
Chaac, god, 208c, 209, 211c
Chaco Canyon, New Mexico, United States, 190, 192, 193c
Chaerephon, 77c
Chalice Hill, 33, 36c
Charles V, King, 232
Cheops (Khufu), pharaoh, 88c, 89, 90c
Cheops, pyramid of, Egypt, 50, 59, 71, **88-91**, 88c, 89, 90, 90c, 92, 170, 212c
Chicana, labyrinthine building, Isla del Sol, 255c
Chichén Itzá, Yucatán, Mexico, **196-201**, 196, 197c, 198c, 199, 199c, 203, 203c, 247c
Chindia Tower (Sunset Tower), Romania, 62, 69c
Cholula, pyramid of, Mexico, 212c
CIA, 185
Cieza de León, Pedro, 256
Citadel, Teotihuacán, Mexico, 212c
Città di Castello, Umbria, 56
Columbus, Christopher, 195
Conical Tower, Great Zimbabwe, Africa, 116, 118c
Conner, Mount, 176
Cook, James, 176
Croesus, King, 75
Cromwell, Oliver, 33, 40
Cuzco, Peru, 248, 248c, 253
Cyclops, ship, 195

D
Daedalus, architect, 82, 83, 83c
Davenport, David, 150
David, King, 134
DC-3, airplane, 195
de Acosta, José, 255
de Belalcázar, Sebastián, 232
de la Nada, Pedro Lorenzo, 225
de la Vega, Garcilaso, 248
de Quesada, Gonzalo Jiménez, 232
Dead Sea Scrolls, Israel, **138-141**, 139, 139c, 140c, 141
Death Valley, California, United States, 186, 186c
Delphi, Oracle of, Greece, **72-77**, 72c, 73, 74c, 75, 76c
Delphine/Daphne, prophetess, 73
Dinsdale, Timothy, 21
Diodorus, 75
Diquis, river, 230
Domingo, Frank, 93c, 94
Dorset County, United Kingdom, 38, 40
Douglas, Janet (the Grey Lady), 22
Dràcul, Vlad, see Vlad III
Dracula, **62-69**, 62, 62c, 64, 64c, 66c
Dragon, Order of the, 62
Dunn, Christopher, 90
Durrington Walls, United Kingdom, 30
Dushara, divinity, 147
Dzoosotoyn Elisen, desert, 159

E
Earl Beardie, 22
Easter Island (Rapa Nui), Chile, 9, 12, 168, 170, **262-267**, 263, 263c, 264, 264c, 266d
Eastern Airlines, 195
Einstein, Albert, 11, 13
El Caracol, Chichén Itzá, Mexico, 196, 198c
El Castillo, see Kukulkán, pyramid of
El Dorado, Brazil, **232-233**, 232, 233c
El Rey, Chalcatzingo, Mexico, 220
El-Deir ("the Monastery"), Petra, Jordan, 147, 148c
El-Khazneh, Petra, Jordan, 143, 143c, 147
Essenes, sect, 139
Eternal Army, see *Terra-cotta Army*

268

Eumenes II, King, 77c
Euphrates, river, 203
Europa (daughter of king of Tyre), 82
Evans, Arthur, 82, 84c
"Extraterrestrial Highway," Nevada, United States, 182

F
Fagan, Garrett, 71
Fajada Butte, Pueblo Bonito, United States, 190
Fawcett, Nina, 232
Fawcett, Percy, 232, 233c
Fisher, Steven, 264
Frederick II, King, 59, 59c, 61

G
Galanopoulos, Angelo, 78
Gaochang, Xinjiang, China, 159c
Gate of the Sun, Tiahauanaco, 256, 259, 260c
Gavrinis, tumulus of, Island of Gavrinis, Brittany, 49c
Gebre Meskel, King, 103c
Gedi, ruins of, Kenya, **112-115**, 112, 112c, 115, 115c
Genghis Khan, 159
Geoffrey of Monmouth, 29, 34
Gilboa, Mount, 131Giza plateau, Egypt, 13c, 59, 89, 90, 92, 94c, 95c, 170
Glamis Castle, Scotland, **22-27**, 22, 23c, 24, 24c, 25c, 27c
Glamis, monster of, 24
Glastonbury Abbey, Glastonbury, United Kingdom, 36c
Glastonbury, Somerset, United Kingdom, **32-37**, 32, 33, 33c, 34, 34c, 36c
Göbekli Tepe, Turkey, **124-129**, 124, 124c, 126, 126c, 128c
Gog, oak, Glastonbury, United Kingdom, 33, 36c
Goseck Circle, the, Germany, **42-43**, 42, 43, 43c
Goseck, Burgenlandkreis, Germany, 42
"Goshintai," Yonaguni, Japan, 166
Governor's Palace, Uxmal, Mexico, 208c, 209, 211c
Gran Cenote, Tulum, Mexico, 204c
Grand Gallery, Pyramid of Cheops, 90c
Great Bath, Mohenjo-daro, Pakistan, 150Great Enclosure, Great Zimbabwe, Zimbabwe, 116, 118c
Great Pyramid, Egypt, see Cheops, pyramid of
Great Stele, Axum, Etiopia, 98, 100, 100c, 101c
Great Zimbabwe, Zimbabwe, **116-121**, 116, 116c, 118c, 121c
Groom Lake, salt flat, 182
Group of Crosses, Palenque, Mexico, 225, 225c
Group, Cemetery, Uxmal, Mexico, 209
Gruta dos pezinhos ("Cave of the Little Feet"), Mato Grosso, Brazil, 232
Guinevere, wife of King Arthur, 36c

H
Hagar, Stansbury, 209, 210
Haifa, Israel, 130c
Halys, river, 75
Hangar 18, Area 51, United States, 182, 184c
Har Megiddo, Israel, **130-133**, 130c, 131, 132c
Harappan civilization, 150, 152c, 203
Harare, plateau, Zimbabwe, 116
Havell, Robert Senior, 28c
Henry II, king, 34
Hephaestos, god, 73
Heraklion, Crete, Greece, 82
Hercules, 38
Herodotus, 88c
Highlands, Scottish, 19

Hikmet, Nazim, 12
Hitler, Adolf, 232
Holles, Denzil, 40
Holmes, Gordon, 21
Holy Grail, 32, 33, 36c, 61, 139, 143
Homer, 83c
House of Pigeons, Uxmal, Mexico, 209
House of the Old Woman, Uxmal, Mexico, 209
House of Turtles, Uxmal, Mexico, 209, 211d
Hoyle, Fred, 29
Huibers, Joan, 122
Hunab Ku, god, 196

I
Incas, 218, 234, 242c, 243, 245, 247c, 248, 248c, 253, 255, 255c, 256
Indians, (Amerindians), 232, 248, 255
Indra, god, 150
Indus, river, 150, 152c, 203, 264
Inti, god, 245c, 247c
Intihuatana (the "Sun Stone"), Machu Picchu, Peru, 243, 245, 245c
Inverness, Scottish Highlands, 19
Irvine, Malcolm, 19
Isaac, 53c, 104
Isla del Sol, Bolivia, 12, 255, 255c

J
Jacob, 104
Jayavarman VII, King, 174c
Jericho, West Bank, 126
Jerusalem, Israel, 59, 59c, 134, 135c, 136, 139, 141
John Paul I (Albino Luciani), Pope, 56
John Paul II (Karol Wojtyla), Pope, 56
John XIII (Angelo Roncalli), Pope, 56
Joseph of Arimathea, 33, 36c
Joshua, 131
Josiah, King, 131
Judith, Queen, 100, 101c
Jurassic Coast, Dorset County, United Kingdom, 38

K
K2, mountain, 159
Kakadu National Park, Australia, 181c
Kalasasaya, Tiahuanaco, Bolivia, 256, 258c, 259, 260c
Kaleb, King, 103c
Karachi Museum, Pakistan, 152c
Karamay, China, 159
Karen, sailing stone, 186, 186c
Karnak, Temple of, Egypt, 131
Kata Tjuta, Australia, 176
Kercado, tumulus, Carnac, France, 44
Kerlescan, alignment, Carnac, France, 44
Kermario, alignment, Carnac, France, 44, 46c
Khafra, see Khefren
Khefren (Khafra), pharaoh, 92, 93c, 94, 94c
Khefren, pyramid of, Egypt, 89, 90, 92
Khmer, empire, 170c, 174c
Khor Virap, monastery of, Monte Ararat, 123c
Khufu, see Cheops
Killaraus, mountains, 29
Kimberley, region, Australia, 180c
Kimura, Masaaki, 166
King's chamber, Pyramid of Cheops, Egypt, 89, 90c
Kircher, Athanasius, 79
Knights of the Round Table, 36c
Knights Templar, 50, 53, 61, 136
Knossos, Palace of, Crete, Greece, **82-87**, 82, 83c, 84, 84c, 86c, 87c
Kolosimo, Peter, 237
Kosok, Paul, 234
Kriz Hill, 70c
Kukulkán (El Castillo), pyramid of, Chichén Itzá, Mexico, 196, 197c
Kukulkán, god, 196, 197c

L
La Venta Park Museum, Villahermosa, Mexico, 219c, 220c
La Venta, Huimanguillo, Mexico, 218, 219d
Lalibela, Ethiopia, **104-111**, 104, 105c, 106c, 107, 110c, 111c
Lalibela, King, 104, 105c, 110c
Landa, Diego de, 203
Las Bolas, stone spheres, Costa Rica, **230-231**, 230, 230c
Lazar, Bob, 182
Le Ménec, alignment, Carnac, France, 44, 45c, 46c, 47c
Lee, Ang, 161cLi, mountain, 162
Lindsay, Clan, 22
Loch Ness Centre, 19
Loch Ness, monster (Nessie) and lake of, **18-21**, 19, 19c, 20c, 21
Lockheed Corporation, 185
Lopez, Andrea, 232
Lothrop, Samuel, 230
Lucius II (Gerardo Caccianemici), Pope, 56
Luftwaffe, 40
Lyon, Sir John, 22

M
Machu Picchu, Peru, **242-247**, 13c, 242c, 243, 245, 245c, 247c
MacKay, Mr. and Mrs., 19
MacNab, Peter, 19, 19c
Madhya Pradesh, region, India, 156
Magog, oak, Glastonbury, United Kingdom, 33, 36c
Malcolm II, King, 22, 27c
Malindi, Kenya, 112
Mandara, mountain, 172
Mané-er-Hroek, monolith, Carnac, France, 45
Manio "Giant," Carnac, France, 44
Maoling, Shaanxi, China, 162c
Marine Sulphur Queen, ship, 195
Marshall, John, 154c
Martin Mariner, hydroplane, 195
Mato Grosso, Brazil, 232, 233c
Mauch, Karl, 116
Maya, 13, 13c, 196, 197c, 198c, 199, 200c, 203, 203c, 204, 204c, 209, 210, 211c, 212, 218, 220, 225, 225c, 226c, 229c, 230
Mayol, Jacques, 168
McAllister, Jim, 186
Menelik, emperor, 136
Menkaure (Mycerinus), pyramid of, Egypt, 89, 90, 92
Merlin, magician, 29, 32
Meru, mountain, 170c
Mile Long Avenue, Glamis Castle, Glamis, United Kingdom, 23c
Minos, 82, 83c, 84, 84c
Minotaur, 82, 83c, 84
Moai, "Paro", Easter Island, Chile, 263
Moai, "the Giant", Easter Island, Chile, 263
Moai, Ahu Ko Te Riku, Easter Island, Chile, 266c
Moai, Easter Island, Chile, 9, 168, 170, 263, 263c, 264, 266c
Mogui Cheng, aka Sulumuhak, Xinjiang region, China, **158-161**, 159, 159c, 161c
Mohammed el-Hamed, 139
Mohenjo-daro, Pakistan, **150-155**, 150, 150c, 152, 152c, 154c, 264
Monomotapa, King, 116, 118c
Monument 56 (Mono que mira el cielo), La Venta, Mexico, 222c
Monument 77 (the Governor), La Venta, Mexico, 222c
Morgan le Fay, 32
Moses, 100, 134, 140c
Mosque of the Three Corridors, Gedi, Kenya, 115cMosque, Great, Gedi, Kenya, 115
Mount of Olives, 141

Museo Nacional De Antropología (National Museum of Anthropology), Mexico City, 214c
Museum of Israel, Jerusalem, Israel, 139
Museum, Archaeological, Delphi, Greece, 74c
Mutitjulu, Australia, 179c
Mycerinus, see Menkaure

N
Nabatei, people, 143, 147
Namarrgon, 181c
Namondjok, 181c
Nancy, sailing stone, 186, 186c
National Library, Rio de Janeiro, 232
Nazca Lines, plain of, Peru, **234-241**, 234, 234c, 237, 237c, 239c, 240c
Nazca, tribe, 234, 237, 239c, 240c
Nebra, Germany, 42
Nebuchadnezzar, King, 134
Necho II, Pharaoh, 131
Nellis, Air Force Base, United States, 182
Nemean lion, 38
Nessie, see Loch Ness, monster
Nevada, desert, 182, 183c, 185
Newspaper Rock, Canyonlands National Park, Utah, United States, 192c
Nile, river, 92, 203
Noah, 122, 123
Noah's Ark, Turkey, **122-123**, 122, 123c
North Portal (or Portal of the Covenant), Cathedral of Notre Dame, Chartres, France, 53, 53c
Notre Dame de Chartres, see Our Lady of Chartres, cathedral
Nourlangie Rock, Australia, 181c
Nunnery Quadrangle, Uxmal, Mexico, 208c, 209, 211c

O
Obodas I, King, 147
Ogilvy, Clan, 22
Okinawa, Island of, Japan, 166
Olmecs, civilization of, **218-223**, 218, 219c, 220, 221c, 222c
Omphalos, stone, Delphi, Greece, 73, 74cOsmanagic´, Semir, 71
Our Lady Mary of Zion, Church of, Axum, Ethiopia, 100
Our Lady of Chartres, Cathedral of, France, **50-55**, 50, 51c, 53, 53c, 59, 61

P
Pacal, King, 225, 226c, 229c
Pacal, King, mausoleum of, Palenque, Mexico, 225, 226c, 229c
Pachacútec, Inca emperor, 248
Pachamama (Mother Earth), 252c
Palace, Palenque, Mexico, 225
Palenque, Chiapas, Mexico, **225-229**, 225, 225c, 226c, 229c
Palmar Sur, Costa Rica, 230
Panamerican Highway, 234, 234c
Parker Pearson, Mike, 29
Paul VI (Giovanbattista Montini), Pope, 56
Pelota ballfield, Chichén Itzá, Mexico, 196, 199, 199c
Pelota ballfield, Uxmal, Mexico, 209, 211c
Pennsylvania State University, 71
Peter II (Peter the Roman), future pope, 56, 57
Petra, Jordan, 104, **142-149**, 143, 143c, 146c, 147, 147c, 148c, 199, 247c
Petrie, Flinders, 90Pillars of Hercules, 78
Plato, 78
Plutarch, 73, 75
Poenari Castle, Romania, 62
Poike, volcano, 263c
Polia, Mario, 232
Polo, Marco, 159

269

Ponce monolith, *aka* Ponce Stele, Kalasasaya, Tiahauanaco, 260c
Ponce Stele, *see* Ponce Monolith
Ponce, Carlos, 260c
Poseidon, god, 78, 82, 84
Posnansky, Arthur, 259
Proust, Marcel, 9
Pueblo Bonito, Chaco Canyon, United States, 190, 190c, 193c
"Puma Punku," Tiahauanaco, 256, 256c
Puna Pau, quarry, Easter Island, Chile, 266c
Puuc, architectural style, 208c, 209
Pyramid of the Dragon, Visoko, Bosnia, 70c, 71
Pyramid of the Dwarf, see Adivino, Uxmal
Pyramid of the Feathered Serpent, Teotihuacán, Mexico, 214, 214c, 217c
Pyramid of the Magician, see Adivino, UxmalPyramid of the Moon, Teotihuacán, Mexico, 212, 212c, 214, 214c, 215c
Pyramid of the Moon, Visoko, Bosnia, 70c, 71
Pyramid of the Sun, Teotihuacán, Mexico, 212, 212c, 215c
Pyramid of the Sun, Visoko, Bosnia, 70c, 71
Pythia, prophetess, 72c, 75, 77c
Python, monster, 74c, 75

Q
Qin Shi Huang, emperor, 162, 162c, 164, 164c, 165c
Qin Shi Huang, mausoleum of, see Xi'an, pyramid of
Queen Mother of England, 22, 27c
Queen of Sheba, 116, 136
Queen's chamber, Pyramid of Cheops, Egypt, 90c
Quetzalcoatl, god, 197c
Quetzalcoatl, Temple of, Teotihuacán, Mexico, 217c
Qumran, West Bank, 139, 139c, 140c, 141
Quwwat-ul-Islam, New Delhi, India, 156, 156c

R
Racetrack Playa, Death Valley, United States, 186
Raft Point, Australia, 180c
Ramhai, negus, 101c
Rano Raraku, volcanic crater, Easter Island, Chile, 263, 263c, 264c
Rapa Nui, *see Easter Island* Reiche, Maria, 234, 234c
Renders, Adam, 116
Road, Ring, Yonaguni, Japan, 167c
Robert II of Scotland, 22
Roggeveen, Jacob, 263, 264
Rongo-Rongo, tablets, Easter Island, Chile, 264
"Room of Tears," Cenote Aktun Ha, Roswell, New Mexico, United States, 182
Royal Geographic Society, 232
Ruz Lhuillier, Alberto, 225, 226c
Ryukyu, archipelago, Japan, 166

S
"Sacred Area," Yonaguni, Japan, 166
Sacsayhuamán, Cuzco, Peru, **248-253**, 248, 248c, 252c, 253, 253c
Sahara Desert, 116, 118c
Sailing Stones, United States, **186-189**, 186, 186c
Saint Adomnán of Iona, 19
Saint Apollinaire, stained-glass window, Cathedral of Notre Dame, Chartres, France, 53, 53c
Saint Columbanus, 19
Saint Cornelius, 47
Saint George, 104, 107, 110cSaint Malachy, 56, 57c
Saint Mary Chapel, Glastonbury, United Kingdom, 34
Saint Michael, Church of, Glastonbury, United Kingdom, 32, 34c
Saint-Michel, tumulus, Carnac, France, 44
Sak Aktun, Yucatán, Mexico, 204c
Saladin, sultan, 143
San Lorenzo Tenochtitlán, Mexico, 218
Santilli, Ray, 182
Santorini, island, Greece, 78, 79c, 84c
Sao Paulo, battleship, 195
Saramago, José, 13
Sarasvati, river, 150
Saul, King, 134
Saxony, Germany, 42
Schmidt, Klaus, 126
Scotland, 19, 19c, 22, 24c
Serra do Roncador, Mato Grosso, Brazil, 232, 233c
Shaanxi, region, China, 162, 162c
Shakespeare, William, 22
Shiva, divinity, 173c
Shona, African people, 116, 116c
Sighişoara, Romania, 62, 64c, 68c
Silk Route, 159, 159c
Smithsonian Institution, Washington, 218
Snefru, pharaoh, 88c
Socrates, 77c
Solomon, King, 131, 134, 136, 136c
Solomon, Temple of, Jerusalem, Israel, 116, **134-137**, 134, 135c, 136c, 141
Sphinx, Giza, 13c, 89, 90, **92-97**, 92, 93c, 94, 94c, 95c, 170
Squadron 19, of U.S. Air Force, 195
Statue 5 (*La Abuelita*, "the little grandmother"), La Venta, Mexico, 222c
Stavenger, ship, 195
Stele of King Ezana, Axum, Ethiopia, 98, 98c
Stirling, Matthew, 218
Stoker, Bram, 62, 62c, 64, 64c, 66
Stonehenge Riverside Project, 29
Stonehenge, United Kingdom, 13c, **28-31**, 28c, 29, 30, 30c, 42, 71, 126
Strathmore, Patrick, 22, 24
Stuart, Lachlan, 19
"Sultan's Palace," Gedi, Kenya, 112c, 115
Sulumuhak, see Mogui Cheng
Sundial, large, Glamis Castle, United Kingdom, 24c
Super Constellation, airplane, 195
Superfort C-54, airplane, 195
Suryavarman II, King, 172

T
Ta Prohm ("Old Brahma"), Temple of, Angkor, Cambodia, 172, 174c
Taklamakan, desert, 159, 159c
Targovişte, Romania, 62, 69c
Tello, Julio, 234
Temple of Phalluses, Uxmal, Mexico, 209
Temple of the Condor, Machu Picchu, Peru, 245c
Temple of the Cross, Group of Crosses, Palenque, Mexico, 225c
Temple of the Feathered Serpent, Teotihuacán, Mexico, 212
Temple of the Foliated Cross, Group of Crosses, Palenque, Mexico, 225c
Temple of the Inscriptions, Palenque, Mexico, 225, 226c, 229c
Temple of the Sun, Group of Crosses, Palenque, Mexico, 225c, 229c
Temple of the Sun, Machu Picchu, Peru, 245c, 247c
Temple of the Three Windows, Machu Picchu, Peru, 243, 245c
Temple of the Two Windows, Machu Picchu, Peru, 243
Teotihuacán, Mexico, **212-217**, 212, 212c, 214, 214c, 215c, 217c
"Terrace," Yonaguni, Japan, 166
Terra-cotta Army (Eternal Army), Xi'an, 13c, 162, 162c, 165c
Teutonic Knights, 64, 64c
Theater of Delphi, Delphi, Greece, 77c
Theater, Roman, Petra, Jordan, 147
Theseus, 82, 83c, 84
Thom, Alexander, 45
Thompson, Edward Herbert, 203, 204
Throne of the Inca, Sacsayhuamán, Peru, 253c
Throne of the Two Jaguars, Governor's Palace, Uxmal, Mexico, 211c
Thutmose III, pharaoh, 131
Thutmose IV, pharaoh, 95c
Tiahuanaco, Bolivia, 12, 255, **256-261**, 256, 256c, 258c, 259, 259c, 260c
Tiber, river, 56
Titicaca, Lake, 12, **254-255**, 255, 255c, 256, 256c
Titus, emperor, 134, 141
Toltecs, 209
Tomb of Empress Li, Shaanxi, China, 162c
Tomb of Sextus Florentinus, Petra, Jordan, 146c
Tomb of the Urn ("the Court"), Petra, Jordan, 146c, 147c
Tomb, Corinthian, Petra, Jordan, 146c
Tomb, Palace, Petra, Jordan, 146c
Tomb, Silk, Petra, Jordan, 146c
Tor, hill, 32, 33, 34c, 36c
Transylvania, Romania, 62, 62c, 64
Tres Zapotes, Mexico, 218
Tudor IV, four-engine, 195
Tulum, Yucatán, Mexico, 204c, 206c

U
U2, spy plane, 185
Udaygiri, hill, 156
Uffington, hill, United Kingdom, 38, 40c
Uffington, White Horse of, 38, 40c
Uhro, region, China, 159
Uluru, *aka* Ayers Rock, Australia, 13, **176-181**, 176, 176c, 178, 179c
UNESCO, 209, 230c, 234
Upper Cemetery, Machu Picchu, Peru, 247c
Urashima, Taro, 166
Urquhart Castle, Scotland, 19, 19c
Urubamba Valley, Peru, 242c
USS Insurgent, ship, 195
USS Wasp, ship, 195
Uther Pendragon, King, 29
Uvita, Costa Rica, 230
Uxmal, archaeological site, Yucatán, Mexico, **208-211**, 208c, 209, 210, 211c

V
Vatican City, **56-57**, 56, 57, 57c
Vidisha, Madhya Pradesh, 156
Vilcabamba, Peru, 242c
Vimana, flying chariots, 150, 152
Viracocha, civilization, 237, 245
Viracocha, god, 255
Vishnu, god, 156, 156c
Visoko, pyramids of, Bosnia, **70-71**, 70c, 71
Vivian, the Lady of the Lake, 32
Vlad III of Wallachia (*aka* Vlad ?epes, aka Dracùl, Vlad), 62, 64c, 66c, 68c, 69c
von Däniken, Erich, 225, 237

W
Wadi Rum, desert, 143
Wailing Wall, Jerusalem, Israel, 134, 135c
Wandjina, Aborigine gods, 180c
Wetherill, Richard, 192
White Lady, 22
White Spring, 32
Whiting, Michael, 33
Wilde, Oscar, 22
Wilson, Robert, 19, 19c, 21
Wiltshire, Salisbury plain, United Kingdom, 29
Wion, Arnold, 56
Worrorra, people, 180c
Wudi, emperor, tomb of, Shaanxi, China, 162c

X
Xi'an, pyramid of, China, **162-165**, 162, 162c, 164, 164c, 165c
Xi'an, Shaanxi, China, 13c, 162, 162c, 165c
Xingù, river, 232
Xinjiang, region, China, 159, 159c, 161c
Xiuh, family, 209

Y
Yahweh, 134
Yang Xin, Princess, tomb of, Shaanxi, China, 162c
Yanluowang, divinity, 159
Yonaguni, submerged ruins of, Japan, 9, **166-169**, 166, 167c, 168, 168c
York Transport, airplane, 195
Yucatán, Mexico, 206c
Yucatán Peninsula, Mexico, 13, 196, 197c, 203, 204c, 209
Yum Kaax, god, 211c

Z
Zapp, Ivan, 230
Zeus, god, 73, 82
Zoscales, King, 98

PHOTO CREDITS

Pages 2-3 The Science Photo Library/Tips Images
Pages 4-5 Michael Hanson/National Geographic Stock
Page 9 per gentile concessione di Iwan Palombi
Pages 10-11 Foto Scala, Firenze
Pages 14-15 Araldo De Luca/Archivio White Star
Pages 16-17 Giulio Veggi/Archivio White Star
Page 18 right Keystone/Getty Images

Pages 18-19 Mauritius/CuboImages
Pages 20-21 David Doubilet/National Geographic Stock
Page 21 Winfield Parks/National Geographic Stock
Pages 22-23 Dean Conger/National Geographic Stock
Pages 24, 24-25, 26-27, 27 top, 27 bottom Massimo Borchi/Archivio White Star
Page 28 left Imagestate/Tips Images

Pages 28-29 Ken Geiger/National Geographic Stock
Page 30 top Dea Picture Library/De Agostini/Getty Images
Page 30 center Archivio White Star
Pages 30-31 Dae Sasitorn and Adrian Warren/www.lastrefuge.co.uk
Pages 32-33 Jeremy Walker/Getty Images
Page 34 Skyscan/Corbis

Pages 34-35 Antony Spencer/Getty Images
Pages 36 top, 36 bottom Eddie Linssen/Alamy/Milestone Media
Pages 36-37 Wojtek Buss/Agefotostock
Page 39 Adam Woolfitt/Corbis
Pages 40-41 Last Refuge/Getty Images
Page 42 Peter Endig/epa/Corbis
Pages 42-43 Georg Knoll/laif/Contrasto
Page 43 right Archivio White Star
Pages 44-45 Gerard Sioen/RAPHO/Gamma
Pages 46-47 Max Homand/Getty Images
Page 47 Joe Cornish/Getty Images
Pages 48-49 RobertHarding/CuboImages
Page 49 R. Linke/Agefotostock
Page 50 GoPlaces/Alamy/Milestone Media
Pages 50-51 Sylvain Sonnet/Corbis
Pages 52, 53 Photononstop/Tips Images
Pages 54-55 Sylvain Sonnet/Corbis
Page 56 G. Dagli Orti/De Agostini Picture Library
Pages 56-57 Marcello Bertinetti/Archivio White Star
Page 58 G. Dagli Orti/De Agostini Picture Library
Pages 58-59 Antonio Attini/Archivio White Star
Page 60-61 Antonio Attini/Archivio White Star
Page 61 Alfio Garozzo/Archivio White Star
Pages 62-63 Marco Cristofori/Corbis
Page 64 per gentile concessione di Bran Castle
Page 65 German School/Getty Images
Pages 66 top, 66 bottom, 67 per gentile concessione di Bran Castle
Page 68 top S. Vannini/De Agostini Picture Library
Page 68 bottom Bruce Yuanyue Bi/DanitaDelimont.com
Pages 68-69 José Fuste Raga/Agefotostock
Pages 70-71 per gentile concessione di Sam Semir Osmanagich
Pages 72-73 Giulio Veggi/Archivio White Star
Page 73 The Gallery Collection/Corbis
Pages 74-75 Giulio Veggi/Archivio White Star
Page 75 Araldo De Luca
Pages 76-77, 77 top, 77 bottom Giulio Veggi/Archivio White Star
Pages 78-79 Alfio Garozzo/Archivio White Star
Page 79 right De Agostini Picture Library
Pages 80-81 Alfio Garozzo/Archivio White Star
Page 82 Gianni Dagli Orti/Corbis
Pages 82-83 Livio Bourbon/Archivio White Star
Pages 84 top, 84 bottom, 85 Giulio Veggi/Archivio White Star
Pages 86-87 Alfio Garozzo/Archivio White Star
Page 87 top Giulio Veggi/Archivio White Star
Page 87 bottom Livio Bourbon/Archivio White Star
Pages 88-89 Marcello Bertinetti/Archivio White Star
Pages 89, 90 left, 90 right, 91, 92 Araldo De Luca/Archivio White Star
Pages 92-93 Marcello Bertinetti/Archivio White Star
Page 94 Marcello Bertinetti/Archivio White Star
pagg 94-95 Giulio Veggi/Archivio White Star
Pages 96-97 Marcello Bertinetti/Archivio White Star
Page 98 left Dorling Kindersley/Getty Images
Page 98 center Wojtek Buss/Tips Images
Page 99 Jon Arnold Images/DanitaDelimont.com
Page 100 Egmont Strigl/Agefotostock
Pages 100-101 Yoshio Tomii/Agefotostock
Page 101 Egmont Strigl/Agefotostock
Page 102 left Martin Zwick/Agefotostock
Page 102 right David DuChemin/Agefotostock
Pages 102-103 Martin Zwick/Agefotostock
Page 104 Stefan Auth/Agefotostock
Pages 104-105 A. Tessore/De Agostini Picture Library
Page 105 left Archivio White Star
Pages 106-107 JD Dallet/Agefotostock
Page 107 JTB Photo/Super Stock
Pages 108-109 Andrew McConnell/Corbis

Pages 110-111 Michael Poliza/National Geographic Stock
Page 111 top C. Sappa/De Agostini Picture Library
Page 111 bottom W. Buss/De Agostini Picture Library
Page 113 Nigel Pavitt/Getty Images
Pages 114-115 Christine Osborne/Corbis
Page 115 Andrew McConnell/Corbis
Pages 116-117 Robert Harding Images/Masterfile/Sie
Page 117 right G. Sioen/De Agostini Picture Library
Page 118 top Desmond Kwande/AFP/Getty Images
Page 118 bottom G. Sioen/De Agostini Picture Library
Pages 118-119 Robert Holmes/Corbis
Pages 120-121 Robert Holmes/Corbis
Page 121 Colin Hoskins/Alamy/Milestone Media
Page 122 The British Library/Agefotostock
Pages 122-123 W. Buss/De Agostini Picture Library
Pages 124-125, 125 right Vincent J. Musi/National Geographic Stock
Page 126 Vincent J. Musi/National Geographic Society/Corbis
Pages 127, 128, 129 Vincent J. Musi/National Geographic Stock
Pages 130-131 Itamar Grinberg/Archivio White Star
Page 132 top Israel images/Alamy/Milestone Media
Page 132 bottom Antonio Attini/Archivio White Star
Page 133 Walter Bibikow/Agefotostock/Marka
Pages 134-135 Itamar Grinberg/Archivio White Star
Pages 136-137 Historic Map Works LLC and Osher/Getty Images
Page 138 left www.BibleLandPictures.com/Alamy/Milestone Media
Pages 138-139 Itamar Grinberg/Archivio White Star
Page 140 www.BibleLandPictures.com/Alamy/Milestone Media
Pages 140-141 Zev Radovan
Pages 142, 143 left, 144-145, 146-147, 147, 148, 148-149 Marcello Libra/Archivio White Star
Pages 150-151 James L. Stanfield/National Geographic Stock
Page 151 right JTB/Photoshot
Page 152 Robert Harding/Robert Harding World Imagery/Corbis
Page 153 Robert Harding Picture Library Ltd/Alamy/Milestone Media
Pages 154, 154-155 UPPA/Photoshot
Page 156 left Tibor Bognar/Agefotostock
Page 157 Robert Harding Produc/Agefotostock
Page 158 left Dennis Stone/Agefotostock/Marka
Pages 158-159 Xu Summergate/Panorama Stock
Pages 160-161 Fotosearch/Getty Images
Page 161 Wei Xinan/Panorama Stock
Page 162 left JTB Photo/Super Stock
Page 163 Araldo De Luca/Archivio White Star
Page 164 Universal History Arc/Agefotostock
Page 164-165 Araldo De Luca/Archivio White Star
Pages 166-167, 168, 169 Attila Bicskos/Auscape
Pages 170-171 Livio Bourbon/Archivio White Star
Pages 171 left, 172 top, 172 bottom, 172-173 Antonio Attini/Archivio White Star
Page 174 top Livio Bourbon/Archivio White Star
Page 174 bottom Ivan Synieokov/Alamy/Milestone Media
Page 175 Marcello Bertinetti/Archivio White Star
Pages 176-177 Per-Andre Hoffmann/Getty Images
Page 177 right Christopher Groenhout/Lonely Planet Images
Pages 178, 178-179 Peter Carroll/Barcroft USA/Getty Images
Page 180 top Dave G. Houser/Corbis
Page 180 bottom John Van Hasselt/Sygma/Corbis
Pages 180-181 Robert Harding Images/Masterfile/Sie
Pages 182-183 Gerrit de Heus/Alamy/Milestone Media

Pages 184-185 Eva Haeberle/laif/Contrasto
Page 185 courtesy of © NVAHOF Oral History Project Collection
Page 187 Ocean/Corbis
Pages 188-189 Jean-Philippe Delobelle/Bipsphoto/Tips Images
Page 191 Massimo Borchi/Archivio White Star
Page 192 Robert Harding Images/Masterfile/Sie
Pages 192-193, 193 Massimo Borchi/Archivio White Star
Page 195 right Archivio White Star
Pages 194-195 Jim Wark
Page 196 Massimo Borchi/Archivio White Star
Pages 196-197 Antonio Attini/Archivio White Star
Page 198 Antonio Attini/Archivio White Star
Pages 198-199, 199 top, 199 bottom Massimo Borchi/Archivio White Star
Page 200 Imagestate/Tips Images
Pages 200-201 Luis Castaneda/Tips Images
Page 202 left Massimo Borchi/Archivio White Star
Pages 202-203 LucaPicciau/Cuboimages
Page 204 Yann Hubert/Biosphoto/Tips Images
Page 205 Paul Nicklen/National Geographic Stock
Page 206 ML Sinibaldi/Corbis
Pages 206-207 Gavin Newman/Alamy/Milestone Media
Pages 208-209 Antonio Attini/Archivio White Star
Pages 209, 210 top, 210 bottom, 210-211 Massimo Borchi/Archivio White Star
Pages 212-213 David R Frazier/Agefotostock
Page 213 right Antonio Attini/Archivio White Star
Page 214 Diego Munoz/Agefotostock
Pages 214-215, 216-217, 217, 218 Antonio Attini/Archivio White Star
Pages 218-219 Charles & Josette Lenars/Corbis
Page 220 Antonio Attini/Archivio White Star
Pages 220-221 Kenneth Garrett/DanitaDelimont.com
Pages 221, 222 left, 222 right, 223 Antonio Attini/Archivio White Star
Pages 224-225, 226 left, 226 right, 226-227 Massimo Borchi/Archivio White Star
Page 228 Antonio Attini/Archivio White Star
Page 229 left Massimo Borchi/Archivio White Star
Page 229 right Archivio White Star
Page 230 right Peter Langer/DanitaDelimont.com
Page 231 Carver Mostardi/Alamy/Milestone Media
Pages 232-233 Luiz Claudio Marigo/naturepl.com
Page 233 right UPPA/Photoshot
Pages 234-235 Gilles Barbier/Agefotostock/Marka
Page 235 right Yann Arthus Bertrand/Corbis
Pages 236-237 Alexander Pöschel/Agefotostock/Marka
Pages 238-239 Top Photo/Tips Images
Page 239 top Yann Arthus Bertrand/Corbis
Page 239 bottom Top Photo/Tips Images
Pages 240 top, 240 bottom JTB Photo/Super Stock
Pages 240-241 Top Photo/Tips Images
Pages 242-243 Antonio Attini/Archivio White Star
Page 243 Hiram Bingham/National Geographic Stock
Pages 244, 245 top, 245 bottom, 246, 246-247, 247 Antonio Attini/Archivio White Star
Page 249 Cordier Sylvain/Getty Images
Pages 250-251, 252-253, 253, 254 left, 254-255, 256-257 Antonio Attini/Archivio White Star
Page 257 left Kevin Lang/Alamy/Milestone Media
Pages 258, 258-259, 259, 260 top, 260 bottom, 261 Antonio Attini/Archivio White Star
Page 262 left Doug Allan/Naturepl.com
Pages 262-263 Peter Langer/DanitaDelimont.com
Page 264 Gavin Hellier/Corbis
Page 265 Gavin Hellier/Getty Images
Page 266 De Agostini Picture Library
Page 267 BILDGENTUR-ONLINE/Agefotostock

Cover: On Easter Island, the Moai Ahu Ko Te Riku is the only one that is complete. According to tradition, the Moai allowed communication with the Afterlife. © *BILDGENTUR-ONLINE/Agefotostock*

Back cover: The Mayan calendar, in addition to demonstrating the astronomic proficiency of the ancient American people, is linked with apocalyptic prophecies charged with mystery. © *Luis Castaneda/Tips Images*

ISBN 978-88-544-0673-5

1 2 3 4 5 6   16 15 14 13 12

WHITE STAR PUBLISHERS

WS White Star Publishers® is a registered trademark
property of Edizioni White Star s.r.

© 2012 Edizioni White Star s.r.l.
Via M. Germano, 10
13100 Vercelli, Italy
www.whitestar.it

Translation: John Venerella
Editing: Suzanne Smither

All rights reserved. No part of this publication may
be reproduced, stored in a retrieval system or transmitted
in any form or by any means, electronic, mechanical,
photocopying, recording or otherwise, without
written permission from the publisher.

ISBN 978-88-544-0673-5
1 2 3 4 5 6   16 15 14 13 12

Printed in China